Accommodating Muslims under Common Law

The book explores the relationship between Muslims, the Common Law and Sharīʿah in the West post-9/11. The book looks at the accommodation of Sharīʿah Law within Western Common Law legal traditions and the role of the judiciary, in particular, in drawing boundaries for secular democratic states with Muslim populations who want resolutions to conflicts that also comply with the dictates of their faith.

Salim Farrar and Ghena Krayem consider the question of recognition of Sharīʿah by looking at how the flexibilities that exist in both the Common Law and Sharīʿah provide unexplored avenues for navigation and accommodation. The issue is explored in a comparative context across several jurisdictions and case law is examined in the contexts of family law, business and crime from selected jurisdictions with significant Muslim minority populations including: Australia, Canada, England and Wales, and the United States. The book examines how Muslims and the broader community have framed their claims for recognition against a backdrop of terrorism fears, and how Common Law judiciaries have responded within their constitutional and statutory confines and also within the contemporary contexts of demands for equality, neutrality and universal human rights. Acknowledging the inherent pragmatism, flexibility and values of the Common Law, the authors argue that the controversial issue of accommodation of Sharīʿah is not necessarily one that requires the establishment of a separate and parallel legal system.

Salim Farrar is an Associate Professor at the University of Sydney, Australia.

Ghena Krayem is a Senior Lecturer at the University of Sydney, Australia.

Accommodating Muslims under Common Law

A comparative analysis

Salim Farrar and Ghena Krayem

Routledge
Taylor & Francis Group
LONDON AND NEW YORK

First published 2017
by Routledge
2 Park Square, Milton Park, Abingdon, Oxon OX14 4RN

and by Routledge
711 Third Avenue, New York, NY 10017

First issued in paperback 2018

Routledge is an imprint of the Taylor & Francis Group, an informa business

British Library Cataloguing in Publication Data
A catalogue record for this book is available from the British Library

Library of Congress Cataloging in Publication Data
Names: Farrar, Salim, author. | Krayem, Ghena, author.
Title: Accommodating muslims under common law : a comparative analysis / Salim Farrar and Ghena Krayem.
Description: New York, NY : Routledge, 2016. | Includes bibliographical references and index.
Identifiers: LCCN 2016002744 | ISBN 9780415710466 (hbk) | ISBN 9781315867618 (hbk) | ISBN 9781315867618 (ebk)
Subjects: LCSH: Legal polycentricity. | Muslims–Legal status, laws, etc. | Muslims–Civil rights. | Common law. | Islamic law. | Comparative law.
Classification: LCC K236 .F38 2016 | DDC 342.08/5297–dc23
LC record available at http://lccn.loc.gov/2016002744

ISBN 13: 978-1-138-60657-9 (pbk)
ISBN 13: 978-0-415-71046-6 (hbk)

Typeset in Times New Roman
by Wearset Ltd, Boldon, Tyne and Wear

MIX
Paper from responsible sources
FSC www.fsc.org FSC™ C013985

Printed in the United Kingdom
by Henry Ling Limited

Contents

Preface vii

Introduction: law, religion and the challenge of accommodation 1

1 Muslim communities in a multicultural context 10
Introduction 10
Muslim communities in a multicultural context 11
Muslim communities in Common Law countries 16
The rise of Islamophobia and its impact on Muslim communities 22
Conclusion 24

2 Contextualising Sharīʿah in the Common Law world 26
Introduction 26
The perception of Sharī'ah: 'Sharī'ah' debates in Common Law jurisdictions 27
Demystifying the debates 34
Is Sharī'ah 'too difficult'? 46
Conclusion 50

3 Muslims, family relationships and the Common Law 59
Introduction 59
An Islamic marriage 61
Financial entitlements 72
Divorce – ṭalāq *81*
Parenting 86
Conclusion 91

4 Muslims, crime and the Common Law 94
Introduction 94
'Processing' Muslims 95
'Excusing' Muslims: protecting 'honour', performing ritual, 'educating' family and community 109
Conclusion: towards a more 'nuanced approach'? 124

5 Muslims, business transactions and the Common Law 133
Introduction 133
Islamic commercial law 135
Conflicts and choices of law 140
Sharī'ah and Common Law as choice of law – case law 141
Sharī'ah, courts and arbitration 158
Conclusion 160

Conclusion 166

Glossary 177
Bibliography 180

Preface

We began the research for this book in 2012 and in the course of that time, so much has happened. Muslim–non-Muslim relations across Europe, Canada, the USA and Australia were already tense because of a ratcheting up of security fears. We did not think the situation could get worse. How wrong we were. The public beheading of Drummer Lee Rigby in London, the bombing of the Boston Marathon, the assault on the Parliament building in Ottawa, the siege on a café in Sydney, the arbitrary murder of an employee of the NSW Police by a radicalised child, the attacks on offices of Charlie Hebdo, the November 2015 bombings and terrorist attacks in Paris and the killings in San Bernardino, California, have all made a tense atmosphere positively toxic.

We have also seen a concerning rise in Islamophobia in all of these countries as Muslims face a relentless call to condemn and apologise for acts they have nothing to do with and in fact contravene their Islamic values and beliefs. This has been made even more difficult by a poisonous public discourse that allows politicians and 'shock-jocks' to suggest that Muslims are not welcome and even should be placed on a database! This is not to mention the unfurling tragedies in the Middle East, the refugee crisis and the collective sense of pain and hurt Muslims feel when they see so many of their brethren slaughtered, in often horrific ways.

It seems as if unless governments, politicians, academics and communities work together to address problems of discrimination and social exclusion as well as radicalisation, we are moving inexorably towards a state of affairs not seen since the likes of World War II. This book represents our small contribution towards that collective effort.

We have lots of people to thank who have helped on us our literary journey. First, we would like to thank our employer, the University of Sydney Law School, which has provided a sanctuary and safe haven, not to mention a collegial atmosphere, for two Muslim academics to reflect, write on and discuss with fellow academics without fear or favour some of the most controversial issues of the day. Second, we would like to thank our colleagues who read through and commented on earlier drafts: Ron McCullum and Mary Crock, Patrick Parkinson, Simon Butt, Mathew Conaglen and Kevin Walton from the Sydney Law School; and Dr Farah Ahmed from Melbourne University's Faculty of Law. Third, there are our research assistants, Helen McCue, David Drennan, Chris Frommer, Tamana Daqiq and the several interns from the Centre for Asian and Pacific Law without whose hours spent trawling through and identifying relevant case reports and empirical data across four jurisdictions, this work may never have got off the ground.

Last, but certainly not least, we must thank our families for their unstinting support and tolerance of late nights and working weekends. We dedicate this book to them and ultimately thank the One who made this all possible.

حَسْبُنَا اللَّهُ وَنِعْمَ الْوَكِيلُ

Allāh suffices us and is the One upon whom we ultimately depend

Ghena Krayem
Salim Farrar
Sydney Law School, 16 December 2015

Introduction

Law, religion and the challenge of accommodation

The law should not make accommodation for injustice, it will be said. Further the very idea that society can be split up into different groups abiding by different legal standards challenges the very unity and cohesion of a country. So the arguments will go, and they can be very persuasive.

(Roger Trigg, *Equality, Freedom and Religion*, 2012a: 7)

In the literature of Prophetic sayings (*Ḥadīth*), Prophet Muḥammad relates the story of the holy man, Jurayj (Al-Bukhārī, Ḥadīth No. 3436).[1] Jurayj was a pious worshipper of God and a follower of Jesus. He had a simple hermitage built in the mountains and used to go there to retreat, pray and reflect. He was particularly fond of prayer and would dedicate himself day and night in optional prayer and remembrance of his Lord. One day, his mother called for him while he was in prayer, and he said to himself, 'My Lord, my mother, or my prayer?' He continued praying. The following day, his mother came again and requested he come out to see her. He continued praying. She came a third day and for a third time, Jurayj ignored her request and continued praying. Upset and angry, Jurayj's mother supplicated to God, imploring, 'O Allāh, do not let him die until he sees the faces of prostitutes'.

Envious of Jurayj's reputation for piety, some of the local people also then began to plot against him and convinced a beautiful prostitute to try and seduce him. She failed, but subsequently became pregnant with a local herdsman, gave birth to a child and claimed Jurayj was the father. The people who used to visit Jurayj felt angry and betrayed. Without confirming or properly investigating the rumour, they impetuously tore down Jurayj's hermitage, tied him up and brought him to the public square to be punished. Before punishment was administered, Jurayj requested for the child to be brought to him. Jurayj then placed his finger on the infant's stomach and asked him the identity of his father. To the astonishment of those present, the infant mentioned the herdsman. Now aware of their grievous error and unjust actions, the people kissed Jurayj, released him and offered to rebuild his hermitage out of gold. He turned them down, asking that they rebuild it exactly as it was (out of mud).

The parable of Jurayj, though related from events taking place two thousand years ago and a society vastly different from our own, informs some essential truths which transcend time and place and which send echoes into our troubled present. Other than noting that a mother's prayers are always answered, the story warns of religious excess, of wrong priorities, of misinformation and disinformation – of community intolerance and of rash response. More optimistically, it also tells us not to abandon hope and that justice wins out in the end.

Religious dedication, in particular dedication to Islām, is problematic in contemporary times in the secular West. If we believe public opinion polls, the majority of these societies are becoming less religious and not more; so it must appear 'odd' that ethnic minorities, especially Muslim groups, are more religious and adhering more to their faith than before. The fact that some groups who claim to follow the same faith then kill and maim innocent people on their streets in the name of religion makes it yet more perplexing. Donald Trump's plans to prohibit Muslim immigration into the USA, 'Anti-Sharīʿah' bills in state legislatures, anti-Muslim marches and voluminous popular newspaper columns on how incompatible Muslims are to a 'Western' way of life, make almost any attempt to address social exclusion and discrimination against Muslims, or religion generally, as practically fanciful.

Even fanciful projects, however, must be attempted sometimes because of what is at stake.

We hope that our book will form part of the discussion on deciding appropriate responses to the complex questions these issues raise. Importantly, we hope that it will take discussions down the path of cooperative, socially inclusive and integrative models of Muslim–non-Muslim relations, rather than the confrontational and poisonous 'clash of civilizations' (Huntington 1996) thesis which has been heard continuously ringing in the ears of legislators and policy makers in the West since the events of 9/11.

There are a number of authors who have made important theoretical and policy contributions on Muslims in the West post-9/11. There is also comparative sociological work that is revealing important and useful insights.[2] We also note a number of important works in particular subject discipline areas, especially in Islamic Family Law (Macfarlane 2012; Bowen 2010), and in particular jurisdictions (Griffith-Jones 2013). As one might expect, there is also a burgeoning literature on radicalisation, terrorism and Muslim engagement in the criminal justice system; as there is on Muslims in business and finance. So far as we can see, however, there are no works as yet which have attempted to draw all of these different strands of the debate and subject areas together and across jurisdictions. Also our work incorporates a discussion and analysis of the law itself, of case law, and how judges have purported to deal with religious questions in a secular context. This issue is important, not just because it demonstrates the capacity, or otherwise, of Common Law Courts to resolve issues where problems of litigants are rooted in understandings of Sharīʿah. It is also important for symbolic reasons, as it sends out a message to Muslims – perhaps those with more 'separatist' inclinations (see Chapter 2) – that there is no need for a system of parallel Sharīʿah courts (if they ever claimed as such; see Chapter 2).

Also, unlike the majority of these works, we also approach these legal, political, philosophical, moral and social issues from a stance of 'critical subjectivity' and experiential knowing (Heron and Reason 1997). As academic lawyers, as practising Muslims, as migrants and locals, of different genders, ethnicities and nationalities, we live and participate within multiple communities – often simultaneously. We understand intuitively the pain, exclusion and significance of racist, sexist and Islamophobic comments and behaviours – as we do the fear, confusion and uncertainties when questions of Islām and Sharīʿah are raised. We also have our preferred responses to these issues that originate in our subjective circumstances and particular interpretations of Islām. As Sunnis, and traditionalists, our 'take' on Islām may not be shared by other Muslims, particularly those from more 'liberal' or conversely 'separatist' perspectives (see further Chapter 2). Nevertheless, we would argue that our views are sufficiently 'mainstream' for policy makers to take notice and which they can ill afford to ignore.

Not only is our understanding of Islām important, but so also is our interpretation of 'law'. For many, religious law, such as 'Sharīʿah', is not 'law' so-called, but religion and applies only in the moral sphere, if at all. Discussion of the accommodation of Muslims or of Sharīʿah, then, is not a legal question but a political one, worked out by communities and their representatives in elected parliamentary or council chambers.

We view 'law' to mean a 'norm' and, like critical legal scholars, an 'expression of power'. But rather than see law necessarily as an instrument of oppression – though in many cases it may be – fundamentally, we view 'law' as 'emancipatory' – it *empowers* and protects human beings, it does not just control or seek to guide them. Law can be also both secular (with a small 's') *and* religious. The latter seeks to guide and lift an innate human instinct to aspire to that which is greater than itself and to release the human soul from its shackles of temporality. The former provides the space in which that human soul manifests its desire for release, without necessarily preferring one religion or interpretation of religion over another. Not all, of course, would share such a religious construction or approve the interrelationship between religious and secular law. We would argue, however, that this conception of law is consistent with a liberal understanding of the function of law as the mechanism to protect and promote moral and personal autonomy (Raz 1988). The point of law in a liberal democracy is to protect individual freedom and to *enable* the human being to make choices, including *religious* choices, in their conception of the 'good life'. 'Religious' law, so long as its application does not deprive others of their choices, can therefore coexist with 'secular' law and need not be in conflict; one can help serve the other.

We also see 'law' as an act of symbolism – a reflection of the norms, or values of a particular society. Our contemporary societies are heterogeneous, comprised of communities from a variety of ethnic, cultural, linguistic and religious backgrounds; and, given the flows of migrants and global refugee crisis, are likely to become even more so. If law is symbolic of our collective values, then it should reflect that heterogeneity rather than wallow in a fossilised imagination of a society's 'glorious past'. That means adapting to the values of newcomers, and recognising the values of suppressed peoples, especially minorities, past and present. This does not mean *deference to*, but rather respect and recognition of difference so that we *all* weave our threads into the fabric of law. Law must be socially inclusive and seen to be so, lest it becomes illegitimate in the eyes of those whom it seeks to govern.

'Law', then, in this conception, is necessarily pluralist. Our conception of law acknowledges the multiplicity of norms in our lives that jostle for priority and some of which will not be found in a posited 'State' Law. Indeed, we may regard such non-posited norms as more important and it would be curious if we did not call that 'law'. We may call these a 'higher law', 'natural law', 'cultural law' or 'religious law' – but those norms are still *law* because of the guiding force they play in our lives (Hooker 1975; Chiba 1989; Davies 2005; Tamanaha 2000). The issue, of course, is what happens when norms collide and how contemporary governments and courts in our liberal democratic and secular contexts should respond. And that is the topic of our book as it relates specifically to Muslims.

The methodology of our study is both comparative and contextual. As we have just sketched out, we believe the problem of 'acceptable' religious expression and how it relates to Muslims is a global issue, and not just a local one. Jurisdictions, therefore, can learn from each other, analyse the particular issues occurring in one jurisdiction and compare in the other. In so doing, we can build up, inductively, a more accurate multifaceted picture of the both the problem we confront as well as the lessons to be drawn. We can also begin the process of formulating more workable policies that address the real problem rather than the ones people commonly, and often wrongly, perceive as the problem.

While much has been written of the pitfalls of comparative analysis and the dangers of promoting legal reforms simply on the basis of successful outcomes elsewhere – the so-called legal 'transplant' (Legrand 1997; Watson 1974), this is less of a problem in our study. We are not comparing 'oranges' with 'lemons'. Epistemic problems are more likely when one compares one legal tradition with a different legal tradition, such as between the Common Law legal system and the Civil Law legal system. We cannot be sure that we are comparing like with like (though there are various techniques to try and make sure that you do). The danger is less, however, where comparisons are between jurisdictions that belong to the same so-called 'legal family' and here the family of 'Common Law' (Glenn 2010; David and Brierley 1978).

These jurisdictions share, to varying degrees, a legal tradition founded on English law: its historical concepts and orientating values; the use of juries and the separation between the tribunal of fact and of law; special procedural devices, such as writs and pleading; a special role for professional lawyers and advocates and, of course, a special place for the trial itself. There is not a single philosophy of the Common Law, other than each case is decided on its facts, and interpreted within the narrow confines of a principle elucidated from a trail of previous cases decided within a particular court hierarchy; and that where there are no clear answers, courts may also look to matters of public policy (Shepherd

2009). In their determination of 'hard cases' (Dworkin 1988), certain concepts frequently emerge, such as 'reasonableness', 'certainty' and 'fairness', but they are not necessarily peculiar to the notion of 'Common Law', but an important feature of Common Law decision-making which we elaborate upon further in our conclusion.

That is not to say that the dangers of false comparisons are not still present, especially when one considers the diversity of the Common Law legal family. It is for this reason we have not included within our comparative analysis the 'Asian' Common Law jurisdictions, such as India, Pakistan, Malaysia and Singapore, even though they have considerable Muslim populations and engage frequently with Sharīʿah matters. In one sense, they are a particular study in their own right because of their common colonial histories, struggles for development and Muslim majorities or considerable Muslim minorities.

Instead, our focus is the major 'Western' Common Law jurisdictions: Australia, Canada, the UK and the USA. Their traditions are closer, being economically and politically developed, generally English-speaking, and without the same flavour of recent anti-colonial struggle. Muslims are also, relatively speaking, a small minority in these countries, particularly in the USA (see further, Chapter 1), and are especially vulnerable to 'tyranny of the majority'. Muslims rely more on the courts than representatives in legislative assemblies in these countries to protect and defend their rights. This makes decisions of the courts, for current purposes, a very important area of study.

But 'Western' Common Law jurisdictions have important differences too. Australia, Canada and the United States have federal legal structures which distinguish between federal law and state law. The UK, on the other hand, while it has a unitary legal structure, is not *unified* as Scotland, England and Wales, and Northern Ireland have their own separate jurisdictions (and systems, in the case of Scotland). Australia, Canada and the USA all have written constitutions which all empower the judiciary to subject the legislatures to its particular terms. The UK, however, is without a written constitution and Parliament remains sovereign, meaning that the courts cannot override Parliament's legislative will. Canada and the United States have their own domestic Bills of Rights, with their particular histories, emphases and doctrines of interpretation. The UK is a party to the European Convention on Human Rights and, since the Human Rights Act of 1998, has incorporated the Convention rights into domestic law and applies the jurisprudence of the European Court of Human Rights. Australia does not even have a Bill of Rights, though it has a few limited rights in its written constitution, and two of its state legislatures, Victoria and the ACT, have drafted their own Bills of Rights that apply to their particular jurisdictions. Canada, Australia and the UK (obviously) are also part of the Commonwealth and, in addition to being constitutional monarchies, frequently refer to judicial precedents from each other's jurisdictions. The United States, on the other hand, is a republic and refers to decisions from the Commonwealth in only very rare cases.

Given these differences, any general conclusions we draw need to take into account local nuances, especially the emphases placed on the 'establishment of religion' (USA), multiculturalism (Canada) and, in the UK, the impact of European jurisprudence.

As we have mentioned, our comparative analysis is contextual and not reliant on case analysis alone. This is for a number of reasons, but primarily because judicial decisions do not operate in a vacuum; they are the product of a particular political, cultural and social environment. Also it is down to epistemic reasons, as in some subject areas there may be only one or two cases in each jurisdiction or no cases at all. We would gain little illumination discussing just one case. It should be remembered that we are also discussing the situations in jurisdictions as a whole and not simply the role of the courts, though given the relative inability of Muslims to influence legislative majorities, that role is a very important one.

Our book is called '*Accommodating* Muslims under Common Law' which clearly implies that the concept of 'accommodation' is fundamental to our thesis. Our use of this terminology, however, is not necessarily for normative purposes. Rather, it is a term that we read – and we ourselves have used (Farrar 2011; Krayem 2014) – in academic and political discussions, over the extent to which the state has and should recognise different aspects of Muslim identity and the Muslim's legal code, the Sharīʿah. Unfortunately, the connotations and implications of this term have often been left unscrutinised and deemed unproblematic.

The New Shorter Oxford English Dictionary (1993) offers the following definitions of 'accommodation': 'something which supplies a want or ministers to one's comfort'; 'room and provision for the reception of people'; 'an arrangement of a dispute; a settlement; a compromise'; 'adaptation, adjustment'; 'self-adaptation; obligingness; a favour'. We would argue that these boil down to three basic meanings: 'compromise', 'adaptation' or 'favour', which present three alternative approaches as to the role of law in the regulation of Muslims' identity and their place within the broader society. We would also argue that all three of these approaches have been applied by courts and legislatures across our jurisdictions and subject matters.

The term 'compromise' implies that there is a two-way communication process in which 'Muslims' – a complex label as we discuss in Chapters 1 and 2 – and the 'State' agree on the acceptable boundaries of religious expression, as it applies to Muslims. In that agreement, each 'side' foregoes aspects of its self-identity and expression. In the words of the former Archbishop of Canterbury, Rowan Williams, this is a *transformational* process in which

> we are prepared to think about the basic ground rules that might organise the relationship between jurisdictions, making sure that we do not collude with unexamined systems that have oppressive effect or allow shared public liberties to be decisively taken away.
>
> (Williams 2008a)

For Muslims, perhaps, this might mean sacrificing the practice of some elements *optional* to their religious worship as opposed to those that are *obligatory* (see further, Chapter 2). For the State, it means it sacrifices its neutrality, and provides the means for those obligations to be performed and removes obstacles that affect their performance, by providing exemptions or opt-outs, for example.[3] From an Islamic perspective, the problem, as we discuss in Chapter 2, apart from very clear matters mentioned explicitly in the Qur'ān and the Prophetic Sunnah and where Islām's top scholars have managed to agree, there exist competing interpretations, including whether a matter is optional or obligatory. The problem is that it then offers to a court, for instance, a choice as to competing interpretations and who is the Common Law Court, a secular construct, to prefer one interpretation over another? Moreover, if it does prefer one interpretation, is it not *colonising* the 'other', denying the Muslim the opportunity to self-identify? This is a reoccurring theme that emerges in particular from our discussion of family and business law in Chapters 3 and 5.

The second term 'adaptation', simply means 'change' but contrary to the first meaning, that change is unilateral on behalf of the state. It does not require anything of the Muslim community. Yet, it remains transformational of the state as it incorporates those aspects of Islām and Sharī'ah it deems compatible. The problem here, as with the first, is that the state offers a preferred view of Islām but it says nothing about the criteria through which this is done.

The third term 'favour' implies that it is the state which is doing all the adapting and is not obliged to recognise religion or a religious community, such as Muslims. Rather, it offers its patronage and, in *quasi*-regal terms, dispenses privileges rather than rights. This then no longer becomes part of a discourse of equality – or even of citizenship – with the position of religion, and of Muslims, subject to the whims and caprice of government. On the one hand, this has some advantages for Muslims as they can remain as they are without needing to adapt to the society around them. On the other hand, their status is rendered fragile and subject to the political mood. In symbolic terms, this concept is also negative for it reinforces a sense of 'otherness' rather than a sense of belonging.

The implications of accommodation as 'favour' are evident across our chapters, but particularly in the 'Sharī'ah debates' in Chapter 2 and the discussion of Muslims in crime in Chapter 4. In Chapter 2, the legal recognition of Muslims and of Sharī'ah is presented as asking for *special treatment*, although like Jurayj, what they actually want is the freedom to do what is legally available for them (and all other citizens) to do – no more, no less. In Chapter 4, accommodation as 'favour' manifests in two respects. First, in the securitisation of Muslims, the freedoms of Muslims are deemed to be only a privilege, rather than a right, so they can be restricted or taken away completely. Second, in the application of the Criminal Law, reference to Muslim identity and Sharī'ah is constructed as an 'excuse' which, in an increasingly uncompromising environment, governments, legislatures, judges and juries are less willing to afford them. The Criminal Law protects the public square and lays down foundational values. As such, people asking for 'excuses' on the grounds of who they are, is deemed divisive, a threat to the unitary state and too fundamental a challenge to what is 'common' in the law.

The challenge of 'accommodation', for the state, in all three senses of this word, is that it jeopardises the secularity and neutrality of the liberal state. By acknowledging Islām, and particularly preferred interpretations of it, the state is no longer the impartial provider and governor. In the spirit of that liberal tradition, therefore, we might expect the Common Law Courts across all of our jurisdictions to maintain a strict detachment from religion and religious interpretation. They will not accommodate Sharīʿah because the law is the 'law' and it is up to Muslims to ensure they come within it. There is no negotiation or agreement, but it does not mean the law is thereby *imposed* on Muslims. Rather, they *navigate* their way around legal obstacles and reinterpret or plough more deeply into their tradition, where appropriate, to ensure that it 'fits' with the current legal and constitutional framework.

Again, we see evidence of this process in our discussion of family and business law in Chapters 3 and 5. The problem with this approach, however, is that it assumes the state is neutral and secular. But as Roger Trigg informs: 'Secularism is never neutral, but always takes a view about the proper place of religion' (Trigg 2012a: 5). Moreover, the state does not operate in an historical vacuum as it has already provided religious exemptions and opt-outs for historically assimilated religious groups. A 'neutral' approach also assumes Muslims will have the financial and intellectual capital to be able and afford the lawyers to craft their own 'carve outs' and navigate the system. As our discussion in Chapter 1 will show, however, Muslims, generally speaking, are amongst the most marginalised and impoverished communities and, therefore, are at a great disadvantage in comparison with others. A neutral approach is more likely to reinforce the unequal status quo.

If we revisit our conception and function of law, as well as our immediate objects, it becomes readily apparent that the concept of 'accommodation', because of its contextual and varied connotations, is possibly not up to the task. If we want to address religious excess and extremism, it is unlikely to succeed unless Muslims are motivated to believe that they are an integral part of the society they live in. Our working concept needs to promote their personal and moral autonomy – their freedom – whereas accommodation has a predilection to dictate, neglect or control. We suggest 'recognition', the active *incorporation of norms* (Woodman 2001: 2), is more appropriate as it reflects and respects human dignity, which is said to underpin the Universal Declaration on Human Rights, as it is based on a mutual 'knowing'. As Muslims, it also happens to reflect a Qur'ānic mandate: '"O" people! You have been created as male and female, and made into nations and tribes that you may *know* each other.' (Qur'ān, 49:13)

The overall argument we advance in this book has both descriptive and normative aspects. First, we argue that Sharīʿah and Common Law are *not* inherently incompatible with each other. They are both 'law' in the sense they represent and communicate a set of 'norms' that operate at both an individual and a community level. Both are 'open-textured' and subject to interpretation which enables boundaries or ground rules to be worked out to the mutual satisfaction relevant communities. We address this argument in our foundational Chapters – 1 and 2.

Second, when we move to actual recognition in the courts, we will argue that there is much evidence of compatibility. The pattern, however, is inconsistent reflecting the complexity and varied connotations of 'accommodation'. In part, this reflects also the nature of the subject matter and the contexts in which the cases arise, as it does the individualistic nature of Common Law decision-making. It further reflects the values of the time in a context of securitisation. This argument is traced through our substantive chapters on family (Chapter 3), crime (Chapter 4) and business (Chapter 5).

In the conclusion, we address normative considerations and questions of policy. We will suggest that 'accommodation' is not enough and that, as liberal democratic societies, we should move towards a notion of 'recognition'. Not all forms of religious or Islamist identity, of course, should be recognised. But like many other behaviours with which the Common Law deals, we argue that it should be filtered by judge or jury through determinations of 'reasonableness'.

Notes

1 There are different narrations of this *Ḥadīth*. See Al-Bukhārī, *Al-Ṣaḥīḥ*, Ḥadīth No. 3436, Kitāb Aḥādīth Al-Anbiyā', in Ibn Ḥajr Al-'Asqalānī (1986), *Fatḥ Al-Bārī*, Vol. 6, Dār al-Diyān Lil-Turāth, Cairo, at 549; Al-Bayhaqi, *Kitāb Al-Adab*, Vol. 1, at 309.

2 See Jocelyn Cesari, *Why the West Fears Islam: An Exploration of Muslims in Liberal Democracies* (New York: Palgrave Macmillan, 2013); Dagistanli, S., Possamai, A., Turner, B.S. and Voyce, M., *Sharia in Australia and US.* ARC Discovery Project 2013–2016.

3 This would be similar to the tests that have been applied to 'manifestation of religion' under Article 9(1) of the European Convention of Human Rights. Here, the European Court has drawn a distinction between acts of worship or devotion that are 'aspects' of a particular religion or belief, from those which are merely 'motivated by it'. See further, *X* v. *United Kingdom* [1984] 6 EHHR 558; *Arrowsmith* v. *UK* [1978] 3 EHHR 218; and *Williamson and Others* v. *The Secretary of State for Education and Employment* [2002] EWCA Civ 1926. See also, the discussion by Robin Griffith-Jones, in *Islam and English Law* (2013), pp. 9–19.

1 Muslim communities in a multicultural context

> There is a growing understanding that the incorporation of Muslims has become the most important challenge of egalitarian multiculturalism.
>
> Tariq Modood (2009: 166)

Introduction

Muslim communities have been at the forefront of recent debates about multiculturalism, so much so that it may be argued that the future success of multiculturalism will depend upon how it deals with the 'Muslim' issue. This refers to the presence of Muslim communities in secular Western liberal democracies, such as those considered in this book: the USA, UK, Canada and Australia. More particularly, it refers to their 'accommodation' and the understanding of accommodation that Muslims deserve 'favour' or 'special treatment'. For some, Islām is inherently incompatible with the West and any accommodation that attempts to afford special treatment to Muslims will necessarily be socially divisive. However, it is the argument of this book that research indicates the exact opposite. Muslim communities are seeking out ways to integrate more with mainstream society, including with the legal system.

We will begin the chapter by exploring the issue of multicultural accommodation and the challenges faced by states who attempt to respond to the needs of its diverse cultural and religious groups. We will question the assumption often made about the neutrality of a secular state and consider the different types of approaches to secularism that a state can adopt. We argue that contrary to the often-held view that multicultural policies divide and destabilise society, these policies can lead in fact to greater social cohesion and transform both the mainstream and the minority communities.

We often speak about Muslim communities as if they are an homogenous group or one community, identical in nature and speaking with one voice. So when one person or group acts or speaks, to say that Sharīʿah, for example, should be recognised officially, then it is assumed that this is what the entire community desires. Whilst it may be tempting to talk about 'the' or 'a' Muslim community, to assert a singular and cohesive Muslim 'community' would be not only a distortion but also inaccurate. This is especially true of Muslims in the minority context because of a multiplicity of Muslim ethnicities arising from their patterns of immigration. This chapter, therefore, will attempt to provide insights on the various Muslim communities in the UK, USA, Canada and Australia in terms of their size, ethnic and cultural make-up, immigration patterns, age, location, education and workforce participation. Although there are similarities, each jurisdiction has its own particular ethnic make-up and social environment that might impact on the role Sharīʿah plays. This is critical because in order to explore more deeply the potential role of Sharīʿah and the need for governments to consider how or whether they should recognise certain of its aspects, we need to understand more about the Muslim communities themselves in each of our particular jurisdictions.

Finally, the chapter considers the broader context of these communities, looking at the impact of the 'War on Terror' and the subsequent rise in *Islamophobia*. In all four countries, Muslims have reported negative sentiments and attacks against them simply because of their faith. This is not just in the form of random attacks on Muslims but also in the tenor of the general public discourse with politicians and the media contributing to a poisonous environment leaving Muslim communities feeling they are under siege. These sentiments also affect any discussion about the 'accommodation' of Muslims and pose one of the great challenges for the future of multiculturalism.

Muslim communities in a multicultural context

Each of the four countries discussed in this book can be described as a multicultural state because of the great diversity of their populations. Canada prides itself as the first country to adopt multiculturalism as official policy. It is home to people from over 200 different ethnic origins and speaking more than 200 different languages (Government of Canada 2015). Australia also has a population that comes from 200 different birthplaces and speaks over 200 different languages, making it one of the most culturally and linguistically diverse places in the world (Racismnoway n.d.). There is no doubt that both the USA and the UK are similarly multicultural in terms of their demographic make-up.

However, there are many challenges that come with being part of a multicultural state, not least of which is the challenge faced by the state when dealing with calls for accommodation or recognition of the diverse practices of the various groups that come within it. As we will discuss in Chapter 2, the recognition of Sharīʿah has been one such challenge. However, the presence of these Muslim communities raises more issues than simply accommodating Sharīʿah. It also relates to their status as a minority group within a multicultural state, as we shall now explore in more detail.

Multicultural citizenship

Accommodating the practices, laws and principles of minority groups is a challenge for any state. Historically, the response of states to such a task was to place the obligation on minority groups to assimilate into the majority culture and society. This meant abandoning any different practices they may have had. However, as demonstrated in this book, this has not in fact occurred. Rather, states have had to deal with the demands made by minority groups for recognition and accommodation of their cultural and religious identity (Baumeister 2003: 396).

Many have long articulated a basis for minority rights to be recognised to supplement traditional human rights in liberal societies (Kymlicka 1996: 6). They argue that the state actually privileges the majority and makes decisions that reflect their norms, thereby questioning the assumed neutrality of the state (Kymlicka 1996: 51). The classical nation state, Koenig argues, is 'considerably less secular and certainly less neutral than is often assumed' (Koenig 2005: 232). This is because the practices of the minority are seen as different (Baumeister 2003: 397) and perceived as 'other', (Addis 1991–92: 619), whereas the dominant cultural understanding and experiences tend to universalise themselves as the 'inevitable norm for social life' (Addis 1991–92: 619).

One of the main arguments against adopting multicultural policies in liberal democratic states is that it is inconsistent with liberalism's focus on the individual. Whilst it is true that there is an emphasis on the individual within liberalism, the individual is not valued at the expense of a shared community (Kymlicka 1989: 2). Part and parcel of individualism is the freedom to make choices, and cultural membership allows individuals to make sense of their lives, not only by providing these choices but also by making them meaningful. Kymlicka contends '(c)ultures are valuable, not in and of themselves, but because it is only through having access to a societal culture that people have access to a range of meaningful options' (Kymlicka 1996: 83). However, members of minority cultural communities may face disadvantage with respect to the 'good of cultural membership' because their culture is not recognised or accommodated in the same way as is the majority culture. It is the rectification of such disadvantage that requires and justifies the provision of minority rights, and obligates a state to take into account and accommodate the various cultural communities that reside within it (Kymlicka 1989: 2). This is certainly how many Muslims feel in the countries that we have considered throughout this book and as later chapters will demonstrate.

Therefore historically, migrant groups were expected to assimilate – in the sense that they were to conform to the existing cultural and political norms – it was hoped that over time 'they would be indistinguishable from native-born citizens' in their way of life. If a group was perceived incapable of assimilation, they were excluded from entering the country (Kymlicka 2007b: 71). However, by the 1970s things started to change as countries such as the USA, Canada and Australia adopted more tolerant approaches, acknowledging the differences of the many different groups that had become part of the state. This policy or approach is often referred to as 'multiculturalism' and it encompasses a broad range of policies that aim to provide 'some level of public recognition, support or accommodation to non-dominant ethnocultural groups' (Kymlicka 2007b:

71). To varying degrees, each of the Common Law countries have grappled with the implications of adopting multicultural policies.

Can such policies lead to civil instability?

There is an increasing fear that multiculturalism 'produces separateness and is counterproductive to social cohesion' (Vertovec and Wessendorf 2005: 21). In particular, the criticism is that liberal multiculturalism fragments society, undermines its stability and ultimately erodes our ability to act collectively as citizens (Kymlicka 1998: 15). The argument is that recognition and accommodation of diversity means that cultural groups will remain as separate entities without developing any common bonds between them (Kymlicka 1998: 15). Kymlicka disagrees, arguing that 'there is no inherent trade-off between diversity policies and shared citizenship policies' (Kymlicka 2007a: 39) because the aim should not be to achieve a 'standard homogenizing model of citizenship'.

No doubt, there still are important policies designed to promote overarching national identities and loyalties, such as official languages, core curricula in schools, citizenship requirements and state symbols, just to name a few (Kymlicka 2007b: 83–84). However, we would argue that liberal democracies should adopt multicultural policies to transform and supplement such nation-building policies so that they do not exclude minority groups (Kymlicka 2007b: 83).[1] This is a central argument that will be explored throughout the book, as it is argued that attempts at seeking some form of official recognition or accommodation of Muslims are attempts to try to fit into the mainstream legal structure and framework, rather than an attempt to set up a separate parallel system. This is evident in our later chapters which consider the ways in which Muslims are doing this in the areas of Family Law, Criminal Law and business transactions.

In fact, it is our argument that accommodation promotes integration into the larger society and not self-government by different groups (Kymlicka 1996: 31). In demanding greater recognition or accommodation, these groups aim to modify the institutions and laws of the mainstream society to make them more accommodating of difference (Kymlicka 2007b: 11). By creating a pluralistic public space, civil society is strengthened (Fielding 2008: 31). It allows minority groups to more actively participate in civil society and reciprocate the tolerance shown towards them (Fielding 2008: 50). If minority groups are alienated, then they are more likely to 'withdraw into their ghettoized communities' (Fielding 2008: 45–46). As will be discussed in Chapter 2, this potential alienation can lead to an increase in Muslim groups adopting separatist approaches and not engaging with the broader community.

We agree with Kymlicka that successful accommodation, in the form of recognition and as a process of mutual knowing, is transformative of both the mainstream society and the minority group. It is a two-way process that requires the mainstream society to adapt itself to minority groups, just as those groups must adapt to the mainstream (Kymlicka 1996: 96). In this way, it is accepted that culture is not static but adaptive and that cultural hybridism is the normal state of affairs (Kymlicka 1996: 101). It is important to remember that such policies are not about entrenching or preserving a particular culture, rather they are supporting the institutions that are 'of importance for those cultures to be sustained and to develop naturally' (Beck 2004: 6). In the context of the argument in this book, this is a critical point. For as difficult as the question of religious accommodation of Sharīʿah may seem for our Common Law countries, we will demonstrate that recognition can assist in the integration of Muslims into official institutions and legal processes. Indeed, the empirical research conducted by Modood in the UK lends support to such an argument. He finds that 'hybrid identities' in Britain are part of a movement of inclusion and social cohesion, not fragmentation (Modood 2007: 185). Studies across Europe have shown that the institutional recognition of minorities has had a positive impact on processes of integration (Vertovec and Wessendorf 2005: 26). It is argued that without such inclusion and accommodation, such minority groups might leave these public institutions and set up their own, leading to further isolation and marginalisation (Kymlicka 1998: 45).

Where does religion fit in?

The discussion so far has focused mainly on migrant cultural groups and multiculturalism, but the question is whether it applies equally to religious groups within diverse states. While it is true that religious groups can concurrently be migrant groups, the Muslims groups can also include quite established communities made up of citizens born in the state.

In their treatment of established Muslim communities, multicultural theorists have tended to focus on particular cultural or ethnic identities, such as Pakistani Mirpuris in the UK city of Bradford or Yemenis in the UK's second city of Birmingham. They have routinely ignored the religious dimensions of these identities (Koenig 2005: 220). They have worked instead on the assumption the State must remain neutral and that can only be maintained through a 'secular' approach to multiculturalism. The problem, however, is that this does not take into account the historical bias and religious inflection of Christian and Jewish traditions already embedded in the laws and state practices over generations. The notion that the state is neutral is a misnomer (Parekh 2006: 189). Continuing to ignore religion and the religious aspects of a Muslim's identity in the formulation and delivery of multicultural policies, therefore, runs the risk of (unintentionally) discriminating against Muslims. As Modood notes, 'in a society where some of the disadvantaged and marginalised minorities are religious minorities, a public policy of multiculturalism will require the public recognition of religious minorities' (Modood 2007: 187).

However, before public policies and debates can take into account the particular needs of religious minorities, there needs to be an understanding of the importance of religion in the life of the individual. This requires a rebuttal of the prevailing view that sees religion as being in conflict with liberalism and a clarification of secularism as an integral element. As we intimated in the

Introduction, secularism does not necessarily imply a 'religion free' public space. While such 'hard' secularism is the favoured interpretation in the laic democracies of continental Europe,[2] the English-speaking Common Law democracies examined in this book traditionally have felt more comfortable with the articulation of religious expression in the public domain. Rather, they prefer a 'soft' or 'thin' secularism in which no religious grouping is favoured over another.[3] 'Neutrality', in this perspective, therefore, entails a more nuanced and subtle examination of the State treatment of minorities and of the ways in which State rules, laws and practices may have differential impact upon cultural groups because of their religious practices. Recognising religious particularity does not negate the essential tenets of multiculturalism. On the contrary, it gives a revitalised meaning and relevance to the lives of those groups for whom religion is an essential defining feature.

A retreat from multiculturalism: a backlash against Muslims

More recently, there has been strong criticism of multiculturalism. Even world leaders such as Angela Merkel and David Cameron have made comments about the failure of state multiculturalism (Helm *et al.* 2011). This has led many to believe that multiculturalism is in retreat. Such comments have been largely directed towards Muslims, with many people questioning whether Muslims can fit in to a liberal democratic framework (Kymlicka 2007b: 124). Despite this, Kymlicka maintains that there has been 'a baseline level of recognition and accommodation for immigrants ... as an inevitable and legitimate aspect of life in a liberal democracy' (Kymlicka 2007b: 128). The question remains, however, why there is a growing perception that the needs and demands of Muslim communities cannot fit into a liberal democratic framework. Modood writes, 'Muslims have become central to the merits and demerits of multiculturalism as a public policy' (Modood 2007: 4). This is interesting given statistically, Muslims make up a very small part of the population.

The reasons for such a backlash are many and varied but an important factor is the perceived threat that 'locally settled Muslims might collaborate with external enemies of the West' (Kymlicka 2007b: 125), thus posing a security threat to the state. This, in turn, is fuelled by the West's anxiety about 'the other', where diversity is something to be feared, not admired. Islām is conceived as the other 'culture' or civilisation most at odds with and therefore the most threatening to society (Vertovec and Wessendorf 2005: 14).[4]

For others, multiculturalism is seen as giving preferential treatment to Muslim communities. According to Joppke, multicultural policies are all about the State accommodating Muslim groups with very little expected by these groups in return (Joppke 2004). He argues that the retreat from multiculturalism is because of the unilateral direction of multicultural recognition and that: 'Muslims are to be given their public law exemptions, but they are not asked to give anything in return' (Joppke 2004). We would argue that there is no evidence of Muslims having been given a special licence. In fact, the research suggests the contrary

(Macfarlane 2012; Krayem 2014) and that Muslims are seeking accommodation within the official system by integrating their processes and beliefs without asking for any exemption.

It is such views that have led many to believe that Muslim groups are incapable of integrating. Thus Sartori asks: 'Am I mistaken, in maintaining that the Muslim immigrant is, for us, the most distant, the most foreign and thus the most difficult to integrate?' (Vertovec and Wessendorf 2005: 12). Parekh contends that Muslims actually pose no major problem to multicultural accommodation as they ask for ways to be accommodated within the existing structure (Parekh 2006: 190). As the rest of this book will demonstrate, Muslims want to live in accordance with both their religion and the laws of the state. This is strongly supported by recent research that found 'high levels of religiosity were positively associated with stronger national belonging and a sense of Muslim integration' (Dunn *et al.* 2015: 4).

Central to understanding questions of accommodation is the need to understand the Muslim communities themselves. The next part of the chapter will consider the basic demographics of the Muslim communities in each of the countries examined in this book.

Muslim communities in Common Law countries

Size and composition

Muslim communities in each of the jurisdictions make up a very small percentage of the total population. They make up 0.9 per cent of the total population in the USA, 5 per cent of the British population, 3.2 per cent of the Canadian population and 2.2 per cent of the Australian population.[5] Whilst these numbers are set to increase in the future, they should still remain relatively small. For example by 2030 in the USA, the Muslim population is projected to rise to 1.7 per cent, in the UK to 8 per cent and in Canada to 6.6 per cent (Pew Research Center Forum on Religion and Public Life 2011: 158). This projected increase is believed to be driven principally by immigration but also by present-day high birth rates among Muslim communities (Pew Research Center Forum on Religion and Public Life 2011: 15).

In terms of Muslim demography, they vary based mostly on historic migration patterns and immigration policies during the mid-twentieth and early twenty-first centuries. Among the four countries considered, the Muslim-American community is unique in that it comprises two major groups: the African-American and the immigrant Muslim communities. Approximately 37 per cent of the Muslim community is born in the USA (Pew Research Center 2011). Their racial, cultural, socio-economic and historical circumstances differ widely (Halim 2006: 243). The immigrant Muslim community comes from over seventy-seven different countries. In fact, the Muslim-American population is the most racially diverse religious group in the country with African-Americans making up the largest contingent at 35 per cent. White Muslim-Americans constitute some 28 per cent of the population, with Asians next at 18 per cent, Hispanics 1 per cent and 'other' at 18 per cent, with the majority of these being first-generation migrants (65 per cent) (Younis 2009). More than one-third of the foreign-born population come from Arabic-speaking countries in the Middle East and North Africa. The second largest group are from South Asia, including Pakistan, India, Bangladesh and Afghanistan (Pew Research Center 2007).[6]

In the UK, the presence of British Muslims has been noted in sixteenth- and seventeenth-century literature but it was not until the middle of the last century, following the collapse of the British Empire, that large numbers of Muslim migrants began to arrive in Britain, with many of these from South Asia, especially Pakistan and India. The number of Muslims born in the UK almost doubled between 2001 and 2011, with 47 per cent of Muslims born in the UK (Office for National Statistics 2013: 1). Muslims in the UK are also ethnically diverse with two-thirds of Muslims (68 per cent) coming from an Asian background. Muslims identifying as Bangladeshi account for 15 per cent of the Muslim population, while some 10 per cent are reported as being Black/African/Caribbean/Black British (Office for National Statistics 2013: 8–12).

In Canada and Australia, Muslim migration only really began in the 1960s and 1970s, although there is a history of Afghan migration to Australia in the nineteenth century when the 'Cameleers' helped in both exploration and later transportation in Australia's arid interior (Jones 1993: 87–104). Australia has a high migrant population and is one of the world's most culturally and linguistically diverse countries. Although the majority of migrants to Australia still come from the UK, the 2011 Census reported that the total number of number of Australian Muslims was 476,000, or 2.2 per cent of the total population with the majority, 61.5 per cent, born overseas (Hassan 2015: 17). The most frequently cited country of birth for Australian Muslims is Australia, with 38 per cent of Australian Muslims born in Australia. In terms of ancestry, 42 per cent of the Muslim community claim to be of Lebanese origin, 28 per cent claim Turkish ancestry and a growing number claim African ancestry, including 5 per cent Somali (Krayem 2014: 58). There are approximately 1,000 Indigenous Muslims in Australia (Department of Immigration and Citizenship 2009: 77).

In Canada, there has been a rapid increase in migration of foreign-born Muslims from a population of 1,000 in 1961 to just over a million at the last census in 2011 (Pew Research Center Forum on Religion and Public Life 2011: 137). Twenty-eight per cent of the Muslim population is born in Canada and, like the other countries, Canadian Muslims come from over sixty different ethnic groups with South Asians being the largest group at 36 per cent followed by Arabs at 25 per cent (Hamdani 2015).

Age

Muslim communities are young communities in the sense that in all four countries Muslims are younger than the national average. In Canada, the average age for Muslims is twenty-eight years compared to thirty-seven years for the general population. Nearly one third of these (34.9 per cent) are aged between 25–44 compared with 30.5 per cent of non-Muslims (Pew Research Center Forum on Religion and Public Life 2011: 137). In America, Muslims are also quite young in comparison to the national average with 30 per cent of Muslim Americans falling in the 18–29 age bracket, compared with 21 per cent of the general public (Euro-Islam.info n.d.).

A similar picture emerges in the UK where Muslims are young compared with other religions with nearly 50 per cent of Muslims in the 0–49 age group. Of these, 48 per cent are under twenty-five. Younger people are more likely than older people to identify as Muslim. Eight per cent of people aged under twenty-five identified as Muslim in 2011 compared to 5 per cent in 2001 (Office for National Statistics 2013: 1). Also 33 per cent of the Muslim population was under fifteen years of age compared with 19 per cent of the non-Muslim population (Muslim Council of Britain Research & Documentation Committee 2015). Muslim Australians are also significantly younger than the average Australian population, with almost 40 per cent under the age of twenty compared with 27 per cent of non-Muslims (Hassan 2009: 5). These figures indicate that in all countries Muslims are younger than the national averages and are concentrated in the more economically productive years of the lifecycle.

Where do Muslims live?

In general, the majority of Muslims in all four countries live in large urban settings. In America, Muslims have settled in all American cities and across the country. The majority of Muslims live in New York, Los Angeles, Chicago and Detroit/Dearborn (Pew Research Center 2007).[7] Similarly, the majority of Canadian Muslims live in large urban settings with a large number living in the Greater Toronto area (in the province of Ontario), constituting some 7.7 per cent of the total urban population.

Also in the UK, there is a concentration of Muslims in a number of urban areas and major cities with 76 per cent of the Muslim population living in four regions – London, West Midlands, the North West and Yorkshire and The Humbar (Muslim Council of Britain Research & Documentation Committee 2015). London has the highest proportion of Muslims at 12.4 per cent for all age groups and this population is more ethnically diverse than in other areas (Office for National Statistics 2012).

In Australia, the Muslim community is also heavily concentrated in urban areas with the majority concentrated in Sydney and Melbourne. Sydney has a Muslim population of 3.9 per cent and Melbourne has a Muslim population of 2.9 per cent. Together, these two cities constituted 78 per cent of the total population of Muslims in Australia (Hassan 2015: 20–22).

Participation in the workforce/economy

Apart from America, there is a trend across our countries for Muslims to have a higher rate of unemployment than the national average, although there is also evidence of higher rates of self-employment and engagement in small businesses. Furthermore, income levels are also generally lower for Muslims than the national average.

For instance, in relation to employment and compared to the general population, only 41 per cent of Muslim Americans are employed full-time, although the rate of self-employment and small business owners (24 per cent) is higher than the rate for the general population (21 per cent) (Younis 2009).[8] As for income, the Muslim-American family's annual income is similar to the American general public, at less than $30,000 (35 per cent) or between $30,000 and $49,999 (24 per cent) (Euro-Islam.info n.d.).

In contrast, Canadian Muslims are the most disadvantaged economically. They occupy the lowest income bracket (earning $30,000 or less annually) and earn less than other religious groups (Beyer 2005: 185). In regards to employment, Canadian Muslims have a higher rate of unemployment, at 13.9 per cent, than the national average which stands at 7.8 per cent. Muslim Canadians have the highest rates of unemployment than any other faith group in Canada (Hamdani 2015).

In the UK, the 2011 census noted that 55 per cent of Muslims had the lowest levels of economic activity among all religious groups (although the reasons given were that they were mainly students [30 per cent], or because they were looking after the home or family [31 per cent]) (Office for National Statistics 2013: 12). It is worth noting that the unemployment rate for Muslims at 7.2 per cent is nearly double the rate of the rest of the population (Hamdani 2015: 58).[9]

Across all age groups, employment rates for Australian Muslims were lower and the unemployment rates significantly higher than those of non-Muslim Australians. Muslim teenagers' unemployment rate was 26 per cent compared with 14 per cent for non-Muslim Australians (Hassan 2009: 9–10). While Muslim Australians are more likely than non-Muslim Australians to have a university degree, they are significantly under-represented in the high-paying and more prestigious professional and managerial occupations. On the other hand, they are over-represented among labourers and in the skilled blue-collar occupations (Hassan 2009: 10).

Education

In terms of education, Muslim Americans compared well with the general American population. For instance, 32 per cent of Muslim Americans had a high school diploma compared with 30 per cent of the general population and 14 per cent versus 16 per cent had graduated from college. There was a slightly higher average of graduate study completion with 10 per cent of Muslims compared to 9 per cent of the general population completing graduate study (Pew Research

Center 2007).[10] The Muslim Americans survey by Gallop also reported that among the female religious groups in the United States, Muslim American women are one of the most highly educated, second only to Jewish American women (Younis 2009). In terms of religious education, there are approximately 150 Islamic Schools, all registered with the Islamic Foundation of North America. This organisation provides curriculum and religious education resources for the study of Islām, Arabic and Muslim-themed literature (Euro-Islam.info n.d.). There are three Islamic religious education options available for Muslim students in full-time parochial schools, providing weekend or evening classes that supplement a secular education programme, or home schooling. The estimated 1,500 mosques in America run education programmes for the children and young adults in their communities. In general, these programmes are offered on the weekend or in the evening and there are many summer schools and camps offered as well which are attended by the community. At the postgraduate level, there are now several institutions offering courses in Islamic Studies (Euro-Islam.info n.d.).

In the UK, the Mayor of London Report noted that in London, Muslims aged 16–24 have lower qualification levels compared with their peers in the general population (Dawn 2006). Whilst 25 per cent of the Muslim population have a tertiary qualification which is only slightly lower than the national average, Muslim communities lag behind other faith groups in other areas of education (Hamdani 2015: 60–61). The vast majority of Muslim youth attend community or non-faith based schools, but there are an estimated 111 Muslim schools in Britain, catering for about 14,000 students. These range from small schools in private homes and mosques to expensive and substantial schools educating over 2,000 children (Tan 2011: 62). A sizeable number of Muslims also attend church schools (Ipgrave 2010: 6). The education of Muslim children in the UK is characterised by underachievement and social inequality (Ipgrave 2010: 9). Evidence indicates that they are suffering academically, culturally and linguistically. A high proportion of Muslim schoolchildren leave British schools with low grades or no qualification. The studies note, however, that Muslim students appear to perform better in schools with larger populations of Muslim pupils even when these are poorly resourced (Shah 2014).

In Canada, the Canadian Muslim population is well-educated, with 45 per cent of Muslims having a university degree compared to a national average of 33 per cent (Environics Research Group n.d.: 64). Among religious groups, Muslims figure second after Christians with 68 per cent having post-secondary education and only 4 per cent with less than eight years' education (Beyer 2005: 185). Muslim men have only marginally higher levels of post-secondary educational achievement (81.5 per cent) than women (81 per cent) (Beyer 2005: 190). A report by the Canadian Council of Women showed that in 2011, among Canadian Muslim girls and women fifteen years of age and older, 56.7 per cent had gone on to higher education, including diplomas and degrees (Hamdani 2014).

In Australia, as in Canada, the vast majority of Muslim youth are enrolled in public schools, although some attend other faith-based schools. In recent years,

Islamic education has become the fastest growing sector among independent schools (Morris 2007). More Australian Muslim men and women complete high school, and a significantly higher proportion of Muslim men have a university degree compared with their non-Muslim compatriots. The 2011 ABS data confirms that a higher proportion of Muslim males have a postgraduate degree (17.9 per cent) than all Australian males (13.9 per cent) (Hassan 2009: 6; Hassan 2015: 50). The 2011 Census also revealed that Australian Muslim women actively pursue higher education with comparable rates to the national average (Hassan 2015: 50). Research shows that Muslims are optimistic about economic and social potential educational advancement in Australia, and are especially active in seeking education and economic opportunities (Centre for Muslim Minorities and Islam Policy Studies 2009: 28).

In summary, since the 1960s, there has been rapid growth in Muslim migration (largely from South Asia and the Middle East, though with increasing numbers from African countries in recent years) and a subsequent increase in the Muslim population across our four countries. Muslim populations are expected to rise further, principally due to high birth rates (especially in Canada and Britain). In demographic terms, the Muslims in three of our countries have predominantly immigrant backgrounds. The United States is unique in this regard, with a significant population of African-American converts in addition to the immigrant Muslim community. Muslims in all countries tend to live in large urban areas and capital cities. They are younger than the national average and are better educated, with the exception of the Muslims living in London. Apart from in America, Muslims in all countries have a high rate of unemployment and in all countries there is a trend to be self-employed above the national average.

We would suggest the above facts indicate a strong economic and social case for governments in each of our countries to better recognise Muslims as a group. While still relatively small in overall population terms in each of our countries, the numbers are still significant, especially given the youth and concentration of Muslims in urban centres. The higher rates of unemployment and lower rates of home ownership also indicate a degree of marginalisation and social exclusion that warrants concern. While higher levels of education appear to buck these trends, this could be a double-edged sword given that education does not appear to lead to greater shares of the economic pie.

It is obvious that these communities do not exist in a vacuum, and are seriously affected by the political and international discourse. This often places Muslims in the spotlight and affects their ability to integrate into mainstream societies. One of the most significant current issues has been the rise of Islamophobia. We will now turn to consider this issue and its impact on Muslim communities.

The rise of Islamophobia and its impact on Muslim communities

There is increasing evidence that Muslims suffer discrimination on grounds of their association with Islām or as a result of *Islamophobia*: 'an exaggerated fear, hatred, and hostility toward Islām and Muslims ... perpetuated by negative stereotypes resulting in bias, discrimination, and the marginalization and exclusion of Muslims from social, political, and civic life' (Wajahat *et al.* 2011).

Islamophobia has its historical roots in the early Muslim migration to Europe in the fourteenth century when a mostly Christian population demonstrated hostility towards Islām. It also developed momentum in the colonial encounters, well described in Edward Said's analysis of Orientalism (Said 1978). In modern times, prejudice against Muslims in Western countries has become a feature of life post-9/11, but there is no doubt that these sentiments existed well before those attacks in the United States and our other three countries.

Following the 9/11 attacks and the subsequent War on Terror (WOT) initiated by the USA and endorsed by the UK, Australia and Canada, terrorist attacks have accelerated exponentially over the past two decades and directly affected attitudes in our four countries. The Bali bombings and London Underground attacks in 2005, the Boston Marathon bombings and the decapitation of Drummer Lee Rigby in London 2013, and the assault on Parliament Hill, Ottawa, 2014, and the emergence of Dā'ish, the so-called Islamic State, have all generated a climate of fear in our countries. In 2015, the situation was exacerbated with the Charlie Hebdo and Paris attacks and, in December 2015, the terrorist killings in San Bernardino, California. For understandable reasons, concerned citizens of Australia, Canada, the UK and USA worry about this extremist Islamism and if all Muslims might be potential terrorists.[11] As we will argue in the next chapter, these versions of Islām are far from the mainstream. Yet, it is largely the actions and words of such extremist groups that occupy the airwaves and public discourse. This makes the case for legal recognition of Sharī'ah and of Muslim identity an even more difficult case to make.

Scott Poynting and Barbara Perry argue that as a result of these attacks:

> ethnic minorities associated with Islam in most Western countries have experienced increased negative attention from the media, police and security forces, and indeed from agitated citizenry. There has been a concomitant increase in anti-Muslim or 'Islamophobic' hate crime, racial vilification and discrimination.
>
> (Poynting and Perry 2007)

In all four countries, there has been an increase in security-related expenditure and security legislation in response to the events of 9/11 and the more recent Islamist terrorist events in each country. While there have been some community programmes, such as the National Action Plan in Australia and other similar programmes in the UK, in general, countries have spent considerably more financial resources on security measures than on building community harmony. For example, the prominent Australian Muslim community leader Samier Dandan, writing in criticism of the government's $1 billion deradicalisation programme, commented that 'the focus of the government's strategy seems to rest heavily on how best it can strip people of their rights in the name of security' rather than looking at the wider social, economic and political issues (Siegel 2015). These laws and their impact will be considered in more detail in Chapter 4.

The externalisation of Muslim identity ('they call us "Muslim"') and, as we have seen, the securitisation of Muslims post-9/11 across our four countries, far from distancing secular Muslims from their faith, have had the reverse effect. Wilson and Grant note:

> The interesting polemic is that behind the backdrop of 9/11 and other media expressing negative views towards Islam, a significant number of nominally cultural or secular Muslims have still rallied closer under the flag Islam, when they could have chosen to step back.
>
> (Wilson and Grant 2013)

We suggest that the external imposition of a social identity as a result of securitisation, together with social and economic marginalisation, discrimination and exclusion of Muslims, has made their Islām more personally relevant. More problematically, in some cases the Islamic aspects of their identity have become a reactionary force in which violence and radical interpretations of Islām and Sharīʿah are no longer unappealing. The stories and psychological dynamics of Muslims in prison,[12] not to mention the constant trickle of Dāʿish recruits from schools and universities in the UK and Australia, illustrate that failures to properly recognise Muslim identity can have very serious repercussions.

In fact, Muslim communities in all four countries have described feeling both defined and targeted by these laws. Recent research in the Australian context by Cherney and Murphy suggest that these laws have had a profound impact on Muslim identity and leave many Muslims feeling targeted (Cherney and Murphy 2014). In the UK, research indicates similar findings. Choudhary and Fenwick argue that these laws are not experienced in isolation (referring to their experiences of Islamophobia and discrimination) and contribute to Muslims feeling as if they are treated as a suspect community. They continue that 'while some Muslims are responding to this through greater engagement, in challenging the misperceptions about them, many more report feeling increasingly alienated and isolated' (Choudhary and Fenwick 2012: 70).

We would argue that these sentiments can potentially push Muslims to retreat into separatist silos in which they can harbour extremist views (we discuss this further in Chapter 2). This can have a devastating impact on both Muslim communities and the broader society, marginalising Muslim communities as the 'other'. According to Tariq Ramadan, Muslims in these countries need to respond by actively participating in society and confronting their particular challenges by developing 'a rich, positive, and participatory presence' in their societies (Ramadan 2004: 225). Clearly, the rise in Islamophobia will make this an even greater challenge.

Conclusion

This chapter has considered the place of Muslim communities in the USA, the UK, Canada and Australia. Each one of these countries can be described as multicultural; each having a significantly diverse population drawn from all over the globe. With such diversity, comes the important question of how a secular, liberal democratic state should respond to the differing norms, practices and principles of such diverse groups.

Despite the recent backlash against multiculturalism, particularly as it relates to Muslims, we argue that policies of multiculturalism and accommodation, in the form of recognition, are transformative for both minority groups and the broader society. Contrary to the argument that multiculturalism is divisive and leads to state instability, we argue that such policies will more likely result in greater social cohesion and a stronger civil society with accommodation generating a more pluralistic and inclusive public space.

We also alluded to conceptual deficiencies surrounding notions of multicultural accommodation and their neglect of religion or religious groups. This is particularly important given that one of the key challenges for multiculturalism is how it responds to Muslim minority groups. In this way, we question the neutrality of the state and of secularism. We maintain in the context of Muslim communities in the Common Law countries explored in this book, that it is imperative to discuss the role of religion and religious groups and to seek out ways for their accommodation.

We need understanding of some of the key characteristics of Muslim communities in our respective countries to know how best to approach accommodation. This includes the preliminary definitional question: who are the 'Muslim Community'? It is not a homogenous grouping and is in fact composed of a very diverse collection of communities coming from multifarious cultural, ethnic, linguistic and socio-economic backgrounds. In each of our countries, they form only a small percentage of the overall population. This is an important corrective given that popular perceptions typically overestimate the size of the Muslim population and therefore its concomitant impacts on broader cultural changes in society.[13]

The Muslim communities are generally young, in urban centres and well educated. But they also suffer from socio-economic disadvantage. It is this disadvantage which can have a negative impact on integration and social cohesion, especially given the promise and expectations which follow from education. Furthermore, as discussed in this chapter, the problem is exacerbated by increasing rates of Islamophobia from the media, politicians and elsewhere. While some commentators describe a scene of Muslims 'under siege', these circumstances have also opened up opportunities for Muslims to reflect on their religious identities and question how that relates to their sense of belonging. The 'real menace', as Charles Taylor describes it, is the spectre of failed integration, feelings of alienation and the reconstruction of counter-identities by young people who have lost their original culture but cannot succeed in society because of a lack of skills or discrimination (Taylor 2009: xiv).

It is to this reconstruction of a counter-identity, the role of religion and Sharīʿah on Muslim identity formation, that we turn in the next chapter.

Notes

1 According to Kymlicka there is no evidence to support the claim that multiculturalism promotes ethnic separateness or impedes immigrant integration, rather it allows difference to be respected and accommodated while simultaneously facilitating the integration of immigrants into a larger society.
2 See further, Lorenzo Zucca, *A Secular Europe: Law and Religion in the European Constitutional Landscape* (Oxford: Oxford University Press, 2012).
3 See further, Roger Trigg, *Equality, Freedom and Religion* (Oxford: Oxford University Press, 2012a). See also, Trigg, 'Religious freedom in a secular society', *International Journal for Religious Freedom*, (2012b) 5 (1): 45–58.
4 Refer to Samuel Huntington, *The Clash of Civilizations and the Remaking of World Order* (New York: Simon & Schuster, 1996).
5 This equates to 476,000 according to the 2011 Census (Australian Bureau of Statistics 2012).
6 See also The Chicago Council on Global Affairs 2007.
7 Ibid.
8 See also Euro-Islam.info n.d.
9 Within the London borough of Tower Hamlets, around one-half of all Muslims were economically active (52 per cent) compared to around two-thirds (67 per cent) of all people. Overall, Muslims in London face numerous barriers to employment. These include educational underachievement, discrimination, and lack of affordable and appropriate childcare, lack of suitable training, travel costs and housing costs.
10 See also The Chicago Council on Global Affairs 2007.
11 For a list of US terrorist attacks, see 'Terrorist attacks and related incidents in the United States', compiled by Wm. Robert Johnston, last updated 16 February 2016, at: www.johnstonsarchive.net/terrorism/wrjp255a.html (accessed 6 April 2016).
12 See further, Gabriele Marranci, *Faith, Ideology and Fear: Muslim Identities Within and Beyond Prisons* (London and New York: Continuum, 2009); and Akil Awan, 'Transitional religiosity experiences: Contextual disjuncture and Islamic political radicalism', in T. Abbas (ed.), *Islamic Political Radicalism: A European Perspective* (Edinburgh: Edinburgh University Press, 2007).
13 The IPSOS MORI Poll in 2014 found Britons overestimated the size of the Muslim population in the UK by 16 per cent, Americans overestimated by 14 per cent, Australians by 16 per cent and Canadians by 18 per cent. See Alberto Nardelli and George Arnett, 'Today's key fact: You are probably wrong about almost everything', *Guardian*, 29 October 2014.

2 Contextualising Sharīʿah in the Common Law world

> In the West, the idea of shariʿa calls up all the darkest images of Islam ... It has reached the extent that many Muslim intellectuals do not dare even to refer to the concept for fear of frightening people or arousing suspicion of all their work by the mere mention of the word.
>
> (Ramadan 2004: 32)

Introduction

In Chapter 1, we considered the Muslim communities in Australia, Canada, the UK and the USA and their demographic make-up. We also examined the multicultural context of each of these countries and discussed the question of accommodation in respect to the diverse cultural and religious groups, both by the state more broadly as well as by the legal system. We argued in the Introduction that Common Law, in the abstract, and in liberal democratic theory, is sufficiently flexible and broad to encompass a variety and plurality of legal cultures and, importantly, ought to do so.

In this chapter, we examine the other side of the coin and discuss in what ways, if at all, Muslims who follow their own legal code, the Sharīʿah, are capable of coexisting and integrating within Common Law frameworks. This issue has been the subject of heated debate and given rise to a number of false accusations about Muslims wanting to implement all of Sharīʿah as well as misconceptions about the meaning of Sharīʿah itself, including the understandings that Muslims have of it. These debates, at least in recent years, have taken place against a backdrop of fears of terrorism. They have generated a febrile climate in which any mention of Sharīʿah produces almost mass hysteria and 'moral panic' that preclude the possibility of any accommodation.

We begin this chapter by setting out those perceptions of Sharīʿah that have appeared in media debates and political commentaries. We then proceed to 'demystify' those debates through a doctrinal and contextual discussion of the meaning of Sharīʿah and its practical understandings in our diverse Muslim communities. We will argue that the capacity of Muslims to integrate within the fabric of the Common Law depends upon their interpretation of the Sharīʿah. While there are interpretations that support the dominant media and political discourse, these are extreme and fail to account for the richness and the breadth of the Islamic legal tradition. We maintain that one can be a 'good' Muslim and follow the Sharīʿah, in both letter and spirit, and at the same time participate as equal citizens in a liberal democratic state under the Common Law. It may entail adaptation and selection of some opinions over others, but it will not require rejection of Sharīʿah as both Islamist extremists and the dominant media discourse suggest.

The perception of Sharīʿah: 'Sharīʿah' debates in Common Law jurisdictions

There is no doubt that the issue of accommodation of Muslims in our Common Law countries, at least in a legal context, has focused on 'Sharīʿah', in particular on its perceived incompatibility with Western liberal democratic secular societies. The public discourse has been filled with politicians and public commentators of all persuasions making statements about the role of Sharīʿah, often with little knowledge of what Sharīʿah actually is or how Muslims relate to it. For example, one recent Australian senator in an attempt to explain Sharīʿah and why it apparently contravened the Australian constitution, said: 'Well I think, um, when it comes to, um, sharia law, um, you know to me it's um … it obviously involves terrorism. It involves a power that is not a healthy power' (AAP 2014). 'I want to see their full allegiance, not 50 per cent, to the Australian Constitution and Australian law. It is one law for all. That is the Australian law full stop' (ABC News24 2014).

To say that the debates have been sensational and dramatic would be an understatement, as the discussion below will demonstrate. Whilst this has taken place in each of the four countries at various times over the last twenty years, it is important to note that the UK and Canada have both had a similar experience of a more intense public debate in response to a particular proposal.

United Kingdom

Debates in the UK, as elsewhere, have centred on the fear of a parallel Sharīʿah jurisdiction and the possibility of Muslims dispensing their own civil and criminal forms of justice. In the post-9/11 and post-7/7 years, these fears famously came to a head in 2008 when the then Archbishop of Canterbury, Rowan Williams, articulated his thoughts in a public lecture and canvassed the possibility of applying a religious law in the legal context of the UK (Williams 2008a). In considering this question, the Archbishop suggested that there could be greater room for the application of Sharīʿah or Islamic law, particularly in the areas of family law and financial transactions, although he acknowledged some 'anxieties'. He concluded by calling for a more nuanced debate about the role of Islamic law in Britain (Williams 2008a).

The public response to that call was vitriolic.[1] Many demanded his resignation as head of the Anglican Church. Modood commented:

> Many people (wilfully or otherwise) misunderstood Rowan Williams' position and thought (sincerely or otherwise) that he was sanctioning the stoning of adulterers, hand-chopping for theft and beheadings for apostasy. Even some of those who recognize that he was not doing so still argue that … granting anything to Muslims in this area would encourage extremists and unreasonable demands and propel the entire society down a slippery slope to the Talibanisation of British law.
>
> (Modood 2008)

Conservative politicians took the opportunity to frame the Archbishop's call for closer engagement as an example of a failed socialist past and a natural consequence of outdated and inappropriate social policies of multiculturalism. David Cameron, then Conservative opposition leader in the UK, said applying Sharīʿah was the: '… logical endpoint of the now discredited doctrine of state multiculturalism, seeing people merely as followers of certain religions, rather than individuals in their own right within a common community' (BBC News 2008).

Rather than being viewed in terms of inclusion, possible accommodation of Sharīʿah was deemed to be divisive and ultimately oppressive. Populist news headlines intimated and the subsequent 'One Law for All' campaign against Sharīʿah law advocated that women, in particular, would be victimised if decisions of Sharīʿah tribunals received the sanction of English law (One Law for All n.d.).[2] 'Religious authorities' were misogynistic 'by definition', even at an unofficial and informal level (One Law for All n.d.). For them, the answer was not to negotiate with Muslims on how to accommodate their legal code within current legal frameworks of English law but to exclude religion from the public sphere altogether (Modood 2008).

However, there were those who supported the Archbishop and the issues of engagement he articulated. Madeleine Bunting, the Associate Editor of the *Guardian* newspaper wrote,

> contrary to the torrent of ineptitude and naivety, there was a rationale behind the archbishop's remarks. Shariah has become the totemic issue for both Muslims and non-Muslims … Williams has squarely put the issue in the public domain to be debated.
>
> (Bunting 2008)

Some academics also sought to clarify the debate. T.J. Winters noted:

> Dr Williams, far from recommending some kind of parallel law for Muslims, was pointing out that informal religious tribunals which already exist on a limited number of civil – never criminal – matters, in a way which is entirely legal under arbitration laws, should be more systematically brought under the regulation of the legal system. He was not commending greater separateness, or an expansion of Muslim courts – quite the opposite.
>
> (Winters 2008)

For decades, the Muslim community has 'developed a strategy whereby methods of Muslim dispute resolution would operate unofficially' (Fournier 2004: 25).[3] These Sharīʿah 'courts', typically referred to as Sharīʿah councils or tribunals (Bano 2012), tend to comprise several scholars or imāms who sit together (usually in a mosque) to decide a case. Each follows a particular procedure that involves making an application to the council and completing a form setting out the details of their case. Councils try to mediate between the parties, but if unsuccessful, they proceed to deal with matters of divorce and/or property settlement. Such councils deal with over 500 cases annually. The majority of applications are made by women.

Notwithstanding media stories to the contrary, these councils have never been recognised as part of the British legal system. They have only moral as opposed to legal authority as it is up to the parties to decide whether or not to comply with their recommendations (Thomson 2007). Nor have there been any proposals to amend legislation to make them part of the British legal system, with the exception of a small but vocal minority (Anthony 2014).

The only council or tribunal that has any authority according to English law is the Muslim Arbitration Tribunal (MAT), which operates under the Arbitration Act, 1996 (UK).[4] The MAT was established in 2007 and touted as 'an important and significant step towards providing Muslims with a real opportunity to self-determine disputes in accordance with Islamic Sacred Law' (Muslim Arbitration Tribunal 2015). The MAT is an attempt to harmonise the application of both English law and Islamic law without any radical change to the existing legal framework; its decisions are binding in exactly the same fashion as any other private arbitration under British law (Lepore 2012: 669).

Notwithstanding its limited pretensions, the MAT has also received negative press coverage implying, like the coverage of the Sharīʿah councils before it, that a parallel Sharīʿah jurisdiction was forming under the approving eye of the UK Ministry of Justice. The latter repudiated this claim and issued a rapid 'clarification' stating that the MAT has always operated within the legal framework of England and Wales, and had its decisions enforced pursuant to English law (Muslim Arbitration Tribunal 2015). The Ministry further stated that 'Shariah law is not part of the law of England and Wales and the Government has no intention of making any change that would conflict with British laws and values' (Hickey 2008).

The Sharīʿah Councils continue to be controversial. In 2011, Baroness Cox tabled the 'Equality Bill' seeking to limit the legality of Sharīʿah law operating in England and Wales, particularly as it applied to women.[5] She argued that Sharīʿah law processes victimised women and were 'utterly incompatible with the legal principles upon which this country is founded' (Malik 2011). Although the 'Equality Bill' failed to pass, there has been little let-up in the anti-Sharīʿah sentiment. In 2014, a petition was submitted to the Ministry of Justice titled 'Ban all Shariah Law in the UK', stating that 'People residing in this country should abide by British law' (UK Government and Parliament 2014). The petition received over 21,000 signatures. The Government responded by stating clearly,

'Sharia "law" has no jurisdiction in England and Wales and the Government has no intention to change this position' (UK Government and Parliament 2014). It went on to state, in a balanced fashion, that there was nothing prohibiting Muslims abiding by principles of Sharīʿah where it would not contradict English law; but there was no place for a parallel system in the UK.

Against the backdrop of terrorist attacks and fears of Islamist extremism spilling over onto British streets, the UK Government appears to have retreated from this balanced approach. Theresa May, the British Home Secretary, in a speech in 2015 outlining the Government's approach to tackling extremism, included a proposal to review the application of Sharīʿah law in the UK (Cranmer 2015). This seems extraordinary given that Sharīʿah is not officially recognised or sanctioned by the State and operates only as an aspect of the private ordering of disputes of which all citizens can avail themselves and which is officially encouraged to prevent logjams in the courts and further avoid tax payers' expense.

Canada

Canada has also been home to heated public debate about the role of Sharīʿah in a liberal democratic state. Like the UK, it has focused on the appropriateness of Muslim bodies offering their own dispute resolution processes informed by Sharīʿah principles. Also like the UK, it has occurred against a backdrop of popular fears of Islamist extremism and from an assumption that Sharīʿah is contrary to Canadian constitutional values of secularism and gender equality.

The debate in Canada goes back to 2003 and a proposal put forward by a Muslim organisation in Ontario, known as the Islamic Institute of Civil Justice (IICJ), which sought to offer arbitration in accordance with Islamic legal principles and Canadian law. This led to sensationalised debates that extended way beyond its borders (Mills 1995).

The IICJ proposed to implement Qur'ānic requirements to guide parties to settle their disputes themselves, by mutual consent, but with the parties assisted by third parties to come to an appropriate agreement. Alternatively, if agreement could not be reached, the service would provide two arbitrators (knowledgeable in Sharīʿah) who would make a decision that would become binding and enforceable under Canadian law (The Muslim Marriage Mediation & Arbitration Service n.d.). This was not a revolutionary proposal, but rather an extension of a facility that already existed under Ontario law. People in Ontario had an existing right to choose arbitration as a means of resolving their disputes, including family law matters (Boyd 2006). Indeed, even faith-based arbitration was permitted under the Ontario Arbitration Act, 1991. For many years, Jewish and Christian groups had set up arbitration boards that ruled in accordance with their religious principles (Korteweg 2008: 436). Muslims were simply availing themselves of an option of private ordering that was already available under the existing system.

The conservative call for similar recognition and inclusion then was drowned out in sensationalist news headlines. Tabloid papers reported: 'Canada allowing

Shariah Barbaric Laws' and 'Canadian Judges will soon be enforcing Islamic law … such as stoning women caught in adultery' (Kutty and Kutty 2004). Newspaper editorials also got in on the act, expressing moral shock that Canadian lawmakers could even consider applying Sharīʿah law in the mediation of divorces when it was 'about the best idea since female foot-binding' (Mallick 2004). While some appeared to intimate that this was a backdoor to implementing Sharīʿah laws against adultery, the vast majority in the media perceived that Muslims were calling for a parallel legal system at the very least. Like the debates in the UK, the construction of this debate was against the backdrop of 9/11 and associated fears of Islamist extremism. The notion was 'Islamic fundamentalism and indeed that faith based arbitration would somehow aid the cause of fundamentalists the world over' (Mallick 2004: 70).

In response, the Ontario Government commissioned a study by former Attorney-General Marion Boyd to consider whether religious-based arbitration should be allowed to continue under the law (Boyd 2004). The consultations and ensuing 'Boyd Report' were comprehensive and represented differing views about having faith-based arbitration as a family dispute resolution process in Ontario. The report concluded that faith-based arbitration should continue and recommended a number of additional safeguards to protect all parties (Boyd 2004: 133). The Ontario Government, however, rejected the findings of the report and amended the law to deny recognition to faith-based arbitration of family law disputes under the Act.[6]

One of the most frequent arguments made against faith-based arbitration was that Islām more generally, and Sharīʿah in particular, disadvantaged Muslim women by treating them unequally (Brown 2007: 532). In fact, a coalition of groups and individuals united to lobby the government to reject faith-based arbitration because of its perceived impact on women. This was a collaborative effort involving the Canadian Council for Muslim Women, the National Association of Women and the Law and the Centre for Human Rights and Democratic Development (Rights and Democracy). This coalition of groups convened workshops and conferences, initiated letter-writing campaigns and invited activists from around the world to publicise what they saw as the negative impact of Islamic law on women's rights (Macklin 2006). Indeed, this coalition ended up comprising over one hundred organisations and individuals (Bakht 2005: 75) and effecting legislative change.

The anti-Sharīʿah momentum continued apace into 2014 and 2015. In 2014, a 'change.org' petition was initiated calling upon the Canadian government to make Canada a 'Sharia-free zone' (Millar 2014). In 2015, the recently deposed Conservative Harper government officially objected to Muslim women wearing a *niqāb* (face covering) during citizenship ceremonies arguing that it was contrary to Canadian values (Maloney 2015). The fact that the Harper government campaigned on an anti-Muslim platform in the 2015 general election and lost to Justin Trudeau's Liberal opposition party, might indicate the anti-Sharīʿah campaigns in Canada have now levelled off.

United States and Australia

The discussion above has shown that the debates on Sharīʿah in the UK and Canada have centred on lingering public responses to specific proposals. In contrast, the debates in the USA and Australia have appeared on a fairly regular and constant basis largely in response to what has been happening in the other countries or to the public opinions of particular individuals. Ghobadzaeh notes the debate has been less specific, including 'a broad arena of calls for developing an Islamic court on the one hand, and using Shariah as an informal mediator body on the other' (Ghobadzaeh 2009: 12). One of the reasons is that unlike the UK, Australia and the USA have not had established 'Sharīʿah councils' and rely instead upon individual imāms to resolve disputes.[7] This means that there has been no perceived need to recognise any particular process.

This has not stopped certain individuals, however, from making a general call for the application of Sharīʿah, such as Kurt Kennedy, the founder and leader of the Best Party of Allāh in Australia (AAP 2005). Some Muslim leaders also suggested setting up a special court or tribunal under Sharīʿah law to deal with divorce matters (Weber 2005).[8] Jamila Hussain, lawyer, academic and then spokeswoman for the Muslim Women's National Network, said that a religious tribunal or court would address the problem suffered by a large number of Muslim women in Australia in securing a religious divorce when their husbands refuse to cooperate. In 2011, the Australian Federation of Islamic Councils (AFIC) also made a submission to the Federal Parliament's Committee on Multicultural Affairs suggesting that certain aspects of Sharīʿah could be implemented in Australia.

Each of these proposals or suggestions has been met with much opposition from various sectors but most notably from politicians and the media. Successive governments in both countries have repeatedly articulated their views about the incompatibility of Sharīʿah and State law. In the Australian context, in 2005 Peter Costello (then Treasurer of Australia) went to great lengths to dismiss any idea of accommodating Sharīʿah in Australia. He stated:

> We will never be an Islamic State. We will never observe Shariah Law … if you want to live in an Islamic republic there are Islamic republics, you might be happier in those countries than you will in Australia.… There is only one law in Australia. It is the law that is made by parliament and it is enforced by the courts. And every person who lives in Australia has to understand this. This is the law they come under.
>
> (A Current Affair 2005)[9]

When the issue of accommodation arose in the UK, the media took the opportunity to ask whether Sharīʿah had a role to play in Australia. In similar fashion to Peter Costello, the Attorney-General Robert McClelland chimed that, 'The Rudd Government is not considering and will not consider the introduction of any part of Shariʿa law into the Australian legal system' (Zwartz 2005).

Over the course of the last ten to fifteen years, politicians in the USA have reiterated the same message. In 2010, the presidential candidate Newt Gingrich opined: 'I believe Sharia is a mortal threat to the survival of freedom in the United States and in the world as we know it.' The Representative of the Republican Tea Party movement, Michele Bachmann, declared Sharīʻah 'must be resisted across the United States'. The former Republican presidential nominee, Herman Cain, also objected to the 'attempt to gradually ease Sharia law and the Muslim faith into our government' (Awad 2012). In 2013, the Florida State Senator Alan Hays even likened Sharīʻah to a 'dreadful disease' requiring vaccination to protect Americans.[10] More recently, the Republican presidential candidate, Ben Carson has expressed the view that a Muslim who adheres to Sharīʻah should not be president of the USA unless they renounce Sharīʻah (Schleifer 2015).

The unequivocal message in both Australia and the USA is that not only is there no room for the application of Sharīʻah, but also that the suggestion itself is a rejection of mainstream values. In the USA, this sentiment has generated a wave of 'anti-Sharīʻah' bills to prohibit the consideration of Sharīʻah in USA courts. While these laws do not make express reference to Sharīʻah, or to Muslims, and refer in fact to 'foreign law', the debates leave no doubt that the target of these laws is Sharīʻah. A 2011 poll found that 30 per cent of Americans believe Muslims want to establish Sharīʻah in the USA (Awad 2012). The fear is that Sharīʻah is taking over the US court system, even in states where the Muslim population is very small. For example, in Oklahoma where only 0.04 per cent of the population is Muslim, a measure was approved in 2010 and supported by mainstream politicians to ban the use of Sharīʻah law in state courts (Lepore 2012: 670).

This fear of Sharīʻah is reflected in the many anti-Sharīʻah campaigns initiated in both countries. 'ACT for America', for example, has been instrumental in advocating anti-Sharīʻah laws across the USA (ACT for America 2015).[11] In Australia, we have seen the rise of right-wing neo-Nazi groups like the 'Reclaim Australia' party who also have called for bans on Sharīʻah in Australia (Ahmad 2015).

Many have attempted to respond to such campaigns and animosity towards Sharīʻah by arguing that Muslims who adhere to principles of Sharīʻah are not a threat to society. They note, in particular, that the accommodation of culture and religion is an integral part of any legal system.[12] Others see such campaigns as 'a calculated beat-up about Shariah law … an attempt to scapegoat Muslims for electoral and other political purposes' (Gould 2006). Regardless of the intention behind these campaigns, their effect has been to block any possibility of expanding the debate on a role for Sharīʻah (Ghobadzaeh 2009: 15).

The reaction from the Muslim community has been diverse and varied, with many expressing their views in the opinion pages of the nation's papers. Soliman, a former president of the Islamic Council of Victoria, wrote that 'Australia is nowhere near ready for Shariah courts any time soon … there have been no calls for a parallel or alternative court system for Muslims in Australia' (Soliman 2008). Akbarzadeh argued that:

> The overwhelming majority of Islamic organisations view Australian law as their protector and appeal to it for redress. Australian Muslims, whether cultural or devout, value the fair-go spirit of Australia. This spirit resonates with their cultural and religious beliefs. It would help us all if we paused to look at values that bind us together.
>
> (Akbarzadeh 2008)

Contrary to the claims of the Sharīʿah ban advocates, the American Civil Liberties Union has stated there is no evidence Sharīʿah law is encroaching on US courts. Rather they note:

> Court cases cited by anti-Muslim groups as purportedly illustrative of this problem actually show the opposite: Courts treat lawsuits that are brought by Muslims or that address the Islamic faith in the same way that they deal with similar claims brought by people of other faiths or that involve no religion at all. These cases also show that sufficient protections already exist in our legal system to ensure that courts do not become impermissibly entangled with religion or improperly consider, defer to, or apply religious law where it would violate basic principles of U.S. or state public policy.
>
> (American Civil Liberties Union 2011)

Demystifying the debates

The discussion above has demonstrated that in each of the Common Law jurisdictions examined in this book, there has been a vigorous public debate and commentary about the role of Sharīʿah. Quite often, it has focused on the question of whether Sharīʿah should be accommodated or recognised by the official legal system. The debates, thus far, have largely been based on generalisations and assumptions that obscure the reality. In fact, much of the opposition and fear has come from a misunderstanding of what is meant by 'recognition' or 'accommodation', let alone an ignorance of the practical diversity, flexibility and meaning of the Sharīʿah itself.

What is Sharīʿah?

'At the most basic level', writes Sherman Jackson,

> shariah is the Muslim universe of ideals. It is the result of their collective effort to understand and apply the Quran and supplementary teachings of the Prophet Muhammad (called Sunna) in order to earn God's pleasure [reward/*riḍā*] and secure human welfare in this life and attain human salvation in the life to come.
>
> (Jackson 2010)

Yet the word 'Sharīʿah' conjures up the most negative of images in the West. In the not-too-distant past, if it was not the punishing of adulterers by stoning and thieves with cutting their hands off, then it was the forced marriages of young girls and the battering of 'disobedient' wives. Now, of course, we have the decapitation of Western hostages, 'apostates' and the burning to death of captured pilots by Dā'ish (the so-called 'Islamic State'), not to mention the enslavement of Yazidi women, all committed in the name of 'Sharīʿah'. As Khalid Abou El-Fadl notes, notions of the Sharīʿah, even of Islām itself, have been hijacked by the extremists.[13]

Given this context and the prevalence of horrific images in our media, it is not surprising that misunderstandings of this much-abused word abound. Linguistically, the word comes from the trilateral route 'sha/ra/^a' which has a variety of meanings, which in their essence mean 'to make clear or apparent' (*bayyana/ awḍaḥa*), or 'to start or begin'. The noun '*shari'ah*' has also been defined as 'a place that leads to water'. The philologist, Al-Layth, continued to define it as: 'What Allāh has made apparent to His slaves in terms of fasting, prayer, pilgrimage, marriage and other matters.' (Lisān al-ʿArab). If we combine these meanings, we can arrive at a working understanding of the term as implying a revealed, divine path comprising a set of rules which, if followed, lead to one's salvation.

Although Muslims believe that the 'revealed path' was finalised and perfected in the guidance given to Prophet Muḥammad, the term 'Sharīʿah' was not exclusive to his nation, for every messenger (*rasūl*) before him, including Abraham, Moses and Jesus, was sent a 'Sharīʿah'. They all had the same monotheistic belief (that God exists without any partner), but had different rules for their time (*Sharā'i*). Prophet Muḥammad mentioned: 'The Prophets are like brothers with the same father, but with different mothers. Their religion is one, but their rules are different.'[14]

Once we understand Sharīʿah linguistically, as a revealed path, and that previous prophets and messengers were also sent rules by God that their followers were meant to follow, a greater intimacy, connectedness and continuity is established between Muslims and contemporary followers of the 'Abrahamic traditions'. Indeed, it establishes linkages with other religious traditions also (as the Qur'ān mentions a prophet was sent to every nation), which is not usually acknowledged. We can say, therefore, that the disciples of Moses and Jesus, for example, were all commanded by God to follow a 'Sharīʿah'. When viewed from this light, far from being divisive and exclusive, the concept of 'Sharīʿah' becomes unifying and a link with people from different nations and traditions.[15]

Sharīʿah as a moral compass

The more abstract definition of Sharīʿah as a 'revealed path' also indicates how it is to operate on a personal and psychological,[16] as opposed to a 'state' level (which is how we have come to understand it since the Iranian Revolution in 1979).[17] That which is revealed acts upon the perfect believer's conscience because it originates from the ultimate 'Law Giver' and shows the path to salvation. Whether the guidance comprises rules that are mandatory, prohibiting, permissive, discouraging or supererogatory, or takes the form of more open-ended principles, they all comprise a holistic guide that bind individuals' consciences. This remains true whether Muslims are leaders or followers, officials or lay-people, traders or customers, families and communities: the Sharī'ah communicates to their conscience in every fact situation they encounter and wherever they are. In a well-known *Ḥadīth* and advice to his companion, Abu Dharr, the Prophet said, 'Obey Allāh wherever you are. If you commit a sin, then follow it up with a good deed which helps to erase the bad. Deal with the people with the best of manners (*ḥusn al-khuluq*).'[18]

The Sharī'ah acts as a moral compass, providing a point of reference and clear direction for the believer. To take the metaphor further, for believers, the Sharī'ah is like the pole star. It remains fixed in the sky, providing a 'true north' from which travellers can navigate through and around obstacles to their eventual destination. On a clear night, when in calm waters, navigating the route with a committed crew over short distances poses few complications. But sometimes, the pole star may be concealed by clouds and its observation obstructed by atmospheric conditions; or the journey may be very long, with intermediate stages full of imponderables. Yet you still know where it is (you have checked with your compass) and have the intellectual tools to realise from where you have come, where you are now and how to best estimate where to go (in our human failings, we cannot presume to know everything).

Importantly, when plotting the journey based on its coordinates, the process will involve the use of reason and effort by experts and lay alike (though each with their own particular spheres of competence). They will determine the most appropriate course given the nature of the terrain, the season, the types of people travelling and in consideration of whatever they expect to encounter. The routes may be multiple, offering a variety of solutions, and all with their particular hazards and uncertainties along the way. Nevertheless, a route must be chosen, based on the most reliable of information (which in itself is a question of human judgement) and decided with precaution, lest one drifts aimlessly or falls prey to dangerous trade winds. All have a choice and all will remain accountable personally for the decisions they make.

Sharī'ah as living law

The 'Shari'a', then, is not simply the 'traditional rules of Islamic law found in medieval textbooks of the various Sunni and Shia schools of Islamic jurists' (Edge 2013: 116). First and foremost, it comprises more than 'Rules of Law', as a Western lawyer would understand them. The Sharī'ah does not distinguish between law and morals. All human action is balanced upon a scale of virtue (*birr*) and vice (*munkar*), with consequences in this life (where the Sharī'ah aligns with the positive law of a state or as a manifestation of Divine Providence) as well as the next for those who fail to carry out obligations (*wājibāt*) and for those who commit prohibitions (*muḥarramāt*). Yet it also sets out acts and omissions that are encouraged (*mandūbāt*), discouraged (*makrūhāt*) and permitted (*mubāḥāt*) in order for the believer to achieve a state of 'perfection' or *iḥsān*.[19]

Unlike 'law' in a Western sense, which is concerned only with setting minimum standards (which in Common Law jurisdictions has been traditionally to set out what you cannot do as opposed to what you must do), the Sharī'ah engages a person's free choice to adopt a 'model personality' in the form and behaviour of Prophet Muḥammad and to thereby copy his Sunnah.[20] In the exercise of that choice, not all choices are equal: priority is given to avoiding prohibitions (*al-muḥarramāt*) and performing obligations (*al-wājibāt*), as this is the best the human being can do to attain safety in the Hereafter.[21] The avoidance of disliked matters and the performance of optional matters for the sake of Allāh add an additional rung in the pious person's ranking in the Hereafter, but are not performed in place of an obligation or avoidance of a prohibition. To prefer an optional deed in place of an obligation, in fact, would be to commit a sin.[22]

Second, the Sharī'ah is not a medieval artefact; it is a living law. Although the Qur'ān mentions that the religion has been 'completed' and 'perfected',[23] this does not mean that the Sharī'ah, as an edifice, was complete in all its details when the Prophet passed away more than 1,400 years ago and evidenced only through the behaviours of the Prophet's Companions (the Ṣaḥābah).[24] The scholars of Qur'ānic interpretation interpreted the above verse to mean only the framework of the Sharī'ah was complete and to which nothing would be added.[25] Its branches (*furū'*), as manifested in the juristic law (*fiqh*) would continue to grow and develop until the Day of Judgement through clarification, interpretation and extension by scholars (*al-'ulemā'*), the 'heirs of the prophets'; through their hermeneutical practices of *ijtihād*.[26] As Imām 'Ali, the fourth Caliph, pronounced, 'the world will never be without one who defends the religion with its evidence' (al-Asfahani 2010: 79), and the Prophet asserted that Allāh will send a 'Renewer' (*mujaddid*) at the start of every century who will rejuvenate their religion.[27] Even if the applied law had crystallised in many Muslim communities, Allāh would send a scholar to breathe fresh life into the religion through not only a reassertion of its basic beliefs and premises, but also to reignite the Sharī'ah as a law of continuing relevance and application in the contemporary lives of Muslims.[28]

Although, historically, some claim that the 'gates to *ijithād*' had all but closed by the beginning of the tenth century and asserted following the sacking of Baghdad in the twelfth century, the reality is that individual jurists (worthy of the name),[29] continued to exercise their *ijtihād* well after that alleged closure (Hallaq 1984). It may be that they did not seek to make famous their own opinions, for they deemed the established 'Schools of Law' (*al-madhāhib*)[30] sufficient for the common person. Yet jurists acknowledged their own continuing obligation to use all of their efforts to determine God's Law in matters that remained uncertain once they attained the highest ranks of Islamic knowledge (*mujtahid muṭlaq*). Even those of lower ranks continued to refine judgements in their particular historical setting, prioritised Prophetic *Ḥadīth*s and extended the sayings of the putative heads of their schools in a process of building, construction and repair akin to juristic 'scaffolding'. This corpus of juristic effort (*Fiqh*) to comprehend God's Law never stopped;[31] developing incrementally from scholar to student down the generations, through authoritative reports in a manner not so distant from the doctrine of judicial precedent familiar to a common lawyer. Although most scholars ceased to interpret the 'legislation' (Qur'ān and Sunnah) afresh, they worked within their own hermeneutical systems of inquiry that were far from 'blind following' (Jackson 2003: 88).

The Sharīʿah in the modern context is also a living law in the sense that community imāms, scholars (*'ulemā'*) and muftis (whether formally appointed by governments or otherwise), provide religious judgements (*fatāwā*/sing. *fatwa*) and answers to questions from their communities on a daily basis, and have been doing so continuously for centuries, in both predominantly Muslim and non-Muslim countries.[32] More often than not, their judgement will be based on the opinions of previous scholars[33] but on occasions, where there is no previous ruling, and they have the applicable scholarship, they may have recourse to their own judgements (*ijtihād*) based upon their perceptions of public interest (*maṣlaḥah*) and necessity (*ḍarūrah*), as seen through an Islamic rather than a secular lens. In some countries, the ability to pronounce *fatwa* is restricted by government legislation (as in Malaysia), but frequently it is left unregulated and this is particularly true in Western Common Law countries where Muslims are a minority.[34] Their authority depends, to a large extent, on the depth of their following as well as the degree of their scholarship.

It is true, therefore, that in the sense already described, the Sharīʿah is a 'jurists' law' and marks a distinguishing feature with the Common Law tradition where jurists have never been accorded a primary 'rule-making' function. That job, particularly in the twentieth and twenty-first centuries, has gone to parliaments, with judges 'filling in the gaps'.[35] In the Sharīʿah, as we see, jurists are given pride of place and act as mediators between the revealed texts (the Qur'ān and Sunnah) and the layperson. They determine what the law is through interpretation – not judges or legislators. Judges (*Quḍā*) are not bound by any system of stare decisis or judicial precedent and merely adjudicate disputes. They do not make law or determine law – they merely find and apply it.[36] The case of legislators in government is more complex as a residual rule-making authority is given to the Islamic ruler and their government as part of the politics of the Sharīʿah (*siyāsa al-Sharī'ah*). This represents an executive function in the implementation of Sharīʿah, however, as opposed to the formulation of any new substantive Islamic content. The latter remains normatively within the sole job-scope of religious scholars, though this has not prevented secular governments from arrogating that function over the centuries, particularly in the modern age, as Muslim governments have sought to 'catch up' with the West.

One of the most common constructions of Sharīʿah has been that it embodies a distinctive ethnic imprint; that it is an 'Arab's law', where rights, privileges, obligations and immunities are reluctantly extended to the non-Arab (*al-'ajami*).[37] While Arabs predominated during Islām's formative stages, and many pre-existing Arab customs were woven into the fabric of the Sharīʿah,[38] Persians, Africans, Asians and Europeans (in Islamic Spain and Muslim Sicily) adopted Sharīʿah as their moral code, helped to formulate its parameters as scholars, and implemented it in government and as administrators. It should also be remembered that the longest ruling dynasty in Islām were the Turkish Ottomans (1389–1922). In fact, the interpretative framework of the Sharī'ah itself facilitated cultural syntheses. Non-Arab cultures wrote their identities into the body of the Sharī'ah through the secondary sources of custom (*al-'urf/al-'ādat*), the presumption of continuity (*al-istisḥāb*) and the residual power given to rulers (*siyāsa al-Sharī'ah*). Ultimately, the ability of a jurist to offer an opinion (*ra'y*) to a question not already specifically addressed in the Holy Qur'ān and Sunnah, but that may have originated in a local context, provided mechanisms for the embedding of local cultural identities within the body of Sharī'ah. Even though the transmission of authoritative Prophetic sayings (*aḥādīth*) eventually had the effect of both limiting the scope of permissible cultural practice[39] as well as trumping local variations of Prophetic behaviour (*sunan*), this was done with a view to ironing out the apparent inconsistencies in expressions of the Revealed Message rather than extinguishing local identities (see Hallaq 2009: 47–48). In some parts of the historical Islamic empire, Sharī'ah and culture operated almost on a symbiotic basis with the latter responsible for social order and for applying conflict-resolution mechanisms (Hallaq 2009: 2003).

The relationship between culture and Sharī'ah is and has been a matter of controversy in Muslim-majority countries. The matter is more complex where Muslims are in a minority, especially where, as in the West, those Muslim cultures are numerous and may have less in common with other Muslim cultures than in predominantly Muslim countries. As we discuss further below, difficult questions arise as to communal and personal identity (Cesari 2013: 49), in addition to the importance of Islām in shaping that identity and the normative role the Sharī'ah should play.

Typologies of interpretation and application

What 'Islām' and 'Sharī'ah' means to Muslims is not free from ambiguity. Unlike Muslim countries where, notwithstanding the inroads of modernist thinking and the influence of petrodollars, particular schools of jurisprudence and of the Islamic creed (*'aqidah*) still predominate, in Western countries Muslims, who come from all over the world, have a multiplicity of religious affiliations. All live side by side, with their own mosques, some with religious schools, their own sets of clerics and their own points of reference and interpretations. There are also increasing numbers of Muslims without any affiliation, particularly those who belong to second- and third-generation migrants, or who have converted to the religion. As a result of refugee and asylum policies, there also exist individuals (and groups) whose beliefs would not be accepted as 'canonical' in their countries of origin (such as the *Aḥmadiyyah/Qadiyāni*), and even thrive in the West.

The reality is a competitive market place of Islamist thought, with each claiming a special insight into human salvation. While such diversity is a feature of liberal democracy, it poses a number of problems when relating or speaking to the Muslim 'community' as there is no single body or authoritative body that can speak for all (a position that obtains at the global as well as the local level)[40] and define the Sharīʿah position definitively. It also gives rise to plural interpretations of text and applications to context that will have differential impacts upon Muslims and their willingness to engage with the surrounding civil and secular society.

In the context of social engagement, we suggest we can group these interpretations into three broad typologies: assimilationist, separatist and integrationist. They are necessarily archetypes and all who claim Islām, but the most extreme, are likely to share one or more of the attributes from different groups. They also have their sub-groups. We use these categories, however, for the purposes of analysis and because they implicitly recognise approaches to accommodation, the running theme of our work.

The assimilationists

Assimilationists are those whom we define as wanting to adopt local customs and ways of life: to 'do in Rome as the Romans do' – whether that is in America, Australia, Canada or the UK. At one end of the spectrum, this approach has little application to questions of religious interpretation. Many of these may not identify first as 'Muslim'. They may not even self-identify as 'religious' but as British Pakistani, Arab-American, Lebanese Australian or African-Canadian, for example. They embrace a secular, national or ethnic identity, while distancing themselves from formal religious expression.[41]

It might be thought that Islām and Sharīʿah have little relevance for 'secular' or 'ethnic' Muslims. They may have little (or no) knowledge of Islamic rules or interest in rooting their behaviours in conceptions of the Sharīʿah. In some respects, they see little conflict with the secular values of the surrounding society because they do not run their lives on religious lines.

But Islamic identity, and Sharīʿah as a framer of that identity, is not unimportant for secular/ethnic Muslims. The cultures of their ethnic origins have Islamic influences and that culture is an inescapable aspect of who they are and their socialisation process. Being members of a family, joining in their celebrations, such as weddings and the ending of the fasting month (*'Eid*) – even if they do not fast – and paying condolences at their funerals, is replete with religious signifiers and rituals. They may commit crimes, go to nightclubs, be covered in tattoos and be enthusiastic members of 'outlaw' biker gangs themselves, but they share in Islām through the patterns of relationship forged with family and friends.

At the other end of the spectrum, however, are those who seek to reinterpret Islām and reform (*Iṣlāḥ*) Sharīʿah in line with local values and customs. They take what is prevalent or 'modern' as the benchmark and where Sharīʿah appears to conflict, they reinterpret the texts accordingly. In contrast with the notion of 'renewal' (*tajdīd*) in which advocates seek to return to what they regard as a 'purist' and 'authentic' form of Islām (see further below), this approach purports to normalise Muslim presence within contemporary environments.

There are many examples of this approach, both historical and contemporary. It includes the approach of Mustapha Kemal ('Atatürk') who, in his drive to modernise[42] and develop Turkey in the 1920s, required Turks to dress like Europeans and to adopt a secular lifestyle. Islām could manifest only in the private, rather than the public sphere. Even here, the regulation of family life was to follow a Swiss/Germanic code, rather than the laws found in Sharī'ah texts. Also, certain aspects of Islamic practice, such as the prayer and the call to prayer, were 'nationalised' requiring Turkish translations of the Arabic.

Contemporary examples originate from what some have called 'liberal Islām'.[43] In these cases, interpretations find a special place for democracy,[44] human rights, gender equality, freedom of thought and human progress. Notwithstanding established conventions and interpretations,[45] texts are reinterpreted as historically or culturally contingent[46] and, in cases of certain sayings of the Prophet, read as apocryphal (see Mernissi 1991).

The separatists

As for separatists, they reject their material and temporal surroundings, and seek truth in the eternal verities of the Islamic creed and actualise it through their applications of Sharī'ah. There are two types of separatists. The first, known as Sufis,[47] advocate a retreat into the moral and spiritual realms, with the purpose of reforming and domesticating their 'inner self' (*nafs*), and cultivating their heart to work in remembrance of Allāh. The surrounding society, whether it be a secular or religious society, whether predominantly Muslim or non-Muslim, is viewed as a prison to be endured with patience but engaged with as a source of heavenly reward. Secular laws are navigated around with the knowledge of the Sharī'ah, gained through engagement with scholarship over the entirety of the period since the coming of Islām, without intermission, as are all obstacles for those who seek a way out of their earthly prison. Their interpretations of the text are not always the most obvious but rationally engage with the literal and implied meanings to accord most with logical dictates underpinning human understanding of Divine Purpose and Divine Attributes.[48]

Rather than retreat into the moral self, the second type of separatists seek to impose themselves on others and implement their interpretation of Sharī'ah, almost in existential and puritanical terms.[49] For them, Muslims can only be called 'Muslims' if the Sharī'ah is put into practice in the surrounding society exactly as they perceive it was during the time of Prophet Muḥammad and his Companions. Any perceived departure from this path is branded a '*bida*' or prohibited innovation and punished. Religious practice is austere and textual interpretation, of both Qur'ān and Sunnah, is rigid and literal. Understanding Divine Purpose is deemed a simple and straightforward affair without need of rational intermediation. Secular 'laws' are not Law and must be disobeyed and secular leaders fought against. There is no engagement with the surrounding secular and liberal societies as they are thought to be indelibly corrupt. Rather Muslims disengage and embark on an active path to implement the literalist Sharī'ah and set up their vision of the Caliphate.[50]

Dāʻish or the so-called Islamic State, provide the most obvious and contemporary example of this type of separatist.[51] The group, which declared a Caliphate in June 2014 to reflect its expansionist and global aspirations, regards its members and those who pledge allegiance to it as the only true Muslims. Formed originally from Al-Qāʻida in Iraq (AQI) in 2013, it cites Usāmah bin Lāden and Abū Mus'ab Al-Zarqāwi as two of its five founding fathers. Its beliefs are almost exactly as we have set out above,[52] only we should add that, like Al-Qāʻida, they believe if you follow, apply or agree to live in a state which does not apply the Sharīʻah, then you are deemed a '*kafir*'/non-Muslim (even if you regard yourself as Muslim), who can legitimately be killed and have their property taken. The only differences between Al-Qāʻida and Dāʻish are strategy, the degree of brutality and the latter's insistence on establishing the Caliphate and the control of territory under its version of Sharīʻah law (see Byman 2015).

A second example of puritanical separatism is provided by Ḥizb ut-Taḥrir, a group which has a significant following in the West, particularly amongst the youth (see Pew Research Center 2010). Ḥizb ut-Taḥrir (HT) was established in 1952 by a Palestinian Judge, Taqiuddin An-Nabahāni. An-Nabahani viewed most of humanity, indeed most Muslims, as misguided and living in a state of ignorance or *jāhiliyyah* (see An-Nabahāni 1998). In modern times, but especially since the fall of the Ottoman Caliphate in 1924, he claimed (as do his successors) Muslims had stopped following the Sharīʻah in all of its details and in particular the precedents of pious ancestors from the first three centuries (*salaf al-ṣāliḥ*). Muslim societies had become corrupted due to poor leadership and had adopted the ways of the West. Their failures to appoint a proper Khalifah (Caliph) to lead them had put them all in a state of sin. The only solution, according to him, was to instigate revolutionary change in Muslim countries and forge a new Islamic leadership marking a return to the Khilafah (Caliphate).[53]

The members of HT are hostile to liberalism, capitalism and its surrounding democratic structures. They regard democracy, in particular, as well as standards of international human rights, as anathema to the Islamic belief system (*'aqīdah*) (Ahmed and Stuart 2009: 38–39). They advocate boycotts of democratic elections because they represent a *kufr* belief system and vest legal and political sovereignty in the people rather than with Allāh (Ahmed and Stuart 2009: 39). They prohibit voting in general elections, participation in local or national parliaments and even the securing of their Islamic rights through the medium of secular law. For them, only an Islamic state (*dawlah Islāmiyyah*) organised and informed through their interpretations of Islamic dogma and *fiqh* is authoritative. Their goal is to set up an Islamic State in its 'pure' form, even in countries which are not formally 'Islamic' or with Muslim populations (An-Nabahāni 1998: 155).[54]

Previous prominent members of the UK branch of HT, such as Omar Bakri and Anjem Choudary, formed their own splinter groups which were later to become proscribed organisations. They openly advocate the implementation of all Sharīʻah (as they view it) wherever there are Muslims and have supported the 9/11 and 7/7 terrorist attacks, jihadist attacks on American bases overseas and more recently the murder and decapitation of English soldier, Lee Rigby. It is important to note that Anjem Choudary, a former solicitor and Chairman of the Society for Muslim Lawyers, who revamped the proscribed organisation Al-Muhajiroun as Islam4UK, was charged in August 2015 for encouraging people to join the 'Islamic State' (Dā'ish) (Koern 2015).[55]

The integrationists

Our third category comprises integrationists who wish to participate in society, but without sacrificing aspects of their religious identity. In other words, they see societal engagement as a 'two-way street' (Kymlicka 1996: 96). On the one hand, like the separatists, they wish to retain their Islamic identity and continue their Islamic practices and customs. On the other, they seek to engage with civic and secular authority in the West and to navigate their interpretations of Islām within existing frameworks. This contrasts with the assimilationists in that they do not follow what is prevalent as a benchmark; that is merely an obstacle to navigate around as opposed to a norm positively embraced. While Muslim minorities endorse and advocate the application of Sharī'ah wherever they may be, it is often interpreted to suit the particular surroundings in which they find themselves. It is this category that we will consider more closely in the final part of the chapter below.

Our first example of integrationists are the 'traditionalists', called as such because they purport to follow the traditional schools of Islamic jurisprudence (the *madhāhib*). Answers to particular questions are addressed by looking at established texts taught in the *madrassahs* (from the established schools of Islamic jurisprudence, such as the Ḥanafis, Shāfi'īs, Ḥanbalis and Mālikis, for example) and global Islamic centres of learning (such as the Azhar in Egypt, the Qarawiyyin in Morocco and the Zaytuna in Tunisia). Where situations appear difficult and fundamentally different for the Muslim minority than they would be in a Muslim country, a *fatwa* is often given by way of a *rukhṣah* or an exception that would permit the act, so long as the *mustaftī* (the one asking for the *fatwa*) complies with its limitations. There are no subject specific boundaries to this approach. Also there is no principled objection to engaging in politics and the legal system, so long as the Muslim works within the confines of *ḥalāl* (the lawful) and avoids *ḥarām* (the unlawful) and tries to secure benefit (*maṣlaḥah*) for the Muslims in the broader community.

The second example of integrationists regards themselves as 'Renewers' or *Tajdīdi*s. For them, the traditional approach of looking at the schools of jurisprudence for all the answers is unsatisfactory. They proclaim a return to the Qur'ān and Sunnah and avoid adherence to any particular school of thought,[56] though the latter remain sources of reference. They approach the situation of Muslim minorities in the West as a problem of *fiqh* and therefore subject to the *ijtihād* and particular reasoning of individual jurists.

Adaptation and 'reconstructing' Sharīʿah

In recent times, a group of these Tajdīdis have combined[57] to produce a new *fiqh* which they call Fiqh al-ʿAqallīyyāt (the 'Law of Minorities'). The purpose of Fiqh al-ʿAqallīyyāt, is to assist in the 'normalisation' of Muslims in the West and help them navigate obstacles posed by the legal system (Hassan 2013: 15). It purports to provide space for the gradual and easy practice of rituals as well as giving Islamic legitimacy to attempts to resolve conflicts between attempts to practice Islām and the local laws and regulations (Hassan 2013: 16). It represents a symbolic attempt to affirm Islamic identity within the political frameworks of a liberal democracy (see More 2010: 4).

One of the leading authorities of Fiqh al-ʿAqallīyyāt is ʿAbdallāh bin Bayyah. For ʿAbdallāh bin Bayyah, the relationship between Muslim minorities and their countries of residence is based on a voluntary contract. It is also based on a commitment to the fundamental values shared between Islām and those embodied within that particular country, such as fairness, justice, mutual respect between peoples, human rights (though their conceptions may differ), pluralism and neutrality between different religious traditions (his construction of secularism). These values are seen as an incident of human nature (a 'natural law'), rather than articulated by a particular religious or juridical voice.[58] Engagement occurs at a shared abstract level that permits negotiation and navigation within one's own religious and cultural frame. Participation in the political and legal system is deemed, therefore, both secular and Islamic at the same time where one works for the common public interest. In case of conflict, the Muslim sides with the Islamic construct (whatever that may be in a particular case), but the relationship between the Islamic Sharīʿah and the secular law is not cast in diametrically opposite terms. Indeed, in many cases, because of their similarities in fundamental value positions, applying the secular law is Islamic. Separatism is not the solution, nor is assimilation; rather, the Muslim minorities integrate into the surrounding society but without sacrificing or compromising their Islamic identities (bin Bayyah 2007: 168; see also, bin Bayyah n.d.a).

Bin Bayyah proposes adherence to the Islamic juridical schools (*al-madhāhib*) and engaging with their rich heritage, including complying with previous opinion, though not necessarily to one School or one particular scholar. Where the Fiqh of Minorities might appear different is in its particular focus on the land of residence and the recognition that not all the rules of the Sharīʿah that would form part of Islamic governance in a Muslim country may be applicable. This includes the specified criminal punishments (*al-ḥudūd*) because of the Prophetic saying: 'Hands shall not be cut off while being in a state of travelling.'[59] The construction and delivery of religious rulings (*al-fatāwā*) is the job of the specialists, the expert scholars: those with years of studying the revered texts and also with an intimate knowledge of the realities in which the meanings of those texts will be realised.[60]

The example of ʿAbdullāh bin Bayyah illustrates that our typologies are only archetypes and the difficulty of finding particular examples that slot perfectly into our categories. In some senses, he cuts across all of our typologies, although he categorises himself as an 'integrationist'.[61] He is assimilationist in his apparent commitment to liberal values, but integrationist in the sense such a commitment is not viewed in conflict with established Islamic and Sharīʿah values. He is a traditionalist in his adherence to established opinion (and very limited application of individual *ijtihād*), but he is a 'renewer' in that he seems to breathe fresh life into the religion through reigniting the Sharīʿah as a law of continuing relevance and application in the contemporary lives of Muslims. However, he is also a separatist in that he is a follower of a Sufi *ṭarīqah* (a spiritual movement) from West Africa.

Representing a bridge between the spiritual and temporal, the contemporary and the traditional, the religious and the secular, the Muslim and the non-Muslim, we view the broad approach (as opposed to particular *fatāwā*) of 'Abdullāh bin Bayyah, and those like him, as the most workable for Muslim minorities in the West and a suitable template of Sharīʿah for governments to refer to in their approaches to accommodation of Muslims in the Common Law world.[62]

Having examined the complexity of the meaning of the Sharīʿah and how it can be interpreted and understood by Muslim communities, both in actuality and normatively, let us revisit the assumptions of the Sharīʿah debates.

Is there really only 'one law' for all?

A common characteristic of all of the public debates in each of the four jurisdictions has been that only one set of laws is applicable and these are the official state laws. This was the reason provided by the Attorney-General of Ontario when amending the law to ensure no recognition of faith-based arbitration in Ontario. It was the same reason echoed by the anti-Sharīʿah advocates in the USA. The law is seen as monolithic and centralised – embodied only in the official state law.

This perception fails to take into account that in many aspects of dispute resolution, various normative orders are in use. Of course, these other orders operate unofficially, outside the official legal system. But for many people, they play a greater role in the resolution of their disputes than the official law. As legal subjects, we do not act merely on the basis of legal prescriptions as identified and interpreted in a formal system. Rather, we act on the basis of the intersecting demands of our own ethical beliefs, our location in a social field, prevailing discourses about right and wrong and any number of more practical considerations (Davies 2005: 97).

For many Muslims, their reference to Sharīʿah operates on this moral and interpretative plane. Their understanding of Sharīʿah provides a moral compass as they navigate their way through the formal legal system and informs their choices open to them within the formal law. It does not operate in parallel or in necessary contestation to the formal law. The Muslim Arbitration Tribunal in England and Wales, mentioned above, provides a clear example of a harmonious integration between Sharīʿah and English law. Similarly, in Canada, the Boyd

Report documents how various faith communities set up processes for the resolution of family disputes (Boyd 2004: 55–68). In particular, within the Muslim community there were examples of these processes already in existence (Boyd 2004: 60). This is also the case in Australia (Krayem 2014) and the USA (Macfarlane 2012). So while public commentary may emphasise the application of official law only, the reality is that people are guided by 'laws' coming from many different sources to resolve their disputes; quite often this does not involve the state or the official legal system. At times, it is the 'unofficial law of the community' that will have a stronger influence on the individual than the 'official civil law of the polity' (Nichols 2012: 2). This does not mean that the official law is unimportant or treated with contemptuous disregard. Rather, it implies people resolve their disputes based on many factors which may lie outside of the official legal system.

Furthermore, as we have argued above, the debates largely assumed that Muslims are asking for official recognition of Sharīʿah or Islamic Law, and a seventh-century version, complete with its corporal punishments. Whilst there may be a very small minority who make such claims, that is by no means the view of the majority of the Muslim communities in our countries. In reality, in the debates described in the first part of this chapter, there was never any suggestion that Muslims were seeking such recognition (Ahmed and Norton 2012: 382). In the UK, for example, Ahmed and Norton found that the Sharīʿah tribunals were mindful of their relationship with the official law and were seeking to interact with, rather than override the official law (Ahmed and Norton 2012: 382). Further, as Archbishop Rowan Williams said, 'to recognise Shariah is to recognise a method of jurisprudence governed by revealed texts rather than a single system' (Williams 2008a). It is not about setting up a parallel legal system or even formal recognition of Sharīʿah at all. Rather, as stated above, it was about whether Muslims were entitled to avail themselves of procedures available under state law.

The assumption that Muslims want a parallel legal system is also at odds with the scholarly opinion many Muslims rely upon that emphasises the importance of abiding by the law of the land. As one Australian academic and scholar argued, Muslim jurists understood:

> that the ultimate authority in any country belongs to the government, and so in a non-Muslim context it is counter-intuitive to assume that individual Muslim, or the religious leaders, can take the law into their own hands when they are not permitted to do so.
>
> (Abdalla 2013: 675)

Is Sharīʿah 'too difficult'?

Earlier discussions alluded to the argument that Sharīʿah cannot be accommodated because of perceived inherent difficulties in applying such principles in a secular state. There are a number of elements to this argument, the first being that the content of Sharīʿah law is so diverse that we cannot ascertain which particular rule of Sharīʿah to apply. This argument assumes the law is necessarily indeterminate because there are choices of interpretation. As such, the argument runs, Sharīʿah cannot provide a basis for decision-making. Yet that is a strange argument to make against applying Sharīʿah when exactly the same argument could be made in the Common Law contexts of adjudication. Most texts of legislation, for example, are 'open-textured' and open to a variety of competing interpretations. Similarly, when case law applies, the ratio decidendi does not simply rise to the surface. Judges have to interpret the facts and reason their way to find the applicable principle. The plurality of possibilities provides flexibility to the judges to interpret the law in light of the present circumstances. It is the same for the Sharīʿah. The plurality of opinion provides for flexibility that the judge can utilise to fit the particular context. The fact that there is a choice enables the most appropriate choices to be made given the fact situation; it does not provide an argument to preclude the making of any choice.

The second element of this argument is that Islamic law is a complex legal framework that 'does not translate appropriately or fairly when utilized in a patchwork fashion' (Bakht 2004: 15). One cannot pick and choose which aspects of Sharīʿah to apply. As the previous section has demonstrated, this is very much dependent on the interpretation given to Sharīʿah. Some interpretations explicitly seek to integrate within existing frameworks and are compatible with both the historical Islamic tradition and contemporary liberal constitutionalism. A state-absorbed Sharīʿah on an integrative model would not make it 'patchwork Sharīʿah' for those who follow it, as the choices made are all Sharīʿah choices.

The third element, and connected to the second argument, is that the application of a religiously based law in a secular society would challenge the neutrality of the liberal state. As we mentioned in the Introduction and Chapter 1, many see religion as a divisive force in society that is at odds with the neutral liberal state (Aslam 2006: 859). They argue, therefore, that 'we should not allow religious groups to apply their own laws and then have the state enforce them' (Dranoff 2005). In this, they assume the neutrality of the secular state while overlooking the religious origins of mainstream law. This is particularly true of American law and the founding of the American Constitution which establishes 'one nation under God' (see Trigg 2012a: 72–82). They also overstate the importance of neutrality to the liberal state and the conceptualisation of law it expresses. While liberal philosophers such as John Rawls and Ronald Dworkin[63] eschew perfectionism (the notion that there is a conception of the 'good life') and that the state should not favour one conception of the 'good life' over another, that view has been challenged by prominent liberal philosophers in recent years, such as Joseph Raz. For him, perfectionism is not inconsistent with key liberal tenets where it promotes 'personal autonomy' and individual liberty. The state, he argues, cannot be neutral in this 'objective good' but must actively promote it by helping or hindering choices which are more likely to achieve this outcome.[64] Applying this to the Sharīʿah debate, it would not be contrary to liberal principles for the state to promote certain understandings of Sharīʿah at the expense of others, so long as those understandings are more likely to promote individual and moral autonomy. The same would be said of any religious conception of the 'good life' and, in that sense, the liberal state remains neutral in its commitment to equality.[65]

Recent world events have left many in the West with the view that Islamic values pose an inherent danger to society. They fear any accommodation would 'provide legal and political ammunition for religious extremists around the world' (International Centre for Human Rights and Democratic Development 2005: 7). Tarek Fatah in Canada, for example, describes it 'like putting a toehold or a bridge hood of Islamic fundamentalism in Canada' and that 'they are trying to get under the radar and bring political Islām by stealth. That is their objective; this is not about anything other than trying to establish authority over a community' (Religious law in Canada 2005). This is also evident in the debates surrounding the legislative bans in the USA on the use of Sharīʿah in courts and the recent protest marches in Australia. Their understanding of 'Sharīʿah', however, is drawn from the puritanical separatist's manual and does not reflect the majority of Islamic scholarship or the integrative approaches we have set out.

The fear that any accommodation represents the first step in some kind of grand plan of so-called Islamic Fundamentalists is a common one. But as Modood argues:

> To avoid discussing and conceding what is reasonable because someone else might later demand something unreasonable is irrational. And to associate a whole group, in this case Muslims, with their extremist elements is a kind of political demonisation that may appropriately be called anti-Muslim racism.
>
> (Modood 2008)

Is 'Sharīʿah' oppressive of women?

The debates discussed above demonstrate that gender concerns with Sharīʿah are paramount and need to be dealt with before any proposal for recognition or accommodation can be publicly accepted. In fact, the campaigns against accommodation have often invoked this argument, most notably in the Canadian context. The main concern was around the issue of consent – that women could not freely choose to enter into such processes because of the pressure placed upon them (Brown 2007: 532). Khan argues that Muslim women experience pressure to conform or risk finding themselves ostracised by their families and communities. This is especially true, according to Khan, for 'women who have concentrated on preserving Muslim culture … and who therefore have few skills with which to survive in the white world' (Khan 1993: 60). These comments suggest that women who adhere to an Islamic way of life are ignorant of, uneducated in and, more importantly, not a part of the wider community. The International Centre for Human Rights and Democratic Development also argued, in its report, 'making religious tribunals readily available and their decisions enforceable under Ontario law will only legitimise women's lack of real choice' (International Centre for Human Rights and Democratic Development 2005: 4). The implication, therefore, is that Muslim women are vulnerable and incapable of making independent decisions.

We would argue that such arguments are paternalistic and objectionable as they deny Muslim women individual agency. They are also open to the same criticisms made of the supporters of faith-based arbitration – that they serve to limit the choices available to Muslim women (Aslam 2006: 850). 'It cannot be assumed', Bakht argues, 'that these women are necessarily duped or oppressed as this would be engaging in the very infantilising of Muslim women that one accuses patriarchal cultures of' (Bakht 2004: 22). For many women, having both the private ordering as well as the option to access the mainstream legal system is precisely what they want; it is not necessarily an either or situation as commonly depicted. Macfarlane's study, for example, found that: 'the overwhelming majority of respondents expressed a desire to be able to continue to access their Islamic traditions in a private, informal system, and also to be able to use the legal process' (Macfarlane 2012: 9). These findings demonstrate that despite the fear that faith-based arbitration was a step towards fragmenting society, it was in fact a step towards further integration.

Many scholars have attempted to address the apparent paradox of supporting multicultural policies which favour the preservation of cultural traditions in minority groups on the grounds of equality when they tend to reproduce discriminatory behaviours on marginalised sub-groups, such as women. Ayelat Shachar, for example, sees the area of family law accommodation as one in which this paradox is most evident (Shachar 1998: 85) (although, as we discuss in Chapter 4, these issues may also be relevant in the Criminal Law context). According to Shachar, this has the potential to disadvantage women as family law is also a realm in which women have been systematically disadvantaged (Shachar 1998: 85). While recognising this potential, Shachar notes that minority groups are not homogenous entities and that 'essential traditions are constantly being redefined', particularly as they interact with outside forces (Shachar 1998: 100, 104). When applied to Muslims and the Sharīʿah, this can be seen in our earlier discussions about the various approaches to modern-day interpretation. Some minority interpretations, particularly those wedded to textual literalism and an ahistorical seventh-century exegesis, are more likely to replicate the behaviours these commentators fear. However, the majority of approaches today engage with the entirety of the Sharīʿah tradition in order to properly serve the public interest, including the interests of Muslim women. In the chapters which follow, we consider in further detail the ways in which Sharīʿah interpretation can have an impact upon Muslim women (favourably and negatively), especially in the areas of Family and Criminal Law. We would argue that what is needed is an understanding of the issues that disadvantage women, and a response that addresses these concerns, while appreciating the importance of religion in their lives. In summary, we need to appreciate that Muslim women exercise agency and can view their faith as a source of empowerment. As Shachar argues, the lives of women are affected by the 'interplay between overlapping systems of identification, authority and belief' (Shachar 2008: 578).

This discussion has demonstrated that the perception of Sharīʿah is intricately linked with the fear that any form of accommodation constitutes a threat to society. This is a common perception across all four countries (with very little sign of that changing). Sharīʿah has been defined in the public eye by narrow and extremist interpretations to the exclusion of other approaches that fit more comfortably within Western societies.

Conclusion

In this chapter, we have argued that Sharīʿah plays a pivotal role in Muslims' personal and social identity, even where they would not formally self-identify as religious. What Sharīʿah means, however, is not self-evident and what matters is how the Sharīʿah is interpreted. Historically, religious scholars and the traditional schools of jurisprudence have restricted authority to interpret God's law to narrow elites. In the post-modern world, authority has fragmented giving rise to a bewildering array of contradictory opinions and positions. Some of these, whom we categorise as 'puritanical separatists', are indeed extreme and their thought is incapable of reconciling with the Common Law or any legal tradition, including established Sharīʿah tradition. While not representative of Muslims generally, their views are influential and make impacts on Muslims in the West. They are also reflected in certain positions taken in the contexts of family, business and crime (which we explore further in Chapters 3, 4 and 5).

The Sharīʿah, however, is also capable of being interpreted so as to enable Muslims to properly and fully integrate into societies governed by Common Law without sacrificing their Muslim and Islamic identities. Whether this is through the mechanism of Fiqh al-ʿAqallīyyāt or through a contextualised application of the established schools, we leave as an open question. We suggest both approaches can be accommodated within the Common Law legal frameworks.

We argue that one of the most problematic aspects of the role of Sharīʿah in these countries is public perception and prevalent assumptions that 'one law for all' means 'no' to all other normative orders; that Muslims want to apply all of the Sharīʿah, including its criminal punishments, and that Islām (and its Sharīʿah) is oppressive of women. In each country, these assumptions have crystallised into a fear that accommodation of Muslims will entail an uncivilised and illiberal parallel legal system that will compete with the official legal system. We have argued that all the evidence indicates the exact opposite. Muslim communities are seeking ways to harmonise their religious practice within the existing legal structure and to avail themselves of the existing avenues of private ordering available to all citizens.

We contend this is a sign of integration and social cohesion, rather than a separatist expression of a 'Ghetto mentality'. As Nichols observes, individuals are 'simultaneously members of multiple communities' and that they 'frequently possess strong citizenship affiliations to a religious group at the same time that they possess a citizenship affiliation to the civil state' (Nichols 2012). These do not have to be mutually exclusive identities as the next three chapters will show.

Notes

1 The next day the Office of the Archbishop issued a statement in response to what they termed a strong reaction by the media to the speech. In this statement they clarified that: 'The Archbishop made no proposals for *Shariah* in either the lecture or the interview, and certainly did not call for its introduction as some kind of parallel jurisdiction to the civil law.' Rather, it clarified that the Archbishop 'sought carefully to explore the limits of a unitary and secular legal system in the presence of an increasingly plural (including religiously plural) society and to see how such a unitary system might be able to accommodate religious claims' (Williams 2008b). However, despite these immediate attempts at clarification, the public debate continued, largely based on the initial reactions to the Archbishop's speech.

2 According to their website, this campaign:

> calls on the UK government to recognize that *Shariah* law is arbitrary and discriminatory and for an end to *Shariah* courts and all religious tribunals on the basis that they work against and not for equality and human rights. The campaign also calls for the Arbitration Act 1996 to be amended so that all religious tribunals are banned from operating within and outside of the legal system.
>
> (One Law for All n.d.)

3 See also: D. Pearl and W. Menski, *Muslim Family Law* (London: Sweet & Maxwell, 1998); D. Pearl, 'Muslim marriages in English law', *Cambridge Law Journal*, (1972) 30 (1): 120–43; D. Pearl, 'Ethnic diversity in English law', in S. Cretney (ed.), *Family Law: Essays for the New Millennium* (Bristol: Jordans Publishing Ltd, 2000); D. Pearl, 'Cross-cultural interaction between Islamic law and other legal systems: Islamic family law and Anglo-American public policy', *Cleveland State Review*, (1985–86) 34: 113–27; S. Poulter, *Ethnicity, Law and Human Rights: The English Experience* (Oxford: Clarendon Press, 1998); I. Yilmaz, *Muslim Laws, Politics and Society in Modern Nation States: Dynamic Legal Pluralisms in England, Turkey and Pakistan* (London: Ashgate, 2005).

4 This will be discussed in the later chapters regarding the resolution of family and business disputes.

5 For further discussion, see R.E. Maret, 2013, 'Mind the gap: The Equality Bill and Sharia arbitration in the United Kingdom', *Boston College International and Comparative Law Review*, 36 (1): 255–83.

6 At the time of announcing the decision of the government to amend the law, then Attorney-General Michael Bryant stated:

> We have heard loud and clear from those who are seeking greater protections for women. We must constantly move forward to eradicate discrimination, protect the vulnerable and promote equality … We will ensure that the law of the land in Ontario is not compromised, that there will be no binding family arbitration in Ontario that uses a set of rules or laws that discriminate against women. This comment reflects a decision that was probably made more for political reasons than policy reasons, as Boyd had devoted a considerable amount of time and attention to considering the impact of these processes on women and had found no evidence that women were being systematically discriminated against. Furthermore, there was no suggestion that faith based arbitration would be

conducted in a manner contrary to the law of Ontario. However, the decision of the government demonstrated how significant the gender concerns were in the public debate about faith based arbitration.

(Ministry of the Attorney General 2005)

7 This is supported by Macfarlane (2012) in the North American context and by Krayem (2014) from her empirical work in Australia.

8 Abdul Jalil Ahmad of the Islamic Council of Western Australia suggested that the court would comprise a board of ten Islamic leaders and that while it would be a 'court of arbitration', it would not take the place of the Australian legal system, as Muslims would not act contrary to law.

9 The issue was again raised in early 2006 when the then treasurer, Peter Costello, in a keynote speech at the Sydney Institute titled *Worth Promoting, Worth Defending: Australian Citizenship, What it Means and How to Nurture It*, spoke out against what he termed 'confused, mushy, misguided multiculturalism' which did not require new citizens to give up culture, language, religion or opinions. In particular he made direct reference to a comment made by a Melbourne imām that Muslims live by Australian law and Islamic law. He stated:

> Our state is a secular state ... There is not a separate stream of law derived from religious sources that competes with or supplants Australian law in governing our civil society. The source of our law is the democratically elected legislature ... There are countries that apply religious or sharia law – Saudi Arabia and Iran come to mind. If a person wants to live under sharia law these are countries where they might feel at ease. But not Australia.
>
> (Costello 2006)

10 This was the rhetorical justification for his co-sponsoring of a Bill to ban Sharīʿah law. See further, Sabrina Siddiqui, 'Florida state senator: Sharia law like disease we should vaccinate against', *Huffington Post Australia*, 2 April, 2013.

11 This fear of Sharīʿah has expanded to include commentary on Muslim professionals working in the law. For example, when a Muslim was appointed to the New Jersey Supreme Court, Governor Chris Christie was asked whether he would bring Sharīʿah to the bench to which the Governor replied:

> Sharia law has nothing to do with this at all. It's crazy! The guy's an American citizen who's been admitted to practice law in New Jersey, swearing an oath to uphold the laws of New Jersey, the Constitution of the state of New Jersey and the Constitution of the United States of America.... This Sharia law business is crap! It's just crazy, and I'm tired of dealing with the crazies!

12 Sebastian De Brennan in response to Costello's comments discussed above, stated:

> As the Canadian experience demonstrates, it is only a matter of time before Sharia law is proposed as a legitimate means of resolving disputes – including family law disputes – as they arise between Islamic Australians. The presence of Koori courts and sentencing circles for indigenous Australians and the fact that much of the law in this land is predicated on the Judeo-Christian legal tradition remind us that there is nothing novel about the interplay and tension between religion, culture and law.
>
> (De Brennan 2006)

13 See further, Khaled Abou El Fadl, *The Great Theft: Wrestling Islam from the Extremists* (New York: HarperCollins, 2005).

A majority of Britons now believe that Islām, and not just Islamist Fundamentalist groups, are a threat to Western liberal democracy. See the recent poll conducted by the *Huffington Post* and reported in the *Independent*: Louis Doré, 'More Britons believe that multiculturalism makes the country worse – not better, says poll', *Independent*, 4 July 2015.

14 Al-*Ṣaḥīḥ Al-Bukhārī*, vol. 4, book 55, no. 652.

15 This also opens up interesting avenues of comparative study of religious laws, given we would expect to encounter a number of similarities upon the above basis.

16 The description in the text is necessarily archetypal and normative, based on the Qur'ānic '*muttaqī*', or 'perfect believer', whose vision of the 'good life' is rooted in the Hereafter and pursues everlasting Heavenly Pleasures rather than the ephemeral attractions of the worldly domain. Muslims, in practice, may have multiple commitments and allegiances, and very little religious motivation or desire to carry out the religion's dictates. See further, Jocelyn Cesari, *Why the West Fears Islam: An Exploration of Muslims in Liberal Democracies* (New York: Palgrave Macmillan, 2013), pp. 50–69.

17 The notion of the 'Islamic State' (*Dawlat al-Islāmiyyah*) was propounded in the 1950s and 1960s by Sayyid Qutb and his followers (the so-called 'Muslim Brotherhood' (MB) (*Ikhwan Muslimeen*) and proceeded Khomeini's Shī'ah revolution and 'Islamic Republic of Iran'. Sayyid Qutb believed that sovereignty rests exclusively with Allāh and that no state has jurisdiction to legislate; that Allāh is the only 'legislator'. He also believed those who pass laws other than through the Qur'ān or through the Prophet are worshipping other than Allāh (see Qutb 2006: 89). The primary obligation of all Muslim rulers, according to him, was to implement all of the judgements in the Qur'ān and Sunnah, without exception and without delay. Where rulers failed to do so, even in one respect, Sayyid Qutb declared them apostates (*murtaddūn*). This declaration included all those who participated in government, in addition to all Muslims who agreed to live under secular law (whether Common or Civil) in non-Muslim countries. He regarded all of humanity as living in a condition of *jāhiliyyah* (ignorance) that existed prior to the Revelation. In some of his works, he claims that all of humanity have committed apostasy ('*Irtiddat al-bashariyyatu bi-jumlati-hā*'); see *Fi Dhilāl al-Qur'ān* (1980), p. 1057. In others, he claims that *all* societies (without exception) are in a state of *jāhiliyyah* and that there is no Islām anywhere; see *Fi Dhilāl al Qur'an* (1980), p. 1057. See also, Qutb 2006: 91 and 93. Writers on the Prophetic Ḥadīth note this is contrary to reports from authenticated collections. In a *Ḥadīth* narrated by Ibn Abi Hatim, the Prophet said: 'I asked my Lord four things on behalf of my Nation. I was given three, but one was barred from me. I asked Him that my Nation would not commit blasphemy in its entirety, and He granted me it.'

The solution, for Sayyid Qutb, was for Muslims to isolate themselves from society to 'purify' (*'itizāl*) (see Qutb 2006: 53) themselves from the corruptions of *jāhiliyyah* until they were in a position to found a 'true' Islamic society (Qutb 2006: 58). At its most benign, Qutbism proposed non-engagement with the legal apparatus of a non-Muslim society and that residence could be only temporary. Muslims could be involved in missionary activity to draw people to the cause, but not to take out 'citizenship' of a country rooted in 'ignorance' and which, in many cases, was hostile to the basic tenets of Islām (as he saw them). So Muslims should not become politicians or participate within secular parties. Nor, clearly, could they become judges, magistrates, lawyers or police officers, the cogs of secular legal authority. For Qutb, such participation rendered a Muslim an apostate deserving of death. Muslims, he wrote, must be autonomous and not subservient to the law of Man (Qutb 2006: 46). Indeed, they were obligated to migrate to the land of *true* Islām (as he saw it); Khaled Abou El Fadl, *The Great Theft*, p. 82. On the position of the traditional Islamic juridical schools on this question and whether there was ever any need to migrate, see Abou El Fadl, 'Legal debates on Muslim minorities: Between rejection and accommodation', *The Journal of Religious Ethics*, (1994) 22 (1): 127–62.

18 This is reported by At-Tirmidhi, in his *Sunan*, Ḥadīth no. 1987.

19 The Prophet described *Iḥsān* as a state in which the believer worships Allāh *as if* he sees him, but in full knowledge that Allāh sees him (*ta'bud Allāha ka-annaka tarāhu, fa il-lam takun tarāhu fa innahu yarāk*). This is part of the *Ḥadīth Jibril* reported by Muslim in his *Ṣaḥīḥ*, Ḥadīth no. 8.

20 In a reliable *Ḥadīth* reported by At-Tirmidhi and Abu Dāwūd, the Prophet advised his Companions, when close to his death: 'I order you to obey Allāh, to hear and obey (the leader) even if an Abyssinian slave so orders. Whoever among you lives (after me) will see many differences. It is incumbent upon you to follow my path (*fa 'alaykum bi-sunnatī*) and the path of the rightly-guided vice-gerents (*al-khulafā'*). Cling to them as hard as you can' (An-Nawawi 2002: 26, Ḥadīth no. 28).

21 In a *Ḥadīth, qudsi* (a saying in which the Prophet reported what Allāh said), the Prophet reported that Allāh said: 'The best that my slave can do to be close and accepted (rewarded) by Me is to perform that which was made an obligation upon him' (*Al-Ṣaḥīḥ* al-Bukhārī, Ḥadīth no. 6502).

22 In devotional matters, for example, prioritising obligations over optional matters would imply that a Muslim should not be praying the optional *Tarāwīḥ* prayers during Ramaḍān if he has not prayed his obligatory Five Prayers.

23 The meaning of the chapter, *al-Mā'idah*, verse 3, provides: 'On this day I have completed your religion for you and perfected My Favour upon you.'

24 The 'Companions' refers to those who met Prophet Muḫammad ordinarily in his lifetime and who believed in him. The generation of the Companions is said to be the 'best of the generations' and the best of the Companions, the four rightly-guided vice-gerents (or Caliphs). When the Prophet ordered (in the *Ḥadīth* mentioned in Note 17, above) those who would come after him to follow the 'Sunnah' of his vice-gerents, this referred to Abu Bakr, 'Omar, 'Othman and 'Ali, by (Sunni) consensus. According to Islamic scholars, this 'following' implied two things: first, imitation of the rulings of these vice-gerents for the *one unable to perform his or her own deductions* from the sources (*liman'ajaza 'an il-nadzr*); second, preference (*at-tarjīḥ*) for the rulings of these four rulers in cases of differences of opinion amongst the Companions (see Ibn Daqīq al-'Id 2012: 149. Note that scholars who died in 702 AH [1302 CE], such as this author, more than 650 years after the time of the Companions, still believed in the ongoing scholarly determination of the rulings [*ijtihād*]).

25 In his concise *Tafsir*, An-Nasafi, states (of the two meanings he refers) that the verse can imply, 'For purposes of accountability, I have completed for you what you need to know among knowing the halal and the haram, with a dependence on the revealed laws of Islām and the rules of analogy *(qawaneen al-qiyās*)' (emphasis added) (An-Nasafi [d. 710 AH] 2008: 306). The explicit reference to the *rules* of analogy, as opposed to the extracted substantive judgement (*ḥukm*) indicates that only the framework or process for deriving judgement has been completed and fixed. The only Sunnis, in Islamic history, to deny a continuing juristic role to develop the *fiqh* (the body of substantive rules of Islām) through analogy were the Dzāhiris who claimed there were only three legal sources in Islām: the Qur'ān, the Prophet's Sunnah and Juristic Consensus (*al-Ijmā'*). The Wahhabis (and 'Salafis'), see below, claimed to follow in their footsteps, and resurrected the works of Daud ibn Khalaf's most famous student, Ibn Ḥazm. The Shī'ah and Ibāḍis (whose adherents predominate in today's Oman) are also opposed to development of the law through analogy, although they still employ their own linguistic interpretations of the authoritative texts with applications to the present.

26 Scholars in the science of the deduction of Islamic rules (*uṣūl al-fiqh*) defined juridical *ijtihād* as the maximum expenditure of effort to interpret a religious question upon which there is no explicit text from the Qur'ān or the Prophetic Sunnah (here, meaning '*Ḥadīth*'). See further, Al-Shirāzi 2006: 136; and Al-Shāfi'i 2005: 110.

27 This *Ḥadīth* is reported by Abu Dawud, in his *Sunan*, Ḥadīth no. 4278.

28 See Mohammad Hashim Kamali, *The Middle Path of Moderation in Islam: The Qur'ānic Principle of Wasaṭiyyah* (Oxford and New York: Oxford University Press, 2015), p. 221.

29 Jalāluddīn Al-Siyūṭī (d. 1505/911) who lived during the time of the Egyptian Mamluks, famously claimed complete *ijtihād*, stating: 'I have now perfected for myself the tools of *ijtihād*.... I say that indicating the blessing of Allāh, the sublime and transcendent, not out of boasting.' See further, J. Al-Siyūṭī, *Sharh At-Tanbih*, vol. 1 (Beirut: Dār al-Fikr. n.d.), p. 16.

30 Technically, there is, and has been, no limit on the number of juridical schools, though for Sunni Muslims (by far the majority), four have come to predominate: the Ḥanafi (after Abu Hanifah [Nu'mān ibn Thābit], d. 150 AH/772 CE); Māliki (Malik ibn Anas, d. 179 AH/801 CE); Shāf'ī (Muḥammad ibn Idris, d. 204 AH/826 CE); and Ḥanbali (Aḥmad ibn Ḥanbal, d. 241 AH/863 CE). For the Shī'ah, the Ja'fari (attributed to Abu Ja'far al-Ṣādiq, d. 198 AH/820 CE) and the Zaydi (attributed to Zaid ibn 'Alī, d. 122 AH/740 CE) schools are the most widespread. The Ibāḍis (after 'Abdullah ibn Ibāḍ, d. 89 AH/708 CE with a presence in Oman, Zanzibar and some areas of North Africa) and the Dzāhiris (after Dāwūd ibn Khalaf al-Dzāhiri, d. 270 AH/883 CE; the school is practically extinct, though deemed a working school according to some) comprise the last of the 'eight schools' defined as 'Muslim' by a global gathering of Islamic scholars convened under the auspices of the Organisation for Islamic Cooperation (OIC). See the *Amman Declaration*, at: http://ammanmessage.com/index.php?option=com_content&task=view&id=91&Itemid=74&lang=en (accessed 8 August 2015). The Ismā'īlīs (a faction of the Shī'ah, headed by the Aga Khan) were formally excluded from this list, but the practical laws of their two sub-factions, the Dawoodi Buhara and the Nizaris, comply largely with the Shāfi'ī and Ja'farī schools, so their particular inclusion was deemed unnecessary.

31 This contests the narrative of the followers of Muḥammad ibn 'Abdul Wahhāb (the 'Wahhabis'), and the modern 'Salafists' who claim that Muslim scholars ceased to guide the Muslim nation who then fell into a state of '*Jāhiliyyah*' (a state of ignorance similar to the state of the Arabs immediately preceding Prophet Muḥammad's 'Call to Islām'). They ignore juridical scholarship from after the first three centuries following the migration, other than those specifically praised by their founder, Muḥammad ibn 'Abdul Wahhab (such as Aḥmad ibn Taymiyyah, Ibn Qayyim al-Jawziyyah and Ibn Ḥazm). According to historians, the Wahhabi doctrines and 'orthopraxy' represented a 'rupture and discontinuity with Muslim society.' See further, F. Gerges, *The Far Enemy: Why Jihad went Global* (Cambridge: Cambridge University Press, 2005), pp. 242–43. The term 'Salafi' harks back to the period of those who lived in the first 300 years after the migration of the Prophet from Mecca to Medina. Following a *Ḥadīth* of the Prophet, they are deemed to be the best centuries since Islām's inception. The group known as 'Salafis' were originally a reform movement (headed by Muḥammad 'Abduh and Rashid Riḍa) at the turn of the nineteenth century which purported to go back to the Qur'ān and Sunnah, rather than be bound by the opinions of the Schools in their respective interpretation. According to Khaled Abou El-Fadl, the 'Salafis' and the 'Wahhabis' became indistinguishable from the 1970s onwards, *The Great Theft*, p. 79.

32 For a good summary of the role of Fatwa, both in history and contemporary times, see A. Black and N. Hosen, 'Fatwas: Their role in contemporary secular Australia', *Griffith Law Review*, (2009), 18 (2): 405. See also, A. Layish, 'The fatwa as an instrument of accommodation', in M.K. Masud, B. Messick and D.S. Powers (eds), *Islamic Legal Interpretation: Muftis and Their Fatwas* (Cambridge: Harvard University Press, 2005).

33 'Traditionalists', a term we use to refer to those who adhere to the schools of jurisprudence, will always follow the 'preferred' previous statement in a school, which is ranked in accordance with the strength of evidence taken from the primary sources

(the Qur'ān and the Sunnah), other than in a minority of cases. According to them, it is prohibited for any '*mujtahid*' or '*muqallid*' (e.g. the layperson) to take any variant opinion without performing an evaluation, including an evaluation of the level of the scholar offering that opinion. Otherwise, rulings become arbitrary and follow one's desires (*hawa'*) in opposition to the religion. See further, M. al-'Aziz (ibn 'Ābidīn), *Sharḥ 'Uqūd Rasm al-Mufti* (Karachi: Maktabah al-Bushra, 2009), pp. 8–9.

34 We do not refer to the position in Asian Common Law countries, such as Singapore, where the giving of any religious rulings or judgements is highly regulated by government and government bodies. See further, T. Lindsey and K. Steiner, *Islam, Law and the State in Southeast Asia: Volume II: Singapore* (New York: I.B. Tauris, 2012).

35 The precise role of the judiciary depends upon the constitutional context, but remains a question of controversy because they are generally unelected. On the American context, see Richard Posner, 'Pragmatic adjudication', *Cardozo Law Review*, (1996): 1. See also, Ronald Dworkin, *Law's Empire* (Cambridge, MA: Harvard University Press 1988).

36 The traditional notion of the *Mujtahid* Qāḍī, who was simultaneously able to determine the Law according to his or her interpretation of the Divine texts and apply it to the facts of a particular case, ceased to reflect the reality centuries ago.

37 In this regard, see in particular the multiple works of Bernard Lewis.

38 See W. Hallaq, *Shari'a: Theory, Practice, Transformations* (Cambridge: Cambridge University Press, 2009), p. 36.

39 The scope of permissible cultural practice is not without controversy. Deference to custom as a default practice or as a norm to justify evasion of Islamic rules met with scholarly rebuke even in the late Ottoman period; see M. al-Kawthari, *Maqalāt al-Kawthari* (Beirut: Dār al-Ahnaf, 1993), p. 290. See also, al-'Aziz, *Sharḥ 'Uqūd Rasm al-Mufti*, pp. 80–81.

40 The Organisation for Islamic Cooperation (OIC) claims to be the global peak Islamic forum, but suffers a legitimacy deficit amongst ordinary Muslims. For further discussion of this potentially important body, see S. Farrar, 'The Organisation of Islamic Cooperation: Forever on the Periphery of Public International Law?' *Chinese Journal of International Law*, (2014) 13 (4): 787–817.

41 See further the empirical research of Jocelyn Cesari (2013: 32–42), carried out with focus groups in America, Canada, the UK and other European countries.

42 The drive to modernise initially took place at the end of the nineteenth century while Turkey remained the centre of the Ottoman 'Caliphate' (as part of the '*Tanzimat*' reforms). These reforms, along with those forced through by Mustapha Kemal, were seen as antithetical to the established Islamic tradition by conservative '*ulemā*'; see al-Kawthari, *Maqalāt al-Kawthari*, p. 290.

43 See C. Kurzman, *Liberal Islam: A Source Book* (Oxford and New York: Oxford University Press, 1998). While this author and others use the term 'liberal' to refer to a particular approach to interpretation of Islamic sources, 'Liberal Islām' is also a particular movement in Indonesia. See further, V. Hooker, 'Developing Islamic arguments for change through "liberal Islām"', in V. Hooker and A. Saikal (eds), *Islamic Perspectives in the New Millennium* (ISEAS, Singapore, 2004); L.Z. Rahim, 'Discursive contest between liberal and literal Islam in South East Asia', *Policy and Society*, (2006), 25 (4): 77–98.

44 See, for example, F. Mernissi, *Islam and Democracy* (Cambridge, MA: Basic Books, 2009).

45 For examples on the role of women, see A. Elewa and L. Silvers, '"I *am* one of the people": A survey and analysis of legal arguments on woman-led prayer in Islam', *Journal of Law and Religion*, (2010), 26 (1): 141–71. See also the works of Amina Wadud.

46 The Sudanese American, 'Abdullahi Ahmed An-Na'im, and his Sheikh, Mahmoud Taha, are good illustrations. See further, A. An-Na'im, *Towards an Islamic*

Reformation: Civil Liberties, Human Rights and International Law (Syracuse, NY: Syracuse University Press, 1990), pp. 52–68.

47 See further, D. Le Gall, 'Recent thinking on Sufis and saints in the lives of Muslim societies, past and present', *International Journal of Middle East Studies*, (2010), 42: 673–87.

48 This is the theological discipline 'ilm al-kalām', or Islamic metaphysics (literally, the knowledge of speech). Its exponents were many, and ran across the doctrinal schools. Fakhr al-Din Ar-Rāzi (d. 1209), was one of the most famous exegetists of the Qur'ān from this tradition. See further, 'Fakhr al-Din al-Razi' 1960–2002, *The Encyclopaedia of Islam*, vol. 2, pp. 751–55.

49 We recognise the historical origins of this term in the Christian religious conflicts of the seventeenth century, but it is applied here in the sense of 'aspiring to a special purity of doctrine and practice' and 'extreme strictness' (see Brown [ed.] 1993, vol. 2: 2420). While the term might be construed with Islamic connotations of *tajdīd* or renewal, it has more derogatory connotations in English.

See further, Abou El-Fadl, *The Great Theft*, p. 46.

50 In addition to Ḥizb ut-Taḥrir referred to in the text, the Wahhābis and the so-called 'Muslim Brotherhood' (MB) movement, otherwise known as '*Ikhwān Muslimeen*', are also representative of this approach.

51 For a recent exposition and refutation of Dā'ish from an Islamic perspective, see Shaykh Muhammad Al-Yaqoubi, *Refuting ISIS: A Rebuttal of its Religious and Ideological Foundations* (Sacred Knowledge, 2015).

52 Their beliefs can be found in various editions of their *Dabiq* online magazine and the book: 'Informing Mankind of the Emergence of the Islamic State'. Full references are included in Al-Yaqoubi, *Refuting ISIS.*

53 Like the Muslim Brotherhood, HT advocate an Islamic State – but 'the Khalifah is the State' (Article 35 of Ḥizbu ut-Taḥrir's *Draft Constitution*. See further, An-Nabahāni, *The Islamic State*, p. 246. In order to justify his position, An-Nabahāni referred to sayings of the Prophet, such as:

> Whoso takes off his hand from allegiance to Allāh will meet Him on the Day of Resurrection without having any proof for him, and whoso dies while there was no *Bay'ah* (pledge of allegiance) on his neck dies a death of *Jāhiliyyah*.
>
> (this *ḥadīth* is narrated by Imām Muslim in his *ṣaḥīḥ*)

He construed this *ḥadıth* to mean that everyone who failed to pledge allegiance to his Caliph, that is the Vice-gerent of Allāh on Earth, would die either as big sinners or as blasphemers. Given, however, that none of the Muslim leaders around the world since 1924 have agreed to appoint a Caliph, the ideology of HT implies that all Muslims who have not made a pledge of allegiance to the HT 'Caliph in waiting' are either in a state of grievous sin or apostates.

54 Advocating the approaches of the Companions of the Prophet, An-Nabahāni stated:

> The Islamic *Shari'ah* is a universal and comprehensive. Therefore, the Muslims never needed to study the laws of the country that they were about to conquer. They never needed to try and accommodate or compromise between the laws they had brought to solve life's problems and the laws in existence within that country. They would conquer a country and introduce the *Shari'ah* as a complete system, implementing Islam from the very first day they entered a country. Their method was radical in the sense that there was no phased approach to implement the system, such as implementing laws A, B, and C but not D, because implementing law D would result in controversy, turn people away from Islam, or was too difficult to adhere to. This type of gradualism did not exist.

55 Another example of these groups is the 'Wahhabis'. Founded upon the doctrines of Muḥammad ibn 'Abdul Wahhāb (1703–1792), their adherents believe they are the

only 'true Muslims'. The Wahhabi mission is (and has been) to rid the world of what they deem *bida'* (innovation) and return to a utopian re-imagining of the time of the Companions. Wahhabi creed and practice has not been known for its tolerance and was extremely violent in its original form. Muḥammad ibn 'Abdul Wahhāb was also openly hostile to the adoption of any customs he categorised as 'non-Muslim' and urged his followers to make visible their dislike and enmity. Although elements of the movement has been tempered through its long relationship with the Saudi dynasty and the Kingdom of Saudi Arabia, the current activities of Dāʿish provide contemporary evidence of a propensity to extreme violence and brutality. For them, violence and killing are seen as 'purifying' and ends in themselves.

Wahhabi clerics have long deferred to Saudi rulers as the necessary price to be paid for the protection and promotion of their creed, but deference does not extend to secular authority or to secular law. Clearly, this limits any engagement with a Common Law legal system. It will also provide some support for vigilante 'justice' which we touch upon in the Conclusion. The values and interpretations of the movement have a number of implications also in family and business contexts which we will explore in Chapters 4 and 5.

56 The approaches of 'Abdallāh bin Bayyah, however, generally reflect the Maliki School and are articulated through Malikite terminologies.

57 The leading proponents of this approach are Ṭāhir Jābir al-ʿAlwāni, Yūsuf al-Qaraḍāwi and ʿAbdallah bin Bayyah. They have their own approaches to Muslim minority questions and important substantive and methodological differences. For further details, see S.F. Hassan, *Fiqh al-Aqalliyyat: History, Development, and Progress* (New York: Palgrave Macmillan, 2013), pp. 57–119.

58 See Hassan, *Fiqh al-Aqalliyyat*, pp. 149–50. These observations are taken from ʿAbdullāh bin Bayyah, *Ṣinā'at al-Fatwa wa-Fiqh al-'Aqallīyyāt'* [The craft of fatwa and the law of Muslim minorities] (Beirut: Dār al-Minhaj, 2007), pp. 167–68.

59 Bin Bayyah reports this *ḥadīth* is narrated by Abu Dawud, At-Tirmidhi and Ahmad with a strong chain of narrators; see bin Bayyah, n.d.b, *On the fiqh of Muslim minorities*, The official website of His Eminence Shaykh ʿAbdallāh bin Bayyah, at: http://binbayyah.net/english/2012/02/20/on-the-fiqh-of-muslim-minorities/ (accessed 11 August 2015).

60 In this matter, Bin Bayyah is in accordance with Khaled Abou El-Fadl, *The Great Theft*. It implies that the giving of fatwa must be restricted to the learned and, by necessity, is elitist; it is not a matter that can or should be democratised.

61 See Bin Bayyah, above, note 58. See also, http://binbayyah.net/english/2014/05/29/advice-from-shaykh-abdallah-bin-bayyah-to-the-muslim-community-of-america-four-obstacles-that-muslims-face-in-america (accessed 10 August 2015).

62 See above at 5, Notes 15 and 16.

63 See J. Rawls, *A Theory of Justice*, revised edn (Oxford: Oxford University Press, 1999), pp. 285–92; Ronald Dworkin, 'Foundations of liberal equality', in S. Darwell (ed.), *Equal Freedom* (Ann Arbor, MI: University of Michigan Press, 1995), p. 191.

64 See Joseph Raz, *The Morality of Freedom* (Oxford: Oxford University Press, 1988) especially Chapters 5 and 6, and pp. 117–24. On a similar note, see Trigg, *Equality, Freedom and Religion*, p. 155.

65 See the Conclusion for further discussion.

3 Muslims, family relationships and the Common Law

> We have seen that Islamic law, far from dissolving, is penetrating into the West through official and unofficial means, contributing to a diversified and evolving law and jurisprudence.
>
> (Giunchi 2014)

Introduction

The Prophet's wife, ʿA'ishah, related that Prophet Muḥammad said, 'The best of you are the best to their wives, and I am the best to my wives.' (At-Tirmidhi, *Ḥadīth* no. 3895). Across the Muslim World, even in the most ostensibly secular of Muslim countries, Muslims have paid very close attention to Sharīʿah family law. Even during colonial times and in the laws of post-colonial Muslim states, when commercial and criminal laws frequently were tampered with and replaced by legislation based on the colonial law (e.g. English or French), Sharīʿah family laws were left almost unscathed. Such was the importance and centrality of Sharīʿah rules relating to the family.

It might be thought that given the diversity of Muslims in the West, and its very secular lifestyles, Sharīʿah has less relevance for Muslim families in these countries. Muslims can utilise a body of secular law to register their marriages, file divorces, seek or challenge custody for their children, and secure appropriate post-divorce financial settlements. Certainly for the Muslim 'assimilationists' we referred to in Chapter 2, they would not regard relying on English or Canadian law, for example, as problematic because they prefer 'doing in Rome as Romans do'. Religion does not occupy a central place in their lives. Even for these people, however, cultural ties remain important and few would seek to marry or divorce in a way that would be unacceptable in their cultural community for fear of ostracism. Indeed, one of the problems we examine in this chapter is the 'limping marriage' and the perceived inability of a Muslim woman to remarry until her husband grants her a divorce in Sharīʿah terms. Relying exclusively on the secular law does not answer her problem. For other Muslims, whether they fall into our separatist or integrationist groupings, resolution of family matters through the framework of Sharīʿah assumes even more importance.

For many Muslims living as minorities in the West and in Common Law countries, therefore, family law remains a central concern (Thompson and Yunus 2007: 361). It is also that aspect of Sharīʿah which appears most in Common Law Courts (Freeland 2006: 228).

Whilst the public focus has been on sensationalised debates[1] saturated in the rhetorical mantra 'one law for all', the reality is that Muslims have had to navigate their way through a plural sea of competing norms and through an unfamiliar legal environment (Yilmaz 2003). Yet this is not a problem unique to Muslims. Other cultural and religious minorities, including Jews, Buddhists, Hindus and Sikhs have their legal traditions that regulate family life and have had to approach the courts. Working within the unitary and secular nature of Common Law, the courts have attempted to fashion solutions for all of them, on a case-by-case basis, responding to their own particular factual situations. Generally, the courts have sought to achieve this by employing 'neutral' Common Law principles of 'reasonableness', 'certainty' and 'fairness'. Also as arbiters of fact and law – putting to one side for a moment the differences between jurisdictions in evidence law – the courts have received expert evidence from 'in' and 'outside' the religious community to determine those aspects of the religious law which bear on application of those principles. Through this process of cultural and legal engagement, the Common Law Courts have had to confront the extent to which they accommodate or legally recognise a religious legal tradition, or at least certain aspects of it.

In the Muslim context, this chapter will show that in many instances Common Law Courts have legally accommodated, in the sense of adapting or coming to a compromise with Sharīʿah family law principles. However, rather than facilitate Muslim self-identification (through Muslim expert evidence), too often the Courts have sought to interpret and define 'Islamic' for themselves, in a quasi-colonial, cultural occupation of the 'other'. In other cases, the courts have not purported to accommodate Muslims at all. They have sought sanctuary in the formal 'neutrality' of the Common Law in the safe application of legal principle thereby, as they see it, distancing themselves from the biases of religious preference. Yet it would be far too simplistic to paint a picture of mutual opposites: of accommodation versus non-accommodation. There are also several cases where courts have taken an intermediate stance by incorporating Muslim expert opinion enabling Sharīʿah legal principles to shape the final outcome. While this may not amount to 'accommodation' in the strict sense we outlined in the Introduction, it offers a more nuanced approach to legal recognition that respects both Muslim autonomy as well as the liberal democratic values underpinning the Common Law.

This chapter cannot attempt to address every aspect of Sharīʿah family law that has arisen in the courts. That is beyond the scope of a single chapter. Rather, it surveys the legal landscape of our chosen jurisdictions and focuses on matters central to Muslim family relations: legal validity of marriage, enforcement of the *mahr* or dowry, validity of divorce and parenting disputes. We begin with marriage.

An Islamic marriage

The concept of marriage, or *nikāḥ*, lies at the centre of Islamic Family Law. Almost every other legal concept in family relations revolves around it (Ali 2000: 151). Linguistically, *nikāḥ* means jimā. Jimā means 'to collect things' or 'sexual intercourse'.[2] In Sharī'ah terms, *nikāḥ* refers to a contract. Islām views marriage as a contract between two people (Lane 2010: 152). However, this should not detract from the religious and spiritual significance of the relationship. Many *ḥadīths* of the Prophet indicate the importance of marriage to an Islamic way of life, such as: 'Marriage is my exemplary way (*sunna*)', those who are averse to my example are also averse to me[3] (Ibn Mājah, Book 9, Ḥadith 1919); and 'There is nothing like marriage for the two who love one another' (Ibn Mājah, Book 9, Ḥadith 1920).

Marriage has five integral elements (*ārkan*): the spoken form (*sighah*), two witnesses, the bride's guardian, a groom, and the bride (Al-Misri 1999: 517). If any of these are missing, the Sharī'ah marriage contract is invalid. In this section, we focus on key issues of capacity to marry, the nature of marriage in Islām, and how Muslims go about marriage in our Common Law jurisdictions and ultimately the intersection of these processes with the official legal system.

Marriage in Common Law jurisdictions

There are many similarities between our four Common Law jurisdictions in the determination of a valid marriage. First, all four jurisdictions determine the acceptable age of marriage at eighteen years, although the United Kingdom accepts sixteen years as sufficient (The Marriage Act 1949 [UK]). Other jurisdictions accept younger marriages with parental consent or court approval. Canada also permits marriages in special circumstances such as pregnancy (Pilon 2001). Other requirements include: a single marital status, mental capacity and not being within the prohibited degrees of relationship.

Statutes also require an officiating party or authorised celebrant (religious or non-religious), signing of documents to signify consent to the marriage, and two adult witnesses. All four jurisdictions mandate registration of the marriage. This can be the most contentious element in validating an Islamic marriage and we will explore it in more detail later in this chapter.

Capacity

Capacity to enter into a marriage is central to the formation of the marriage in both Sharī'ah and Common Law. Both parties must have capacity, and the contract is void without it. The Sharī'ah determines capacity by physical maturity, proximity of blood ties, sanity, voluntariness and various other gender-specific conditions.

There is no minimum age for a contract of marriage, but it should not be consummated if that would cause harm to the putative spouse. While this does raise the issue of child marriage, Hussain notes that has little practical significance.

Most Muslim countries today have legislated to provide a minimum age of marriage (Hussain 2011: 79) and Muslim communities in the diaspora also are not calling to alter the minimum age for marriage.

Also related to capacity is that the parties must not be within the prohibited degrees of affinity. The prohibited degrees of affinity are set out in the Qur'ān and are that 'a person may not marry his or her ascendants, descendants, siblings, nieces and nephews, aunts and uncles, in-laws, step-parents and step-children and their descendants' (Hussain 2011: 80).[4]

These conditions associated with capacity pose no problem for Muslim communities in our Common Law jurisdictions, and in fact are quite similar to the conditions found in the official legal system. We see that many Muslims easily navigate their way to comply with both the religious aspects and legal aspects of getting married. However, there are other conditions that are gender-specific which may not be so harmonious with the official legal system. Namely that Muslim men can marry Muslim, Jewish or Christian women, but a Muslim woman is prohibited from marrying a non-Muslim man (Hussain 2011: 79).[5] Obviously according to the laws of equality in secular states, there can be no such restriction. This means a Muslim woman who chooses a non-Muslim partner can register that union as a 'marriage' notwithstanding community and family objection.

Another gender-specific condition is the permissibility of Muslim men to marry up to four wives. Whilst a prominent feature of the anti-Muslim narrative, polygyny, though permitted in the Sharīʿah, is in fact quite rare and that is largely due to the limitations and conditions the Sharīʿah imposes. A man can marry up to four wives at the same time but must provide for each one equally. This includes accommodation, food, clothing and other ancillary expenses. He must also spend an equal amount of time in the household of each wife. If he does not do this, it is considered an act of injustice without the explicit consent of the other wife (Ministry of Religious Endowments and Islamic Affairs 1983: 184).

Polygyny, or 'polygamy' is against the law in all of our Common Law jurisdictions. It is a criminal offence to contract a marriage whilst being legally married to someone else (see s.94 Marriage Act 1961 [Cth], s.57 Offences against the Person Act 1861 [UK], s.293 Criminal Code [Canada]; all US states have similar laws). In some jurisdictions, namely Canada and some US states, it is also an offence to cohabit whilst being legally married to someone else.

Whilst there has been very limited research done on polygamy in the Muslim communities in our Common Law countries, namely due to the fact that it is against the law, there has been some recent commentary about its growing prevalence. In particular, in the UK it has been described as being on the increase (although without proper research it is hard to be certain of this) (Jaan 2014: 8). In the North American context, Macfarlane relates that taking on 'second wives' was described by some of the research participants as a source of conflict in their relationship (Macfarlane 2012: 127). Obviously, polygamy is not an issue that only affects Muslim communities as it is well known that in the USA context, it is also practised by other communities such as the Mormon community.

So if it is illegal, how does it occur? Muslim men get around bigamy laws by not registering the second marriage and by just having a religious marriage. Given the discussion above, where we have seen that in certain cases, courts have held that religious marriages are capable of being recognised as legal marriages, there is a possibility that even without registering the second marriage they may fall foul of such laws. Even without registration, these relationships may have legal effect in regards to separation, financial entitlements and custody of any children of the relationship.

Whilst some have argued that there may be reasons for changing marriage laws to include polygamous marriages (Parkinson 1996: 309–26), there have not been any proposals for any legislative amendment proposed by the Muslim communities in our Common Law jurisdictions. However, there is no doubt that this is an area that needs to be researched, particularly given the fact that anecdotal evidence suggests that this is an increasing practice in Muslim communities.

Consent and forced marriage

An important aspect of the marriage contract is that both parties have given their consent. While the majority of the Islamic schools of jurisprudence require the bride's marriage guardian, who is usually her father or grandfather, to agree to the marriage, in most cases they cannot coerce or force the bride to enter into a marriage contract (ʿAbd al ʿAti 1995: 156).[6] The consent of both parties is an essential element of marriage. As the Qur'ān mentions: 'Do not prevent them from marrying their (former) husbands, if they mutually agree on equitable terms' (Qur'ān 2:232). The Prophet also declared invalid a marriage of a woman previously married who had refused her consent (Bukhāri, Book 67, Ḥadith no. 64).

The matter of choice is necessary for both parties. This stands in contrast to the common understanding that people have that in Islām women can be forced into marriage. Unfortunately, despite the religious requirement or recommendation for consent, some Muslims still ignore this and compel girls to marry against their will.[7] Ahsan, writing about the UK, argues that although Islām emphasises freedom of choice and consent of the couple, 'the parents, especially those whose norms and values are embedded in family and village customs and traditions rather than in Islamic law, often pressure children to accept.' (Ahsan 1995: 24) This is a clear abuse of Sharīʿah norms along with so-called 'honour crime' with which this is linked and we discuss in more detail in Chapter 4.

Forced marriage is a pressing concern in all of our jurisdictions. Although it is not one that affects Muslim communities exclusively, it undoubtedly exists. Quite often, the motivation behind parental coercion is cultural practice rather than a religious understanding. This reflects the complexity that arises when culture intersects with religious practice. In the UK, a Forced Marriage Unit (FMU) has been in operation for over a decade, dealing with over 1,200 cases on an annual basis. Over a third of these are associated with the Pakistan community (Forced Marriage Unit 2015). The FMU oversees the government's policy on forced marriage including policy, outreach and casework (Foreign and Commonwealth Home Office & Home Office 2013). This includes the operation of the Anti-Social Behaviour, Crime and Policing Act 2014 (UK) which makes it an offence to force someone to marry with a penalty of up to seven years in jail. Many organisations aim to support victims of forced marriage within the Muslim community and promote awareness and education within the community. For example, the Muslim Women's Network UK explains the operation of the legislation and provides a counter narrative from a religious perspective (Muslim Women's Network UK 2015). Similarly in Canada, the Zero Tolerance for Barbaric Cultural Practices Act 2015 was passed to add forced marriage to the Criminal Code. Whilst some groups supported this measure, others criticised its racist tone and questioned whether criminalisation would actually help the victims who often struggled to speak out (Browne 2015). Australia too has criminalised forced marriage under s.270.7A of the Criminal Code (Cth). Although it is difficult to know how many women are affected, researchers suggest that it impacts on women from diverse backgrounds (McGuire 2014). This issue is dealt with at a state level in the USA, with only ten states which criminalise forced marriage (Reiss 2015). Recently, 'Unchained', a non-profit organisation supporting girls and women affected by forced marriage, drew attention to the levels of child marriage in the USA (Reiss 2015). Again, whilst this practice is not sanctioned by Sharīʿah or religious principles, it reflects the continuing influence of patriarchal cultural practices within Muslim communities.

Whilst there have been cases brought under these criminal laws, there are also a few case brought under family laws. In *Essey* v. *Elia* [2013] FCCA 1525, an Australian court was asked to determine the amount of contact a child was to have with its father. In the course of the dispute, the court discovered the marriage had been conducted when the mother was under age and without her consent. The mother's father admitted to knowing both of these facts at the time of marriage (*Essey* v. *Elia* [2013] FCCA 1525 at para. 19).

The court was quick to distance the 'forced marriage' and under-age marriage from Islām. In limiting the father's access to the child, Judge Harman focused on the violence, the harm caused and future potential harm to the child, namely, what was in the 'best interests of the child'. The court noted evidence of the child marriage and lack of consent bore only on these questions. The Judge commented that the evidence:

> is not referred to so as to suggest either any criticism of the Islamic faith or to suggest or accept that the behaviours of the father as referred to are in any way consistent with adherence to belief or practice of the Islamic faith. Far from it. They are simply suggested as representing a most heinous interference in this young girl's childhood.
>
> (*Essey* v. *Elia* [2013] FCCA 1525 at para. 42)

While the Australian court did not recognise the relevance of Islām to the parental dispute and took a neutral approach, a decision of the English Supreme Court has held otherwise. In *Sohrab* v. *Khan* [2002] S.C.L.R 663, the court was asked to declare a 'forced' marriage a nullity. It involved a 16-year-old girl and a 19-year-old man whose parents had arranged the marriage, providing the girl only one week's notice prior to the marriage ceremony. While her consent was given, evidence suggested this was a result of her mother threatening suicide if she did not go through with the marriage. The court held that this 'was more pressure than a sixteen year old girl could bear' and '... was not true consent' (*Sohrab* v. *Khan* [2002] S.C.L.R 663 at para. 23). In holding the marriage a nullity, Lord McEwan offered the following in *obiter*:

> It may be that in the multi-cultural society in which we now live such situations will continue to arise where ancient Eastern established cultural and religious ethics clash with the spirit of twenty-first century children of a new generation and Western ideas, language and what these days passes for culture. There is inevitable tension, and clashes will happen.
>
> (*Sohrab* v. *Khan* [2002] S.C.L.R 663 at para. 85)

While these comments appear to note the relevance of religious values to the outcome – and therefore some degree of accommodation – religion (read the Sharīʿah) is framed as anti-modern ('ancient'), other ('Eastern') and inconsistent with the liberal democratic values of contemporary English society.

Nature of marriage: contract versus registered status

The nature of marriage as either a contract or a status has a bearing on how it is treated at law. One of the recurring themes across all jurisdictions is the intersection of Islamic marriages and state marriages or legal marriages. Here, parties face the prospect of needing to comply with two sets of legal principles to have a marriage that is recognised officially by the state and by the parties and their families. If only the religious ceremony is conducted, the parties run the risk the state deems their marriage invalid. If only a state's legal requirements are complied with, the parties risk their 'marriage' not being accepted by their families or community. We set out below how Common Law jurisdictions have dealt with this particular problem.

How Muslims marry

Not one of our Common Law jurisdictions recognises a purely religious ceremony as a valid marriage. This means that often a couple will ensure that they have a marriage ceremony that satisfies both state law and Islamic teachings. However, as the discussion below will demonstrate, there are instances where courts based on the Common Law presumption of marriage have recognised a religious marriage as a legal marriage. In order for us to understand the marriage cases that come before the courts, it is also important to appreciate the intersection between state law requirements for registration, cultural expectations and religious requirements.

A Muslim marriage, as often practised in Western countries, has a number of stages. First, there is usually an engagement period, which can be as short or as long as the parties agree.[8] This is followed by a religious marriage ceremony known as *ʿaqd qirān* or *Katb Al-kitāb*. At this ceremony, the couple enter into a marriage contract according to Sharīʿah law.[9] Culturally, however, often they are not yet afforded the status of husband and wife until another ceremony takes place, the *walimah*. This is akin to a wedding reception, after which the couple begin living together as a married couple. However, as al-Hibri states, 'The Kitāb ceremony usually precedes the wedding by a period of time ranging from minutes to years' (al-Hibri 2005: 210). Some couples have the *Katb āl-kitāb* or Islamic marriage ceremony and wedding party at the same time, while others will wait up to two years after the *Katb āl-kitāb* before living together. Although they might not be living together, many still regard themselves as husband and wife (which is true in a religious sense) (An-Nawawi 2005: 374). Yilmaz argues that it is the religious marriage ceremony that 'determines the nature of the relationship and is perceived as dominant; the official one is only seen as mere formality' (Yilmaz 2003). It is the date of the execution of the marriage contract, and not the wedding, which determines the marital status of the parties (al-Hibri 2005: 212).

For most couples, they register their marriage at the time of their religious marriage ceremony. Others may try to delay registration until the date of their wedding reception. Both scenarios have implications for the couple. In the first case where the marriage is registered, the couple do not see themselves as husband and wife as they have not had a wedding party. They have not yet moved in together and essentially still live as if they are not married, although technically speaking, they are legally and religiously married. This can cause some issues for the couple if they separate prior to the wedding party. In the eyes of the law (both state and religious), they must get divorced. Whilst at a religious level, this is usually a straightforward process, they may find themselves needing to comply with the statutory requirements of divorce which can take much longer. This is important because in the eyes of many, they cannot form another relationship if they are still married, even if a religious divorce has taken place (Krayem 2014: 140). Others may not register their marriage at all.

Marriage as contract

From a legal point of view, Islām views marriage as a contract between two people, and as Ali notes, all major writers on Islamic law agree that marriage 'according to Islām [marriage] is in the nature of a contract' (al-Hibri 2005: 212). The key elements in the formation of the contract should be distinguished from the rights of Husband and Wife borne as a consequence of the marriage.

These elements include offer and acceptance, witnesses, *mahr* (or dowry) and additional terms as agreed between the parties.

According to Nasir, 'the marriage contract can only be concluded through the two essentials or pillars of offer and acceptance' (Nasir 1986: 42). The law does not insist on any particular form in which this contract is entered into or on any specific religious ceremony, although there are different traditional forms prevalent among Muslims in different parts of the world (Nasir 1986: 42). Pearl notes that this simple form of marriage is almost always accompanied by religious ceremonials (Pearl 1987: 41). These can vary from country to country and culture to culture, and even occur in different languages. The majority of Islamic scholars agree that the contract can be solemnised in languages other than Arabic (Nasir 1986: 42). Regardless of the language, it begins with a statement from the bride or her guardian that means 'I marry you' and an immediate acceptance by the groom of 'I marry her' or 'I accept her in marriage'. The woman is the offeror and the man the offeree (Al-Misri 1999: 517). The spoken words constitute the actual marriage contract, although marriage celebrants encourage the parties to put it in writing, and to include many the details that formed the agreement.

It is also a requirement that there are two witnesses to this contract, to help publicise the marriage (Nasir 1986: 49; Ibn Rushd 1996: 19; Al-Misri 1999: 518). This publicity is important as some jurists argue 'an agreement to keep the marriage secret invalidates the contract' ('Abd al 'Ati 1995: 60). This needs to be understood in light of the fact that publicity was often the factor that distinguished 'legitimate unions from illicit ones' ('Abd al 'Ati 1995: 60).

While an oral contract of marriage is sufficient in Sharī'ah, Common Law jurisdictions require registration for the validity of the marriage. Accordingly, the issue of recognition of the Islamic marriage has been one that has come before the courts in each of the jurisdictions. One might assume if the parties did not comply with the statutory rules governing marriage, the courts would hold that there is no legally recognisable marriage (unless the marriage was solemnised in another country). However, a closer look at several cases in our Common Law jurisdictions tells a different story. In each of the countries, we have instances where only an Islamic marriage was conducted but the court still held that to constitute a legal marriage.

In the USA, the Ohio Supreme Court held in *Ohio* v. *Phelps* (1995) 100 Ohio App 3d 187 (1995) – in the context of a murder trial – that a wife was not compelled to give evidence against her husband. The couple were not married under any US law but married only in an Islamic Marriage ceremony. The court determined their union a 'Common Law marriage' on the basis of a ceremony, a marriage certificate and evidence they lived as husband and wife. Whilst this case was a criminal trial, it still remains quite significant in the sense that a state court formally recognised a an Islamic marriage ceremony without any registration (Freeland 2006: 231).

However, of even greater significance are the cases where the issue is solely about the legal recognition of such marriages. In *Aghili* v. *Saadatnejadi* 958

S.W.2d 784 (1997), the couple went through a marriage ceremony performed by a person unauthorised to solemnise marriages. Also the husband did not sign the marriage licence. After their honeymoon, the husband indicated to the wife that he would not register their marriage unless she relinquished her dowry (*mahr*). The wife, along with the Imām who presided over the ceremony, filed another marriage licence form signed by the Imām as Officiant. The trial judge held the marriage void and dismissed the wife's complaint for divorce. The Tennessee Court of Appeals disagreed with this finding and found that the person who solemnised the wedding 'possessed the authority to administer Islamic blessings' and that although the marriage licence was filed late, this did not make the marriage void.

In another US case *Juma Mussa* v. *Nikki Palmer-Mussa* 722 S.E.2d 608 (N.C. 2012), the husband sought an annulment on grounds of of bigamy – that his wife was married to someone else. The parties had married in late 1997 but in early 1997 the wife had conducted an Islamic marriage ceremony with another man. Soon afterwards, she divorced him Islamically before marrying Mr Mussa. In 2008, the wife sought a divorce from the husband who then claimed that they had not been validly married due to her bigamy. At first instance, the court dismissed the husband's claim for lacking evidence. However, the Court of Appeals of North Carolina, whilst acknowledging that the wife's first marriage ceremony did not meet the requirements for a valid marriage, decided it was not void but voidable, meaning the marriage was valid until annulled by a tribunal. As this had not taken place, the subsequent marriage was deemed bigamous and an annulment granted. In this way, the court recognised the validity of the first Islamic marriage, but not the Islamic divorce. On appeal, the Supreme Court of North Carolina reversed the Appeal Court's decision and reinstated the order made at first instance, namely, that the wife's first marriage did not meet the requirements of a valid marriage. This case reflects the various approaches that courts can take on the question of validity or recognition of religious marriages and the consequence that this can have for Muslim couples.

In the English case of *A* v. *A* [2013] Fam. 51, a couple went through a marriage ceremony in 2002 conducted by an Imām in a mosque registered under s.41 of the Marriage Act 1949. They lived together and had three children. They discovered in 2009 that their marriage had not been registered. Both parties had intended to contract a marriage valid under English law, and asked the court to recognise their marriage. The Attorney-General submitted that the ceremony did not create a valid marriage for non-compliance with the Marriage Act 1949. The court held, however, that while an intention to contract a valid marriage on its own was insufficient, the performance of a 'ceremony' made it a valid marriage. Moylan J concluded, 'The fact that the ceremony was conducted according to Sharia does not mean that the ceremony "as a ceremony" could not be within the scope of the 1949 Act' (*A* v. *A* [2013] Fam. 51, at 97–98). This case is a prime example of legal recognition of a Sharīʿah law marriage and the courts looking to preserve the marital status (and indirectly the reputation) of the couple.

In the Canadian case of *Abdirashid Mohamed Isse* v. *Linda A Said* 2012 ONSC 1829, on spousal support, a question arose as to whether the parties were spouses for the 'purpose of the equalization of property' when they had conducted only an Islamic wedding ceremony according to Sharīʿah law. A marriage licence had not been issued, nor was the marriage registered under the law of Ontario. Section 31 of the Marriage Act deals with circumstances of non-compliance and allows the court to deem a marriage valid if four elements are satisfied: the marriage was solemnised in good faith; there was an intention to comply with the Marriage Act; neither party was under a legal disqualification to contract the marriage; and the parties lived together and cohabited as a married couple (*Abdirashid Mohamed Isse* v. *Linda A Said* 2012 ONSC 1829 at 16). The question in this case was whether 'the marriage was intended to be in compliance with the Marriage Act. The court accepted the wife's evidence that there was such an intention and therefore deemed it valid (*Abdirashid Mohamed Isse* v. *Linda A Said* 2012 ONSC 1829 at 25–26).

This issue of recognition of an Islamic marriage has also arisen in the Australian context. In *Wold* v. *Kleppir* [2009] FamCA 178, a couple had gone through an Islamic marriage ceremony before an Imām who was also a registered marriage celebrant, despite the husband arguing that it was a 'conversion' ceremony rather than a marriage ceremony. The judge rejected the husband's argument on the basis of evidence given by the Imām. The Imām was a registered marriage celebrant and had presided over the ceremony, but had not registered the marriage. The Imām told the court:

> a couple may come to me and they will say 'look we are living in sin, we want to be married, we want to get married quickly so can you just bless us?' so what I will do is for them to be recognised as a couple in the Muslim community I will perform the Islamic rituals, meaning consent from both sides, but it will not be signed. There will be no papers signed.
>
> (*Wold* v. *Kleppir* [2009] FamCA 178 at 30)

The Australian court accepted this as a marriage ceremony, conducted in the presence of an authorised celebrant and declared it a valid marriage pursuant to the Marriage Act 1961 (Cth). At the same time, Barry J reiterated the importance of Imāms registering marriages. He said:

> I propose to add an addendum to this determination on the responsibility of the Imam to comply with Australian law when carrying out his duties in performing ceremonies such as the one performed on this occasion. The Marriage Act imposes penalties on marriage celebrants who do not comply with the procedural requirements imposed in that legislation and this should be made clear to the Imam and to relevant authorities.
>
> (*Wold* v. *Kleppir* [2009] FamCA 178 at 57)

In this way, the court balanced both the need to preserve the marital status of the parties (protecting their reputation in the community), with the need for clarity and certainty in the determination of marriage.

In *Oltman & Harper* (no 2) [2009] FamCA 1360, a couple went through an Islamic marriage ceremony before an Imām who was not a registered marriage celebrant (the marriage was obviously not registered). The wife argued that she had left organising the ceremony to the husband and did not know the true situation. The husband argued that they did not intend to have anything more than an Islamic marriage ceremony, calling it a 'commitment ceremony' for the purposes of legitimating an intimate relationship in religious terms. Relying on s.48(3) of the Marriage Act, the court held that as the wife believed that the Imām was lawfully authorised to conduct the form and ceremony of the marriage (*Oltman & Harper* [no 2] [2009] FamCA 1360 at 65) and there was a Common Law presumption of marriage which the husband had failed to rebut, the parties were validly married.

These cases demonstrate that, in certain circumstances, in all of our Common Law jurisdictions, the courts have been willing to recognise Islamic marriages as having a legal status despite their non-conformity with the statutory regimes. Case law suggests that the Common Law presumption of marriage, the existence of a marriage ceremony, cohabiting as husband and wife, an intention to register the marriage and other such factors, enable subsequent legal recognition under Common Law of a Sharī'ah-only marriage. This is not special recognition of religious marriage, but rather the application of neutral Common Law principles, reflecting an attempt by the courts to respond to the individual cases that come before them.

In contrast, there are also cases where the courts have not recognised Islamic marriages. In fact, these cases reflect the complexities of Muslim marriage practices. For example, in the English case *Al-Saedy* v. *Musawi* [2010] EWHC 3293, the wife sought a decree of divorce on the basis that they had been married in Damascus in 1996. The husband disputed that they had ever been married. Rather, he argued that they had entered into a religious agreement, sufficient in Shī'ah law to permit the parties to live in intimacy without committing unlawful sexual intercourse (*zinā*). The wife argued that no such religious agreement existed in Islam. Bodey J ultimately concluded, following expert evidence on the point: 'It is inappropriate for me to try to determine an issue as to Islamic religious law' while accepting, in the husband's subjective opinion, 'there does exist a status of religious agreement which falls short of marriage' (*Al-Saedy* v. *Musawi* [2010] EWHC 3293 at para. 32). The court held that on the evidence before it, there was no marriage ceremony in Damascus in 1996 and further that their relationship did not justify the application of the principle of the presumption of marriage.

Another similar case arose in the USA. In *Re* the *Marriage of Fereshteh R* and *Speros Vryonis* 202 CAL.APP.3d 712 (1988), a putative wife gave evidence that the couple (the woman a Muslim and the man a non-Muslim) entered into a *mut'a* or temporary marriage in 1982; a form of marriage deemed permissible according to the Shī'ah. The wife claimed that she believed the ceremony (which had only involved the parties themselves) had established a valid and binding marriage. She was unfamiliar with the requirements of US marriage laws. The parties did not cohabit or hold themselves out as a married couple. In 1984, the 'husband' legally married another woman and the 'wife' petitioned for divorce. The trial judge held that whilst there was not a valid marriage, the circumstances were such that the 'woman' was a putative spouse – meaning that she had believed in good faith a valid marriage existed. The 'man' had consented to the *mut'a* and had assured the wife (who was new to the country) that it was a valid marriage. However, the California Court of Appeals found her belief was unreasonable as the alleged private marriage went unsolemnised, unlicensed and unrecorded. Thereafter, the parties did not cohabit, or hold themselves out as husband and wife. Furthermore, the 'woman' could not rely on the 'man's' statement to reasonably believe that she was married. Therefore, there was no legally recognisable marriage.

There are also cases where a marriage certificate has been issued, that is, the marriage was legally registered, but one of the parties seeks an annulment on the basis that there was no marriage in fact. In the Australian case *In the Marriage of Nemer Osman* [1989] FamCA 78, a woman sought a decree of nullity on the ground that her consent to marriage had been obtained by fraud. Both parties describe the marriage process to the court as involving a ceremony called a 'kitāb' – a process 'in the nature of a contract whereby each party solemnly agrees in writing to marry the other' (*In the Marriage of Nemer Osman* [1989] FamCA 78 at para. 5). This had taken place and a marriage certificate pursuant to the Marriage Act issued. However, the parties submitted that under Lebanese Muslim custom, they did not consider themselves man and wife and would not cohabit or consummate the marriage till the holding of another ceremony known as 'erais' (*In the Marriage of Nemer Osman* [1989] FamCA 78 at para. 5). Despite this qualification, the Court deemed the 'kitāb' sufficient to constitute a valid marriage according to Australian law. The court rejected the application for nullity and suggested that it would have been better had the wife availed herself of divorce proceedings instead.

This case demonstrates the difficulty for courts to recognise Sharīʿah marriages when the particular marriage practices are so interwoven with culture, custom and the particular interpretation of the parties. This is also an example where Sharīʿah law and the official law are similar but stand in contrast to the cultural understanding of the law.

In the case of *Najjarin* v. *Houlayce* (1991) 104 FLR 403 similar cultural issues arose, yet the court reached a different result. Here, the parties agreed to go through what the court referred to as a 'kitāb' and at which point a marriage certificate would then be issued. However, the evidence presented before the court by the applicant was that none of the conditions of that ceremony had taken place. The parties had gone to a marriage celebrant, completed and signed the forms for a legal marriage certificate to be issued, after which the husband indicated that he no longer wanted anything to do with his putative wife. Based on the applicant's evidence that there was actually no marriage ceremony according to Sharīʿah (and under Marriage act performed by a minister of religion) then there was no valid marriage. The court, therefore, issued a declaration of nullity.

While the above cases highlight the willingness of the court to validate unregistered Islamic marriages provided certain conditions are met, they also bring to light the Court's unnecessary and at times premature intervention in cases where expert evidence from Islamic scholars should have been sought. The differences in Muslim cultural practices require more nuanced understandings of Islamic practices and of the different interpretations each of the parties present to the court to support their case. The above cases also illustrate that there is nothing in the case law or in the approach of Common Law Courts more generally, that deny Muslims the opportunity to validate their marriages. While there are concerns for clarity and certainty, that is an important principle also coming through in most interpretations of Sharīʿah.

Financial entitlements

This section will consider the financial entitlements that arise between the parties to a Muslim marriage. This mainly focuses on the application of the *mahr* or dowry which, as noted above, is an important factor in a Muslim marriage contract. Generally, it becomes a legal issue upon divorce when the courts attempt to relate the *mahr* to any post-divorce financial settlement between the parties. It is important, therefore, to begin by understanding the general legal framework for property settlement in each of our chosen Common Law jurisdictions.

Jurisdictional comparison

Factors affecting the determination of property entitlements after the breakdown of a marriage are much the same across Australia, the United Kingdom, Canada and the United States. Commonly referred to as the 'four-step model' (Beatty 2014) in Australia, those factors include contributions to the marriage – both financial and non-financial (e.g. homemaker, caretaker of children). Contributions (Family Law Act 1975, s. 79[4]) include initial contributions each party brought into the marriage; contributions during the marriage by way of income, gifts, compensation payments, redundancy packages, improvements to key assets, primary homemaker, caretaker of the children; and post-separation contributions, such as continuing to pay the mortgage, care for the children.

Other factors that affect adjustment to entitlements include: length of the marriage; standard of living established during the marriage; future arrangements for the children, future considerations (Family Law Act 1975, s. 75[2]) such as age, earning capacity and health; and financial resources available to the parties. Finally, the courts ensure that the financial adjustment is 'just and equitable' (Family Law Act 1975, s. 79[2]) in the circumstances. Interestingly in Canada, courts incline towards an 'equal' rather than an 'equitable' division as follows:

> The value of any property that you acquired during your marriage and that you still have when you separate, must be divided equally between spouses. Property that was brought into your marriage is yours to keep, but any

> increases in the value of this property during the duration of marriage must be shared.
>
> (Divorce-Canada.ca 2015c)

The only exception to the above rule pertains to the matrimonial home where there is no adjustment for the person who brings it into the marriage (Divorce-Canada.ca 2015c).

US courts distinguish between 'separate property' and 'marital property' and arguments arise pertaining to financial entitlements canvassed during the divorce hearing (HG.org Legal Resources 2015). In contrast, in Australia, Canada and the UK, the divorce hearing is more an administrative process followed by a short hearing separate to the property proceedings. Accordingly, arguments pertaining to financial entitlements focus entirely on the above considerations and the grounds for divorce (particularly in US cases of 'fault-based' divorces) and do not affect the outcome of proceedings where property is sought.

Mahr

As noted above, a fundamental part of the marriage contract is the *mahr*, or dowry, which is given by the husband to the wife. In a discussion of the *mahr*, it is necessary to explore what *mahr* means in Sharī'ah and, more importantly, its significance to Muslims in Western countries. In the context of financial entitlements, it is also important to examine the way in which the Common Law Courts have characterised the *mahr*.

The marriage payment, commonly known as *mahr* or *ṣadaq*, is the money or property a husband must pay a woman to marry her. It is recommended to be stipulated in the marriage contract according to the Shāfi'ī and Ḥanbali Schools (Ministry of Religious Endowments and Islamic Affairs 1983, vol. 39: 152). The marriage is still valid even if the *mahr* was not mentioned in the marriage contract. According to the Shāfi'ī School, she would be entitled to the amount typically received as marriage payment by similar brides, such as a relative with similar characteristics (Al-Misri 1999: 534). Where stipulated in the marriage contract that the husband will not pay the wife the *mahr*, then according to the Māliki School, this breaches the contract (Ministry of Religious Endowments and Islamic Affairs 1983, vol. 39: 152, Ṣāliḥ 'Abd al-Samee' Al-Ãbi al-Azhar, 2009: 371). The woman is entitled to a 'mahr mithl', but only if the man had sexual intercourse with her after that contract.

There is no maximum amount for the *mahr*. According to the Shāfi'ī and Ḥanbali Schools, there is no minimum either. However, according to the Ḥanafi School, the minimum amount is ten silver coins or their value. Whilst in the Māliki School, the minimum amount is one-quarter of a gold coin (or three silver coins) or their value (Ministry of Religious Endowments and Islamic Affairs 1983, vol. 39: 162, Ṣāliḥ 'Abd al-Samee' Al-Ãbi al-Azhar, 2009: 368). There are significant variations as to how this is actually practised. While for most, it is a monetary amount or tangible material object, like property or furniture, it can also be Qur'ānic or Arabic lessons, a pilgrimage to Mekkah, or a year's rent (Krayem 2014: 147).

Once the marriage contract has been completed, the husband is at liberty to increase the *mahr* and this will be binding according to the Ḥanafi School (Ministry of Religious Endowments and Islamic Affairs 1983, vol. 39: 162). The *mahr* can be composed of two parts: an advance payment and a delayed payment (Ministry of Religious Endowments and Islamic Affairs 1983, vol. 39: 168). In regards to the deferred amount, this is a debt that remains owed by the husband until repaid. If the husband dies before repayment, then the amount will be taken from his estate as a debt owing.

The *mahr* should be given by the husband to the wife. In the event that that bride's guardian accepts it, this can only be permitted if she has given him express permission to take it on her behalf (Ministry of Religious Endowments and Islamic Affairs 1983, vol. 39: 169). If the husband were to divorce his wife before having sexual intercourse, then only half of the *mahr* is due for payment (Ministry of Religious Endowments and Islamic Affairs 1983, vol. 39: 177). This is clearly stipulated in the Qur'ān: 'And if you divorce them before you have touched them and you have already specified for them an obligation, then give half of what you specified' (Qur'ān 2:137).

Since the *mahr* is the property of the wife, she has full right over how it is spent. She is not obliged to spend it on the household expenses, nor on any furniture. The husband is required to spend upon her and the household. This is called the *nafaqah* (Ministry of Religious Endowments and Islamic Affairs 1983, vol. 39: 40). The amount of *nafaqah* is whatever the wife needs to cover her necessities, according to the Ḥanafi and Māliki Schools, as well as some opinions from the Shāfiʿī School. This includes food, clothing and accommodation. It can even include the costs associated with obtaining a maid in the house. If the wife has a servant in her father's home, or she is from a family where wives usually do not perform household duties, then it is obligatory on the husband to secure the services of a maid to perform the cleaning, cooking and other duties in the home (Ministry of Religious Endowments and Islamic Affairs 1983, vol. 39: 44). If the husband is absent, then he is still required to pay her *nafaqah*, according to the Ḥanbali, Shāfiʿī and Ḥanafi Schools (Ministry of Religious Endowments and Islamic Affairs 1983, vol. 39: 50). Therefore, according to Sharīʿah, the obligation of maintaining the household lies with the husband (even if the wife is wealthier than him). Whilst, at a practical level, this may be difficult to enforce in our Common Law countries, for many it is the religious sanction that counts. It also provides a basis for the argument that any arrears in maintenance is a debt on the husband which can be claimed upon divorce (unless she consented to make these payments voluntarily during the marriage).

Common Law approaches to the mahr

In light of the above discussion, the following question arises: if the *mahr* is a gift to be paid by the husband to the wife as part of the marriage contract, then why does it form part of divorce and property settlement discussions? The answer is a complex one not only for the Common Law Courts but also for Islamic scholarship.

Essentially, there are two circumstances that give rise to disputes over the *mahr* in the course of property proceedings. First, the deferred *mahr* which remains outstanding at the date of divorce; and second, the repayment of the *mahr* (or part thereof) to the husband in the event of a *khul'* divorce (i.e. divorce sought solely by the wife). The array of cases before the Common Law Courts indicate varied approaches to the characterisation of *mahr* in the context of property proceedings by both litigants and judges alike. The *mahr* has been characterised in two main ways by the Courts – either as a pre-marital agreement between the husband and wife, or simply as a contract between the parties (separate to the marriage). Each characterisation has its own deficiencies and it is posited that neither approach can provide the standard for all cases.

It is clear that in the North American context, the *mahr* is the most common Family Law issue considered by the courts. The most common observation made is that the courts are inconsistent (Sizemore 2011: 1085; Alkhatib 2013: 88). According to Fournier, the reason for this inconsistency is that 'the migration of *mahr* to Western courts unfolds at the crossroads of several doctrinal fields and disciplinary boundaries – contract and family law, constitutional and Islamic law, public policy and private ordering' (Fournier 2010: 2). It provides fertile ground, therefore, for judicial interpretation and for a variety of approaches. She also argues that once the *mahr* enters that forum 'it is animated by a diverse and often unpredictable set of legal constructs ... it becomes a hybrid and transformed version of what was once described as mahr by classical Islamic jurists' (Fournier 2010: 2). Thus the process of introducing the concept of *mahr* into the court system has a transformative effect, arguably both for the concept itself as well as for its host – the Common Law.

Mahr *as a contract*

Several US courts have sought to rely upon principles of Contract Law to enforce a *mahr* agreement, regarding the agreement akin to a secular promise (Sizemore 2011: 1096). In the Odatalla case (*Odatalla* v. *Odatalla* 810 A.2d 93), the husband argued that the court lacked authority to review the *mahr* agreement under the separation of the Church and State doctrine. The court responded by asking 'Why should a contract for the promise to pay money be less of a contract just because it was entered into at the time of an Islamic marriage ceremony?' (*Odatalla* v. *Odatalla* 810 A.2d 93 at 95). In fact, the court went further to argue that: 'the challenge faced by our courts today is in keeping abreast of the evolution of our community from a mostly homogenous group of religiously and ethnically similar members to today's diverse community' (*Odatalla* v. *Odatalla* 810 A.2d 93 at 96). Neither did the court accept the argument that the terms of the contract were too vague to be enforced. The postponement of the payment was held analogous to a promissory demand note under which the wife could demand the money at any time. Similarly in *Aziz* v. *Aziz* 488 N.Y.S.2d 123 (Sup. Ct. 1985), the court ordered the husband to pay the *mahr* based on a contract despite the husband's claim that it was part of a religious ceremony.

In *Akileh* v. *Elchahal* 666 So. 2d 246 (Fla. Dist. Ct. App. 1996), the trial judge held that the *mahr* was unenforceable because there was no consideration or meeting of the minds as to this term. This was then overturned on appeal as the Florida Court of Appeal enforced it as a contract, with the marriage itself seen as being adequate consideration. Yet the characterisation of the marriage as consideration in the context of Contract Law, or a 'bride price' is arguably at odds with the Islamic understanding of the *mahr*. Hence, while the above cases appear to be examples of state accommodation of the Sharīʿah principle, namely the right of a married woman to her *mahr*, the construction of the Islamic marriage and its elements in arriving at those conclusions, at times reflects inaccurate interpretations on the part of the Court. Furthermore, such reconstructions demonstrate the potential implications for Muslim women when attempting to fit their religious constructs into the 'neutral' principles of the state law.

A prime example of an essential misreading of the Islamic marriage by the Courts was in the case of *Habibi-Fahnrich* v. *Fahnrich* No. 46186/93 1995 WL 507388 (N.Y. Sup. Ct. July 10, 1995), in which the Court deemed the agreement pertaining to the *mahr* as too vague to be enforceable. The court found there was a lack of mutual understanding, a lack of specificity and a lack of clear enforceable terms (Wolfe 2006: 454). Interestingly, in this case the husband was not a Muslim. The *mahr*, therefore, was secondary to the Islamic validity of the marriage itself. According to all Islamic juridical schools, such a marriage would be invalid as the man does not meet the prerequisite requirement of being a Muslim. This is an interesting example of the Court attempting to accommodate one Sharīʿah principle (i.e. woman's right to *mahr*) while overlooking another (although applying equality provisions, that would not be accommodated).

While the above cases deal with the *mahr* agreement as a contract *separate* to marriage, in the Canadian case of *Khaddoura* v. *Hammoud* [1998] 168 D.L.R, 4th 503 (Ont. Ct of Justice, Gen. Div) the court accepted marriage itself as a contract and the *mahr* as a matter arising from that contract. The Court held:

> the extent to which it obligates a husband to make payment to his wife is essentially and fundamentally a religious matter. Because Mahr is a religious matter, the resolution of any dispute relating to it or the consequence of failing to honour the obligation are also religious in their content and context.
>
> (*Khaddoura* v. *Hammoud* [1998] 168 D.L.R, 4th 503 [Ont. Ct of Justice, Gen. Div] at 510)

In this way, the *mahr* was equated with obligations in a Christian marriage, such as to love, honour and cherish. The Court said it was not equipped to deal with matters that are based in religion (Thompson and Yunus 2007: 379).

Hence, it appears that if the courts emphasise the religious aspects of the agreement, despite their characterisation of it as a 'contract', then the conclusion that follows is that as a religious construct they cannot enforce it. It should be noted that Canada has the Charter of Rights and Freedoms which emphasises secularity. However, in this case it seems that the right of 'non-interference' in religion by the state is being misapplied. The only way in which the wife could enforce her right – which is a tangible and objective right – as opposed to 'love', 'cherish' etc – would be through the court. So in effect, taking the secular approach deprived the woman of her religious right and arguably her charter right to 'manifest' her religion.

Unlike the other jurisdictions, the *mahr* has not come up often for consideration in Australian courts. The most significant case in the Australian context is *Mohamed* v. *Mohamed* (2012) NSWSC 852. The parties had an Islamic marriage and entered into an agreement providing the husband would pay the wife $50,000 if he initiated the divorce. The Local Court enforced this as a contract. The husband appealed to the Supreme Court arguing that it was unenforceable on public policy grounds and that the Magistrate did not have jurisdiction to make a decision according to Sharīʿah. The court looked at other Common Law jurisdictions where such an agreement has been held to be enforceable. It held that no determination had been made under Sharīʿah with regards to the divorce but that the magistrate had just determined factually when separation occurred. The husband sought leave to appeal to the Court of Appeal on public policy grounds and this was rejected.

We note the Court decision did not prejudice marriage as there was no legal marriage here in the first place and the legislation already contemplated use of contracts in this sense. Furthermore, the case involved no moral judgement as, from a contractual law perspective, the fact the money was in the form of a *mahr* was coincidental. This case not only has implications for the enforcement of *mahr* in the context of Contract Law, but also illustrates how Islamic marriages, without any registration, can be indirectly recognised by Australian Common Law of contract. It also raises the question as to whether women entering into contractual agreements (drawn up by lawyers), where there is intent to register a marriage, can still protect their rights through Contract Law.

Much like its US counterparts, UK courts have also characterised the *mahr* as an enforceable right arising out of contract, as illustrated in *Shahnaz* v. *Rizzan* [1965] 1 QB 390 and *Quereshi* v. *Quereshi* [1971] 1 All ER 325. However, once again there are instances of accommodation by the Courts that are at odds with general Islamic principles. In *Uddin* v. *Choudhury* [2009] EWCA Civ 1205, the couple had an Islamic marriage contract, but the marriage was neither registered nor consummated prior to breakdown of the relationship. Upon divorce, the wife sought payment of the *mahr* and the husband's father, on his behalf, sought return of the jewellery given to the wife at the time of the marriage. Following expert evidence that, unless stipulated in contract, gifts are not returned and the *mahr* should be paid in full as lack of consummation was not the fault of wife, the court enforced the contract. Bowen argues that this decision contains several acts of recognition of Sharīʿah:

> The Judge ruled that the gifts stay where they are, the mahr comes due, the Islamic contract has English legal force, and the Islamic marriage was validly dissolved. In this sense the decision contain several acts of 'recognition' of shariah by the civil courts.
>
> (Bowen 2010: 425)

Yet the Court did not consider the fact that the divorce was treated as *khul'* (initiated by the wife) under Sharīʿah, in which case the *mahr* or part of it, is not payable to the wife. Also the Court did not consider non-consummation of the marriage which, according to Sharīʿah, could have an impact on how much of the *mahr* is due. Again, we see here an acceptance of some elements of Sharīʿah over others. It could be argued, however, that in this case the shortcomings in interpretation was on the part of the expert rather than the courts.

Mahr *as a premarital agreement*

The second main approach adopted by the courts is the construction of the *mahr* as part of a prenuptial agreement. Obviously, this is subject to the statutory regime of each of the jurisdictions. Assuming such an approach were adopted, then the marriage contract would govern property settlement post divorce. Sizemore (2011: 1093–94) and Siddiqui (2007: 648) argue, in the case of a small *mahr*, that could work unfairness and shortchange the wife upon divorce where, potentially, there is a much larger property settlement. This is critical when considering that in many of the cases discussed above, the parties have sought to convince the court of their particular interpretation of Sharīʿah and the one that best fits their case. Another potential implication of this approach is that it means the courts then may proceed to void the *mahr* agreement because it does not meet the state's statutory standards for prenuptials (Sizemore 2011: 1104).

For Sizemore, it is misleading to view the *mahr* as part of a prenuptial agreement. She writes:

> the *mahr* developed for the sole benefit of the wife, as a way to ease an inequitable marriage custom and prevent financial destitution. In contrast, American prenuptial contracts were formed to protect the commercially superior party from sharing assets with the economically inferior party upon divorce.
>
> (Sizemore 2011: 1104–05)

Furthermore, Muslim couples may not have intended the *mahr* agreement to represent the exclusive post-divorce settlement. As Alkhatib notes, the *mahr* is 'not designed to settle the financial claims of the wife on the husband's estate or to preclude other relief upon divorce' (Alkhatib 2013: 90). Again, this approach demonstrates the difficulty of attempting to fit the *mahr* into a 'one-size-fits-all' category.

Expert evidence

The discussion above demonstrates the importance of courts understanding Sharīʿah. This often will depend on the use of expert evidence. *Uddin* v. *Choudhury* (2009) discussed above, highlights the significant role experts play where an interpretation of Sharīʿah is required. The use of expert evidence has its own complexities. In *Rahman* v. *Hossain* No A-5191–08T3, 2010 WL 4075316 (N.J. Super. Ct. App. Div. 17 June 2010), the New Jersey Supreme Court ordered the wife to return her $12,500 prompt *mahr* because an expert witness said the wife had to return it if she was at fault. Similarly in *Dajani* v. *Dajani* 204 Cal. App. 3d 1387; 251 Cal. Rptr. 871 (1988), where the wife was denied the *mahr* because the court heard testimony that a wife forfeits the *mahr* if she initiates divorce. Yet, as Freeland notes, the Court did not have the opportunity to hear an alternative interpretation. Hence, though the use of expert evidence removes the burden of interpreting Islamic concepts from the Courts, the process and appointment of 'experts' becomes a point of contention. Freeland argues that expert testimony from both sides should be admitted to account for the diversity of Sharīʿah and similarly with Christian or Jewish custom (Freeland 2006: 238). It should be noted, however, that if the Courts were to take into account diverse expert opinion, they can get embroiled in controversy choosing one opinion over another. Accordingly, it may be conducive in such cases to appoint joint single experts to give evidence. In this way, the Courts are relieved from the burden of interpretation of Islamic principles. This also enables a case-by-case approach rather than a generic position which is more appropriate in the context of Islamic marriages.

The *mahr* cases indicate an openness to accommodate Islamic family law principles in the Common Law. That accommodation, however, occurs in two ways. On the one hand, the Courts appear to go beyond formal accommodation whereby they utilise expert evidence by way of Islamic legal experts and scholars. In effect, this allows Muslims to define their own space within the legal system which, we suggest, should be the preferred approach. In contrast, at times the court seems too keen to co-opt Sharīʿah and arrive at its own interpretations. To properly understand Sharīʿah concepts for these purposes, courts need to involve themselves in the interpretation of religious doctrine which they are not qualified to do. Arguably, this approach 'often replaces the parties' original intent with *ex post* interpretations influenced by prospect of economic gain' which can create inconsistent and misleading precedent (Sizemore 2011: 1095). As Sizemore argues, the *mahr* is dealt with differently according to the different Schools of Islamic jurisprudence and that by not taking into account the different Schools of thought 'the court may have distorted the intention of the parties and the meaning of the contract' (Sizemore 2011: 1098). Wolfe also notes this approach is 'overly simplistic assuming a single perspective is correct, not recognizing the enormous diversity of opinion' (Wolfe 2006: 455). It misses the debates and complexities of Sharīʿah (Bowen 2010: 434). In this way, although

Sharīʿah is accommodated, we argue it is 'colonised' and fails to articulate an autonomous Muslim voice.

In practical terms, this inconsistency also deprives Muslims of predictable judicial outcomes (Sizemore 2011: 1103). The way forward, according to Sizemore, is not for American courts to enforce vague *mahr* agreements, but rather to facilitate the American Muslim community to develop marriage contracts with more specific terms (Sizemore 2011: 1106). We suggest, however, that the problems which arise are not the result of a lack of specificity of terms. Rather, it is the complexity of Sharīʿah marriage contracts themselves. This means that there is not a 'one-size-fits-all' approach, and a case-by-case approach is required.

Post-divorce entitlements

For many, any discussion about the financial entitlements of Muslim couples upon divorce is simply about the *mahr* – as if that is the only issue that needs to be resolved. As previously mentioned, and as we will discuss further below, when Muslims seek a religious divorce they will usually access the informal community processes to facilitate a religious divorce. In the UK, this usually means attending a Sharīʿah Council and in the USA, Canada and Australia this usually involves an ad hoc process involving an individual or small grouping of Imāms. Whilst the next part of the chapter will consider the divorce issue, it is important to note that because of the link between divorce and *mahr*, then these processes will usually deal with financial issues. One needs to remember that these processes, and any decisions or agreements that flow from them, are not enforceable in a legal sense. However, many are critical of these community processes because they are perceived as discriminating against women by not giving them as much as they may be entitled to under the general legal process. Many have argued that the issue of financial rights for women post divorce has been a neglected and marginalised part of Sharīʿah (Krayem 2014: 182).[10] First, in our modern context, many women contribute to the maintenance of the household (both financially and non-financially). This needs to be taken into account in post-divorce settlements. Second, there is the often ignored concept of *mut'ah* which refers to the post-divorce financial support or payment given by the husband to the wife (Krayem 2014: 182). There is strong evidence from Islamic jurists and Qur'ānic commentators that this is highly recommended or obligatory, where he separated from her without any reason on her part (Krayem 2014: 183). This area needs urgent attention by current Islamic scholars as well as the Imāms who deal with couples going through the divorce process. They need to ensure that women who seek to resolve these issues outside of the formal legal process are not being disadvantaged by interpretations of Sharīʿah that limit their financial entitlements. This is a far more complex exercise for Islamic scholars as they consider this issue in light of the various schools of Islamic jurisprudence, yet there is no doubt that this will be an emerging issue in the future.

Divorce – *ṭalāq*

Islamic context

In the technical language of the Sharīʿah, divorce means 'separation' and is a husband's right. This is referred to as *ṭalāq*. Doi argues that Islām takes a balanced view about divorce, recognising that:

> When a marriage becomes impossible to sustain, it is better for the parties to amicably separate rather than being miserably bound together ... but on the other hand, it seeks to make ṭalāq a serious business and something abhorrent to Muslims.
>
> (Doi 2006: 83)

The permissibility of divorce in Islām can be traced back to the importance placed on marriage as a contract between a husband and a wife. While the contract is sacred, with great significance attached to its formation and compliance, it also functions as a negotiated agreement by the parties, and one that recognises the right of divorce if one party breaches a condition agreed upon in the contract. However, as noted above, this needs to be balanced with the fact that Islām does not encourage parties to easily tread the path of divorce. Although divorce is generally considered lawful, it is also strongly discouraged, and even prohibited in some circumstances according to some scholars. The Qur'ānic principles encourage people to look beyond the deficiencies of their partner, and seek to reconcile their differences: 'On the contrary live with them on a footing of kindness and equity. If ye take a dislike to them, it may be that ye dislike a thing and Allāh brings about through it a great deal of' (Qur'ān 4:19). There are also numerous Aḥādith that relate to divorce, such as: For Allāh, it (divorce) is among the most hated (*abghaḍ*) of the lawful things (Ibn Ḥajar 2007, Ḥadith no. 912: 186).

Finally, it is important to note that if parties are to divorce, they should do so in an amicable way. The Qur'ān stresses this most for men who divorce their wives: 'A divorce is only permissible twice: after that, the parties should either hold together on equitable terms, or separate with kindness' (Qur'ān 2:229).

There are several ways that a marriage can be terminated according to Sharīʿah. The most common form of divorce is known as *ṭalāq*, and this occurs when the husband seeks to end the marriage. It is an exclusive right of the husband and takes effect upon the husband communicating his desire to divorce the wife. For a valid divorce, it must issue from a husband who is sane and who voluntarily effects it (Al-Misri 1999: 556). The husband may commission another person to divorce on his behalf (Al-Misri 1999: 557). There are three chances given for divorce between a husband wife, after which they cannot marry unless the woman marries another man, consummates the marriage, and the new husband divorces her. A divorce may be effected by either plain, direct words or implied words (Al-Misri 1999: 560).

In the Ḥanafi School of thought, the husband can delegate this right of divorce to the wife, either at the time of the marriage contract, or at a later time; this is called *ṭalāq at-tafweeḍ*. In legal terms, the husband is agreeing to delegate his right to *ṭalāq* to the wife in certain circumstances (Al-Misri 1999: 283). Hussain describes it as existing:

> where the wife has included in her marriage contract a condition that the husband delegates his right of divorce to the wife so that she can exercise it.
> (Hussain 2011: 108)

This right can be delegated to the wife at the time of marriage or afterwards. In these circumstances the wife can initiate the divorce process as a husband would initiate *ṭalāq*.

Divorce can also occur by mutual consent of both husband and wife, on terms agreed by them, without wanting anything from the other, and this is known as *mubara'h*. A wife can also initiate a process known as *khul'*, by agreeing to compensate the husband (it can be a matter of foregoing a portion of the *mahr*) so she can seek to end the marriage. Finally, it is also possible for a court or judicial body to make an order of dissolution of the marriage in certain circumstances, and this is known as *tafreeq'* or *faskh*. Each form of divorce or separation which operates has differing implications as to when the divorce takes effect, and any financial adjustments.

Jurisdictional comparison

Before examining the intersection of Islamic divorces with state law, it is critical to apply a jurisdictional comparison. Essentially, the prerequisite for divorce in all four jurisdictions is a valid marriage (including foreign marriages) and a period of residency (of at least three months) of at least one party in the country in which divorce is sought. In the United Kingdom, there is an additional requirement of having been married for at least one year prior to seeking a divorce (UK Government 2015).

We find the most significant distinction among the Common Law countries in the context of divorce, however, in acceptable grounds for divorce. While the Canadian and Australian jurisdictions have a no-fault divorce system whereby the grounds for divorce need only be an irretrievable breakdown of a marriage and a twelve-month separation period (Divorce-Canada.ca 2015b; Federal Circuit Court of Australia 2014), the United States and United Kingdom still make available other grounds for divorce. These include adultery, unreasonable or cruel behaviour such as violence, desertion, long periods of living apart separately (divorce to be granted with the consent of the parties) and mental illness (HG.org Legal Resources 2015b; UK Government 2015). While there are differences between states, all states in the United States also accept irretrievable breakdown of marriage and irreconcilable difference as valid grounds for divorce under 'no-fault' divorces (HG.org Legal Resources 2015b). The Canadian courts also waive the twelve-month separation period in cases where there is physical or mental cruelty towards one party by the other and in this way allows room for other grounds for divorce (Divorce-Canada.ca 2015b).

Of significance is also the way in which divorce proceedings occur in each jurisdiction. While in Canada, Australia and the United Kingdom divorce proceedings are largely an administrative process that operate separately in relation to children and property, in the United States divorce proceedings are tied in with property and custody disputes and often all matters are finalised in the one trial. Inevitably, this results in adding to the complexity of US divorces cases but also provides an alternative approach.

Intersection of Islamic divorce and official law

The discussion above describes the ways in which Muslims in our Common Law jurisdictions marry and importantly, the way in which they navigate the mainstream legal system. This is also the case when it comes to divorce. Just as an Islamic marriage is important to many Muslims, an Islamic divorce is equally important and Muslim communities in all four countries have established community processes that operate at an unofficial level to help Muslim couples resolve their family disputes. This was discussed in some detail in Chapter 2 where it was observed that in the UK there are established 'Sharīʿah Councils' which deal with matters relating to divorce. These Councils operate at an unofficial level in the sense that their decisions are unenforceable, with the exception of the Muslim Arbitration Tribunal. This complies with the official legal system as well as with Islamic principles of family dispute resolution. In contrast, it was argued that Muslim communities in the USA, Canada and Australia have far more ad hoc processes with individual or groups of Imāms dealing with Islamic divorce processes. The research indicates that, like in marriage, Muslims seek to ensure that they comply with both the religious requirements associated with divorce as well as with the official legal processes.

Islamic divorce comes before the courts in all jurisdictions, although most commonly when one party (usually the husband) seeks recognition of an Islamic divorce obtained in a foreign jurisdiction. In the USA, courts have refused to acknowledge Islamic divorces that take place within the USA unless confirmed by a court of law in another nation. This poses an interesting question – can one of the parties have an Islamic divorce recognised simply by travelling overseas? (Thompson and Yunus 2007: 383). In *Tarikonda* v. *Pinjari* (2009) No. 287403, slip op. at 2 (Mich. Ct. App. Apr. 7, 2009), the couple had been living in the USA for seven years; the husband then travelled to India and pronounced the *ṭalāq*. The Michigan Court of Appeals refused to recognise this as a divorce, holding that the *ṭalāq* was 'violative of due process and contrary to public policy', because effectively it excluded the wife from the proceedings (Kim 2014: 294). The point being that divorces need to be documented or officially recognised for them to be recognised. This case clearly illustrates non-accommodation of Islamic divorce in the USA.

A similar approach is taken in the UK as demonstrated in *Basma Sulaiman* v. *Walid Ahmed Al Juffali* [2002] 2 FCR 427 (UK) where both parties were citizens of and domiciled in Saudi Arabia. The husband had pronounced *ṭalāq* in England in 2001, a day after a petition for divorce had been filed in the English court. This *ṭalāq* was registered with the Sharīʿah Court in Saudi Arabia. The argument made was that the court should recognise this as an overseas divorce within the meaning of the Family Law Act. Munby J did not accept that this was an overseas divorce, despite its registration in Saudi Arabia. Rather, he held that it was obtained in England as soon as it was pronounced and that the legislation provided informal divorces obtained in England otherwise than by proceedings in a court of civil jurisdiction were not recognised (*Basma Sulaiman* v. *Walid Ahmed Al Juffali* [2002] 2 FCR 427 [UK] at 50). Munby J emphasised that this decision had nothing to do with religion, stating:

> Although historically this country is part of the Christian west, and although it has an established church which is Christian, I sit as a secular judge serving a multi-cultural community of many faiths in which all of us can now take pride, sworn to do justice 'to all manner of people'. Religion – whatever the particular believer's faith – is no doubt something to be encouraged but it is not the business of government or of the secular courts. So the starting point of the law is an essentially agnostic view of religious beliefs and a tolerant indulgence to religious and cultural diversity.
> (*Basma Sulaiman* v. *Walid Ahmed Al Juffali* [2002] 2 FCR 427 [UK] at 47)

What that implies is a refusal to accommodate Sharīʿah because of the underlying 'secularity' and neutrality of the Common Law.

These questions have also come before the Family Court of Australia. On the whole, Australian courts do not recognise Islamic divorces. However, there have been instances where one of the parties has sought a divorce in a Muslim country according to the Sharīʿah and then sought to have the divorce recognised by the Australian court. In *Dinal* v. *Tohim* [2009] FamCA 540, the husband obtained a divorce in Egypt and sought to have it recognised by the Family Court in Australia. The wife argued that the Egyptian divorce was not valid as it was not registered in Egypt. The court heard evidence from an Australian Imām that whilst the wife may not be able to remarry in Egypt because the divorce has not been registered, the divorce was still an Islamic divorce and capable of being registered in Egypt. The court accepted this evidence and ultimately recognised the divorce under the Family Law Act 1975 (Cth). It appears, then, in contrast to the United States and the United Kingdom, Australian courts are more willing to recognise Islamic divorces when they occur overseas.

Limping marriages

The most significant issue associated with Islamic divorce in a Western context is that of 'limping marriages' where the husband refuses to give the wife a religious divorce even after a civil divorce has been obtained. The existence of a limping marriage occurs where, for all intents and purposes, the marriage has ended but the woman cannot remarry because she is still 'religiously' married. This is a difficult and perplexing situation for the Imāms with severe consequences for many Muslim women. The Family Law Council of Australia in its 2001 report found:

> For those who find themselves caught between what are effectively two discrete legal systems, the consequences of being divorced under the rules of one system and not being able to be divorced in the other, can be emotionally, financially, and spiritually debilitating.
>
> (Family Law Council 2001: 6–7)

The approach taken by some imāms is that if there is any document or evidence that the husband, in the divorce proceedings, or anywhere else, has consented to a divorce or said that he is divorced, then they will grant the woman a divorce. The Australian Family Law Council (2001) in its report recommended that a final divorce not be granted until the court is satisfied that all impediments have been removed to the other party's remarriage, but these recommendations have not been implemented. Essof also argues that in the Australian context, the Family Law Act should require Muslims to ensure that they have gone through Islamic divorce processes prior to finalising a civil divorce (Essof 2011: 186). While the intention of such recommendation is to encourage the husband to issue the Islamic divorce, we suggest that if such recommendation were implemented it could have the unintended consequence of keeping a woman married under Civil Law and preventing her Common Law right to remarry (at least for women who might see the civil divorce as the one to signify the end of their relationship).

However, the Family Law Council report also observed that there was very little consensus from the Islamic community as to how the government should deal with these issues (Family Law Council 2001: 4). Many would argue that it is not the role of the Family Court, or indeed any secular court, to interfere with or concern itself with the application of religious norms or laws that operate outside its jurisdiction. Whilst this has not been implemented in the Australian context, a similar scheme has been in force in New York (Mahmoudjafari 2014: 1084). Indeed, Alkhatib's research in the USA indicates judicial involvement in applying pressure on husbands to give *ṭalāq* to the wife (Alkhatib 2013: 95–98). An example of this is the case of *Hammoud* v. *Hammoud* 2012 Mich. App. LEXIS 417, 1, 2012 WL 752044 where the trial judge awarded monthly spousal support until the wife received an Islamic divorce. However, the Michigan Court of Appeals overturned this considering the involvement of the court in this manner to be improper because it would using spousal support to punish the husband, thereby treating the parties inequitably (Alkhatib 2013: 102–03).

Other approaches have included bringing the parties together to negotiate and to explain to the husband that keeping a wife in such circumstances is a breach of the fundamental principles of Islām, and this is generally the approach that imāms adopt (Krayem 2014: 198). Another more pragmatic approach adopted in the UK by the Muslim community has been to advise women prior to entering into a marriage contract to include within its terms a clear right to divorce (Badawi 1995: 78). This has resulted in several key Muslim organisations and religious leaders agreeing on a pro forma marriage contract that encourages couples to insert such a term (Muslim Marriage Contract 2008). However, it should be noted that this pro forma contract has been opposed by key religious leaders, particularly some who oversee the operation of Sharīʿah courts in the UK. They objected on the following basis:

> After a thorough study of the document, the Council finds that the proposed contract contains numerous flaws which contradict the Qur'an, Sunna and Ijma' of our previous scholars including the four great imams, despite the fact the document claims to refer to those sources. Moreover, this contract has introduced into the Shariah many elements that are alien to both the text and the spirit of the Shariah (Islamic Shariah Council).[11]

However, reputable scholars from the Ḥanafi School hold different views on this matter. Hartford and Muneeb in their book, *Your Islamic Marriage Contract*, state:

> Upon making a valid marriage contract, the husband 'owns' the right of divorce. Thus it is permissible for him to transfer this right to his wife. In doing so he does not lose the right himself. It is better in this circumstance that the wife stipulates the right to divorce herself under specific conditions: such as if he abandons her. This offers the woman a measure of security. It might be noted that upon receiving the right to divorce herself, for example, after the occurrence of a certain condition, it is completely up to her if she uses it or not.
>
> (Hartford and Muneeb 2007: 11)

Practically speaking, however, there are very few cases of *ṭalāq at-tafweeḍ* or delegated divorce in Muslim communities in the West. Clearly, this is an avenue the community should explore because of the potential that it has in alleviating the difficulties some Muslim women face in obtaining a religious divorce.

Parenting

Islamic context

Upon divorce, custody of the children goes immediately to the mother, on the condition that the children are under the age of discretion (usually around seven years of age). After this age, the child, boy or girl, is given the choice of where to live. This is in accordance with the Shāfiʿī School (Ministry of Religious Endowments and Islamic Affairs 1983, vol. 17: 315). As for the Ḥanafi School, a boy would remain under the custody of the mother until he reaches seven years of age. The girl would remain under her custody until the age of puberty (Ministry of Religious Endowments and Islamic Affairs 1983, vol. 17: 314). Thus, the general approach is that the years of infancy are spent with the mother with the child having an option after seven years of age (Rafiq 2014: 269). However, the wishes of the child are in many cases subject to the principle of the overall welfare of the child which looks at what is in the child's best interest (Rafiq 2014: 270). This approach is arguably compatible with the approaches described below taken by the Common Law Courts, although undoubtedly in an Islamic context the role of religion will feature more prominently in determining what are in the child's 'best interests'.

Jurisdictional comparison

When it comes to determination of residency or custody of children following a divorce or separation, the paramount consideration in all four jurisdictions is the 'best interests of the child' (Divorce-Canada.ca 2015a; Doskow; Nickson 2015; Family Law Act 1975 s.60CC). What constitutes the best interests of the child varies across jurisdictions and interpretations of Courts within those jurisdictions. Some key considerations that are consistently applied, however, include the child maintaining a relationship with both parents and the welfare of the child or the need to protect the child from physical and psychological harm. In Australia, these two considerations form the primary considerations with greater weight being given to the latter consideration (Family Law Act 1975 s.60CC).

Other factors that are considered in determining the best interests of the child include the parenting abilities of the parents and ability to provide for the child; care arrangements prior to separation; the child's relationship with each parent and other people including grandparents and other relatives; the likely effect on the child of changed circumstances; the maturity, sex, lifestyle and background of the child and of either of the child's parents; incidents of family violence, if any, and the wishes of the child. While all jurisdictions take seriously the wishes of the child, in the United States, Canada and Australia those wishes have more standing once the child is closer to twelve years of age. In the UK, the age of the child is less important. Accordingly, the express wishes of the child of any age is given considerable weight (In Brief n.d.). Other jurisdictions, especially Australia, place greater emphasis on the child maintaining a meaningful relationship with both parents and hence the custodial parent's willingness and ability to facilitate that relationship with the other parent is an important consideration. Often, the wishes of the child are expressed through a Court Welfare Officer or an Independent Children's Lawyer (Family Law Act 1975 s.68L).

Australia is also distinguished in that it recognises the right of an Aboriginal and Torres Strait Islander child to enjoy his or her culture (Family Law Act 1975, s.60CC[3][h]). Such consideration also extends to children of other cultures. While other jurisdictions refer to residency or custody whereby the child lives with one parent and has contact with the other parent, Australian legislation imposes 'shared parental responsibility'. There is a presumption of equal shared parental responsibility with respect to the child which often results in the child spending equal or 'substantial and significant time' with both parents unless there are vitiating reasons (Family Law Act 1975). Shared parenting has attracted heavy criticism for shifting the focus from the best interests of the child to the wants of the parent. It has also been criticised for preventing the child from having one stable home and resulted in increased litigation between parties. Nevertheless, in 2014, the UK also introduced 'parental responsibility' into legislation as well as 'child arrangement orders' to replace 'residency' and 'contact' orders with a view to encouraging a 'meaningful relationship with both parents' (Children and Families Act 2014).

Accommodation of Islamic beliefs in parenting cases

Courts have dealt with the issue of Islamic beliefs and practices in many cases dealing with parenting disputes as maintaining a connection with one's cultural and religious practices. They hold that it should be a factor to take into account in determining the parenting arrangements post separation. Sometimes in this context, the religious and cultural factors can be intertwined. In the UK case, in the matter of *A-M* (A Child) [2006] EWCA Civ 1068, the issue was whether the mother could relocate with the child to Holland against the father's wishes. His objection included an argument that the trial judge 'gave inadequate regard to the unusual Muslim socio-cultural element of the case, namely the loss to Y later in life of the great mantle of patriarchal authority' (In the matter of *A-M* [A Child] [2006] EWCA Civ 1068 at para. 10). This related to his Iraqi cultural background and was a prestigious status descending from the child's grandfather. There was an expectation that this would be passed down from eldest son to eldest son. It was argued this would be lost to the child if he was not cared for by the father. Whilst the court considered the father's arguments, and was a matter for which the court would accord the 'respect properly due' (In the matter of *A-M* [A Child] [2006] EWCA Civ 1068 at para. 10), they were outweighed by other relevant factors. This meant that it was in the child's best interests if he was allowed to relocate with the mother. Whilst the argument of the father was based more on cultural factors than religious principles, the case demonstrates the relevance of culture/religion in parenting cases.

Sometimes the court is placed in a difficult position of having to differentiate between the beliefs and practices of an individual parent and that of the faith itself. For example in the Australian case, *Heiden* v. *Kaufman* [2011] FMCA fam 478, the father reportedly expressed a desire that his children should die as martyrs and would make the child watch violent videos, among other arguably inappropriate things. Judge Harman noted that 'this is not a case in which either Islām or the political beliefs of the organisation to which the father belongs ... is at all relevant' (*Heiden* v. *Kaufman* [2011] FMCA fam 478 at 91), and in ordering that the children reside with the mother and have no contact with the father, also stated the matter was 'no way connected with his faith ... it is connected with the underlying disfunction in his view of the world which has no basis in Islām at all' (*Heiden* v. *Kaufman* [2011] FMCA fam 478 at 135). Justice Harman's comments give consideration to the child's connection to his faith although it was not relevant in the particular circumstances.

It proves even more difficult when both parents are Muslims but differ in their practice of their faith. For example, in *Kasun-Stojanovic* v. *Kasun* [2007] FamCA 877, the parents were both Muslims but described as non-practising when they got married. After the birth of the child, however, the mother became more devout and adopted Islamic dress. She also wanted the child to wear the *ḥijāb* and to attend an Islamic school when both matters were opposed by the father. Whilst the judge commended the parents on their ability to reach an agreement to reconsider the matter when the child turned ten, the way in which the judge described the parents beliefs is interesting. The Court stated:

> the parties are both Muslim in faith, yet differ in the depth of the respective beliefs, the wife being fundamentalist. The husband expressed concern that the child embrace what he described as the 'Australian way of life'.... Each must consider and respect the views of the other, but in the result, any decision of this court will be predicated upon her best interests.
>
> (*Kasun-Stojanovic* v. *Kasun* [2007] FamCA 877 at 16)

This demonstrates the difficulties faced by practising Muslims in articulating the importance of their religious practices in a parenting context. In this case, the mother was labelled a 'fundamentalist' for what appears to be simply adhering to her religious beliefs.

In contrast, in the Canadian case *Wafa* v. *Faizi* (2014) CarswellBC 2788, 2014 BCSC 1760 in which the parents also disputed whether their daughter should go to an Islamic School, the Court upheld the decision of the mother to send the child to the Islamic school on the basis that it would assist the child both educationally and culturally. In *Aubrey* v. *Ellerby* [2011] FMCA fam 535, however, Federal Magistrate Burchardt noted:

> it is not the Court's task to make any kind of comparative analysis as to what might be said to be the mutual worth or validity of any religion, including the Muslim one. The question in this case is the best interests of the child.
>
> (*Aubrey* v. *Ellerby* [2011] FMCA fam 535 at 23)

In this case, the mother was no longer practising aspects of the faith, had removed her *ḥijāb* and objected to the father telling the child that it was bad to play with non-Muslims:

> The mother does not wish to lead a more conservative Muslim lifestyle and she is perfectly entitled to do so, just as the father conversely is also entitled

> to lead a conservative Muslim lifestyle should he so desire. The tension, however, between their two positions is plainly a difficult one, and is one in which [X]'s needs to be placed at the forefront.
>
> (*Aubrey* v. *Ellerby* [2011] FMCA fam 535 at 47)

Similarly in *Abney* v. *Paris* [2013] FMCA fam 7, where the mother had reverted back to Christianity, and in a parenting dispute did not want the child to be 'instructed' in the Islamic faith. FM Coker noted: 'that a father or a mother didn't necessarily teach their children how to be a good person or a religious person but rather let the children observe their practises in that regard and that religion was the centrepiece of the father's life. He continued it would be 'to all intents and purposes, impossible to suggest that he and his family not instruct the children in relation to their faith, because it would form a part of their daily lives' (*Abney* v. *Paris* [2013] FMCA fam 7 at 66). It would seem that an important concern of the courts is to allow children to maintain a connection with the religion of both parents and to allow them to learn the tenets of the faith of both their parents. However, the court will place this into the context of what is in the child's best interest.

In the English case *S* (Children) [2004] EWHC 1282 (fam), Justice Baron went to great lengths to understand and appreciate the key aspects of both the Islamic religion and the Jain religion as the mother was a Muslim and the father a Jain. In fact, over five pages of the judgement are devoted to setting out the basic beliefs and practices of the two religions. The issue before the court was the mother's seeking permission to raise the children as Muslims and have the son circumcised. She argued that as a devout Muslim, it was her duty to bring her children up as Muslims. The father was opposed to both (*S* [Children] [2004] EWHC 1282 [fam] at 47). The court accepted that prior to the parents separating, the children were exposed to both religions although growing up in a Jain household. Justice Baron held that each party has the religious duty to bring the children up in their religion and, in this way, they would have the best of both worlds. Furthermore, she held that the children of a mixed heritage should be allowed to decide for themselves which, if any, religion they wish to follow (*S* [Children] [2004] EWHC 1282 [fam] at 83).

Awad argues that in the USA, courts 'refuse to engage in a doctrinal evaluation of the parties' religious child-rearing disagreements' (Awad 2014: 182). This is reflected in the case of *Najmi* v. *Najmi* [2008] – Ohio – 4405, where the mother was Christian and the father Muslim. The court affirmed the trial court's decision to grant custody of the child to the mother and permit her to relocate to another state which the father argued would prevent him from teaching the child about Islam. The court held that a trial court is prohibited from evaluating the merits of religious doctrine or defining the contents of that doctrine. In essence, the court has no authority to decide religious rearing disputes on doctrinal grounds (Awad 2014: 183). Whilst culture and religion may be a factor for the determination of custody, the best interests of the child was the overriding determinant (Awad 2014: 184).

In contrast, it appears that Australian courts are more willing, even in difficult cases, to recognise the importance of the child's religious background. For example, in *Essey* v. *Ella* [2013] FCCA 1523 where there was severe family violence, the Judge said that: 'the child is also from an Islamic background. It would appear that the Mother will continue to support, encourage and facilitate this child's engagement with that rich culture and important element of her identity and sense of self' (*Essey* v. *Ella* [2013] FCCA 1523 at 148). This willingness in Australian courts possibly derives support from the legislation's acknowledgment in the case of Aboriginal and Torres Strait Islander children to 'enjoy their culture'. By extension, the child's right to enjoyment of culture seems to be extended beyond indigenous heritage.

Conclusion

Family law is an area of law that touches most people at some point in their lives. As spouses, parents and children, we all experience some engagement with legal norms and principles of marriage and divorce. As we have argued in this chapter, this is true for Muslims living in our Common Law countries with the added complexity that not only will they need to comply with official legal norms but also with Islamic family law principles. For this reason, Muslims, like other faith-based communities, negotiate or navigate their way through the intersection of the official legal system and their religious beliefs. Put simply, for many Muslims this means ensuring that their family relations are recognised *both* by the state as well as by their religious community.

Often this intersection is seen as undermining the official legal system and any response to calls for accommodation of religious diversity have been usually met with an insistence that there is only one law for all. This fails to take into account the well-documented evidence that Muslims of all levels of religiosity place importance on Islamic principles and access informal community processes when they marry and divorce (Krayem 2014; Macfarlane 2012). However, this does not mean that Muslims ignore or shun the official family law system. Rather, as this chapter has clearly demonstrated, they engage with the legal system and bring matters of marriage and divorce (with Islamic components) before the Common Law Courts. Whilst this might not be true of all Muslims (the separatists as described in Chapter 2 probably would not actively seek to engage with the official legal system), the cases that have been discussed in this chapter describe how some Muslims seek an accommodationist path – actively seeking ways to bring their religious principles into harmony with official legal processes and principles.

This chapter has considered several areas where Muslims have presented before Common Law Courts with family law matters, namely the recognition of religious marriage and divorce and enforceability of the *mahr*. Case law across the jurisdictions illustrates that at present, while the courts are keen to accommodate Islamic family law principles, more often than not the courts have taken either to interpretation of complex Islamic elements of marriage, such as the *mahr* or have opted for one interpretation (i.e. expert or Sharīʿah principle) over another. Such an approach has resulted in diverse and at times contradictory results. At present, the courts' accommodation of Islamic family law principles appears to lack consistency in method and outcome. For example, some courts have attempted to dismiss the religious relevance of *mahr* with a view to applying neutral principles of law. On this basis, they have found the *mahr* to be too vague to be enforceable. On the other hand, when courts have considered the religious significance of *mahr*, they have deemed it improper for a court to enforce as a secular approach requires non-interference in religious affairs. These approaches, we would argue, have led some courts to deprive women of their religious rights, thereby demonstrating that the secular neutral principles can have a detrimental effect on Muslim women. Going forward, a more systematic, refined approach is necessary – ideally with the consultation of Islamic scholars and community leaders and, perhaps, the assistance of jointly-appointed single experts.

This chapter has also argued that courts have taken notice of religious aspects of the issues when applying general Common Law principles. For example, we detailed several cases where Islamic marriages have been recognised by courts based on the Common Law presumption of marriage, even when the ceremony had not complied with the statutory requirements. However, in the divorce context, Common Law Courts have not been as accommodating. In all jurisdictions, there can be no recognition of religious divorces. Parties need to seek out both a religious divorce as well as a civil one.

Whilst the inconsistent approaches taken by courts in our Common Law jurisdictions demonstrate some complexity, Muslims nevertheless are still engaging with the official legal system by bringing their religious matters before them. We would argue that these are Muslims approaching courts as citizens of the state and are seeking accommodation or recognition with the official legal system – a process that undoubtedly will be transformative for both.

Notes

1 See Chapter 2.
2 The word *nikāh* tended to be used by the Arabs to refer to the act of trees coming closer together, that is, 'The trees became drawn, or connected together'. *Lane's Lexicon*: 2848.
3 'The Prophet did not mean by this that it is bad, in itself, not to be married. Rather, it was the Prophet's response to the celibacy practiced by Christian priests in his time.'
4 The prohibition is also extended to relatives that arise out of what Islām terms as foster relations, which refers to the relationship that 'is deemed to come into existence between a woman who breast feeds a child and that child'.
5 Though the application of this ruling varies across different Schools of Islamic law with the Shāfiʿī School, for example, having a very narrow definition where there must be 'continuous ancestry'. The Shāfiʿī School confines the permission to marry a Jewish or Christian woman only if it is known that her ancestors entered the Jewish faith before the coming of Jesus Christ.
6 According to the Shāfiʿī School, the only guardians who may force their charge to marry are a virgin bride's father or father's father. This is only in the case of marrying

her to a suitable match (*kuf'*) and where these guardians comply with the rules of '*adālah*' or trustworthiness.

Ahmad ibn Naqib Al-Misri, *Reliance of the Traveller: A Classic Manual of Islamic Sacred Law*, translated by Nuh Ha Mim Keller (Baltimore, MD: Amana Publications, 1999), p. 522.

7 'The Ḥanafis interpreted the above Hadith as requiring consent of the bride in all cases. The Shāfi'i scholars, while restricting the same Hadith to women who had been previously married, nevertheless deemed it preferable and sunnah to ask for the girl's consent.'

8 The marriage begins with a period of *khuṭbah* or betrothal where the man requests the hand of a woman and she accepts. This can be seen as a mutual promise to marry. This engagement period is usually the time when the couple really get to know one another and can easily change their mind about the marriage. The *khuṭbah* is a promise by a man of his intention to marry a certain woman. It is a sort of agreement that serves as a preliminary to the contract of marriage (*nikāḥ*).

There are differing practices among the various cultural groups about how the engagement is conducted. Some celebrate it with a large party, while others make it known only to a very small and select group of close family and friends, leaving the publicity for a later ceremony. This can vary according to the different cultural practices of Muslims.

9 Once the couple agree that they are ready to marry, they take the next step, which is to negotiate a marriage contract and have an Islamic marriage ceremony. At this ceremony, the couple will officially enter into the marriage contract. Again, there are many different ways that this ceremony is performed, although most are officiated by an imām or religious leader; even though, as discussed above, there is no specific requirement for this in Islamic law. This practice serves to illustrate the religious importance of marriage, with many, even those who are not practising Muslims, seeking some religious sanction to their relationship. Although there are cultural variations, the ceremony begins with the imām reciting Qur'ānic verses, and explaining the marriage contract to the couple. The imām then asks about the *mahr* that has been agreed upon and this is recorded in the marriage contract. The imām then asks about any other terms or conditions agreed upon by the couple, acquires the consent of both parties and then sees that the couple sign the necessary documents.

10 For a further discussion on this see Krayem (2014: 181–86).

11 In particular, they objected to the provision in the contract that delegated a right to divorce to the wife, as they argue that this contradicts Islamic principles.

4 Muslims, crime and the Common Law

> Ordinary people, of course, come in all shapes and sizes and temperaments, and what is required is that you take into account the whole mass of various kinds of people who go to make up the community. Somewhere there is a line to be drawn between people who can be classed as ordinary people and those who are abnormal. You are required to look at the whole class of ordinary people.
>
> (Finlay, J in *R* v. *Saliba* (1986) 10 *Criminal Law Journal* 420)

Introduction

There is no reason why, logically or in principle, Muslims should be accommodated or given recognition under Criminal Law. If we take the content of the Criminal Law as given, and representing serious or 'core' public wrongs such as murder, rape, theft and burglary, Muslims should be held to account the same way as anybody else. To hold otherwise, to carve out exceptions and to particularise on the basis of culture or belief – to do Muslims 'a favour' – would undermine basic ties of civic responsibility and respect for the Rule of Law.

The problem is that we take this content for granted. Putting to one side the notion that 'crime' may be historically and politically contingent,[1] the traditional liberal view is that we are all equally responsible, rational moral agents. In modern democratic political theory, Criminal Law, carrying with it the sanction of punishment, has moral force only on the assumption that its norms have been communicated to all and made the subject of popular participation and discussion. As Anthony Duff describes (Duff 2007: 191–93), the designation of a certain social behaviour as a crime represents a 'moral communication' between fellow citizens; yet many groups and people suffer systematic disadvantage and exclusion from participation in this discourse of citizenship, so upon what basis can they be held morally to account and the Criminal Law deemed 'just'?

As we have suggested in Chapters 1 and 2, while Muslims in our four jurisdictions have integrated in varieties of ways in all aspects of society, they also suffer systematic exclusion, discrimination and marginalisation; increasingly so since the launches of the 'war(s) on terror', the emergence of Dāʿish and the continuing rise of 'Islamophobia'. They have become a community under siege, or at least perceive to be so.[2] Recent trends of 'overcriminalization' (Husak

2008; Lacey 2012) and 'law and order populism'[3] have made Muslims potential targets of the Criminal Law and victims of ever-increasing police powers like never before.

The point and method of seeking 'accommodation' in this context, or going beyond accommodation, we suggest, is not to 'excuse' Muslims or seek 'unilateral favour' for infractions of the Criminal Law. In some situations, as we highlight later in the chapter, it may be necessary to impose exemplary sanctions to express our (by 'our' we include Muslim) collective indignation and denunciation of that conduct. Nor is the point of accommodation to exempt Muslims from procedures that the rest of the population are required to follow. Rather, the objective of our focus is to emphasise the relevance of religious identity as we develop 'more nuanced legal procedures' (Duff 2007: 193) that respond to cultural and religious diversity as well as to the particular social circumstances in which individuals, in our case Muslims, are situated.

This chapter explores the Criminal Law in the context of this security environment and asks to what extent, and in what ways, courts and legislatures have recognised Muslim identity and cultures. It also examines the potential and limitations of cultural evidence and whether there is a place for the 'culture defence'.

Recognising that procedural aspects of the law of crimes and doctrine are interconnected elements of the same machinery of criminal justice (Brown *et al.* 2015: 17), we examine both procedure (in which we include evidence) and the substantive law. We look first at civil or what may be broadly termed as 'participation rights' in the criminal justice context, both pre-trial and at court. In the second half of the chapter we examine the substantive law, focusing on so-called 'honour-related violence' (HRV), religious rituals, parental responsibility and 'Sharīʿah' vigilantes.

'Processing' Muslims

Policing

Policing is the most visible manifestation of a country's criminal justice system. It is also the most vulnerable to claims of illegitimacy and to discrimination. Integral to the notion of the Rule of Law is that all are equal before the Law, so reports of unfair treatment at the hands of the police will impact greatly on how the Police and the system of criminal justice as a whole is viewed and whether the Rule of Law is implemented in practice. Accommodating Muslims in this context, therefore, does not mean giving Muslims preference over others, or refusing to apply the letter of the Law because a potential offender appears to be Muslim. Neither, however, does it mean adopting a position of neutrality whereby police officers will pay no attention to a Muslim's religious or cultural background in the course of stopping, questioning, searching, arresting and detaining suspects who happen to be Muslim. Rather, it asks police officers and policing to recognise the relevance of and be sensitive to Islamic symbols and practices of Muslim suspects in the course of their operations just as they recognise the relevance of age, race and gender. It also implies non-discrimination; that Muslims will not be subjects of 'religious profiling'[4] and deemed 'suspects' because they are Muslim. The presumption of innocence overrides any assumed shared criminogenic traits.

Much of police processing of Muslims, as with all others caught up within the Criminal Justice System, is largely hidden from sight and beyond the control of courts. Police exercise a wide degree of discretion, influenced by legal and non-legal factors as well as their ideas of who most needs to be 'policed' (McConville *et al.* 1991: 14–17). Legality within our different jurisdictions is structured around the concept of 'reasonable suspicion', or 'probable cause' and in theory all stops and searches, arrests and detentions should have factual and objective bases that link suspects to the occurrence of a crime. Although police have codes of practice and operational guidelines that purport to guide how they exercise their discretion in particular and specific fact situations, in practice, there is nothing to ensure that they do. Indeed, operational police cultures (and prejudices) can endeavour to achieve the exact opposite (McConville *et al.* 1991: 14–17).

Muslims enjoy formal equality of the law and are not explicitly targeted by the law or official policy. Nevertheless, as predominantly ethnic minorities and living on the margins of society, they are more likely to be 'policed'. Further, as discussed in Chapter 1 their situation has been exacerbated by security fears. Since 9/11, 7/7 and the Bali bombings, Muslim minorities have been deemed 'suspect communities': put under surveillance, stopped, searched, questioned, arrested and detained in numbers disproportionate to the size of their population. As McCullogh and Pickering have noted, 'race, religion and ethnicity continue to be seen and used as proxies for risk under counter-terrorism frameworks' (2009: 635).[5]

Religious identifiers, in the case of men, have tended to be ethnic, with South Asians and Arabs the usual targets.[6] In the case of Muslim women, suspicion has attached to dress, in particular the '*niqāb*'. Its wearing has been regarded as 'confronting', 'provocative' and a reason to stop. It has alluded to an association with extremist religious groups, whom we discussed in Chapter 2. In continental Europe, security fears coupled with secular opposition to public displays of religiosity has resulted in legislation banning the wearing of *burqa*s and *niqāb*s. In Common Law jurisdictions, legislatures have not gone so far. In Britain, Canada and the United States, they have resisted any ban, regarding its wearing a matter of personal choice but subject to restriction in certain contexts where identification is necessary.[7] Australia has also resisted a general 'burqa ban', but in three jurisdictions (NSW, ACT and WA) police have been given specific powers to remove 'face coverings' to confirm identity.[8] Although these provisions apply equally to wearing balaclavas and helmets, enhanced policed powers were legislated following an intense media campaign and uproar after a false allegation was made that a police officer had, for 'racist reasons', forcibly removed a Muslim woman's 'burqa'.[9]

Studies indicate (Poynting and Mason 2006; Poynting and Perry 2007; Tyler *et al.* 2010: 365) that in terms of police operational practice, there has been little evidence of accommodation of Islamic religious identity across our jurisdictions. Rather, evidence suggests police have targeted and discriminated against Muslims simply on grounds of religious identity. While Muslims tend not to object to greater personal intrusions where clearly justified for security reasons (Tyler *et al.* 2010), such procedural unfairness is likely to be counter-productive in the fight against Islamist terrorism. In recent research conducted by Adrian Cherney, Elise Sergeant and Kristina Murphy on Muslim communities in Brisbane, Melbourne and Sydney, it was found Muslims who felt they were targeted by the police were less trusting of police, less likely to identify with Australia and less willing to cooperate with police. Conversely, they found if police officers went about their tasks paying attention to procedural fairness, these Muslims were more likely to report suspicious terror-related activities and to feel less 'under siege' (Cherney *et al.* 2015).

Coronial investigation

Homicides are categorised as the most serious crimes and deserve the most thorough investigation. Rule of Law and Equality before the Law, not to mention International Human Rights, acknowledge the equality of human life and that all victims, and their families, irrespective of the community to which they may belong, have a right to as thorough an investigation as circumstances permit, to determine the factual cause of death. Because Criminal Law in our four jurisdictions is also constructed as a 'Public' rather than a 'Personal' Law, there is also a public expectation that investigations into unexplained causes of death will be thorough in order to protect community welfare and not just to protect the rights of individuals.

The coronial inquiry traverses this very complex intersection between public welfare and private rights. Accommodating Muslims in this context, as well as Jews, some Christians and Indigenous groups, is not met in the neutral application of existing coronial rules or in the intent of medical examiners to discover the factual cause of death. Rather, it is found in the sensitised manner of its procedure.

According to authenticated sayings of the Prophet, 'Breaking the bones of the dead is like breaking the bones of the living.'[10] Following literal interpretations and popular Muslim perceptions, this would imply the usual autopsy or an invasive examination of the body where bones are broken, organs removed and tissues damaged might be akin to committing such acts on a living person and be prohibited. The body of the human being is to be honoured and respected in death as it is in life.[11]

The investigation of unexplained deaths, especially where a homicide is suspected, clearly is a special context at which the above *ḥadīth* is not unequivocally directed. This has generated interpretative space and diverse interpretations. If we return to our typologies from Chapter 2, the 'separatist puritan', who tends

because of the importance of a fair trial.[19] Even there, the courts have understood Muslim sensitivity and respect for modesty by discussing alternative measures with counsel. Similarly in Canada (*R* v. *N.S.* [2012] 3 S.C.R. 726) the courts have deemed a mandatory requirement to remove the *niqāb* as 'extreme' and a violation of Charter rights to freedom of religion. The Chief Justice of the Canadian Supreme Court has gone so far as to say: 'A secular response that requires witnesses to park their religion at the courtroom door is inconsistent with the jurisprudence and Canadian tradition' (*R* v. *N.S.* [2012] 3 S.C.R. 726 at 735). If a witness has 'sincere religious reasons' (evaluated in a voir dire) in wearing the *niqāb*, she is only required to remove it if: (a) this is necessary to prevent a 'serious risk' to the fairness of the trial, and alternative measures will not remove that risk; and (b) the 'salutary effects' of requiring her to remove the *niqāb* outweigh any 'deleterious effects'. The court further clarified if the witness's evidence is uncontested and credibility is not in issue, she is not asked to remove her *niqāb*.

The courts in England and Wales have taken a similar balanced approach (*R* v. *D (R)* [2013] Eq LR 1034) but have not insisted on any pre-trial inquiry where the 'sincerity' of the witness's religious belief would be questioned (the courts have not been deemed the appropriate forum). The witness is only required to remove her *niqāb* during cross-examination, and even then she is shielded from the gaze of the public galleries by a screen or by way of a live-video link (as has been customary when cross-examining children and other 'vulnerable witnesses').

While one might question the objective value of interpreting facial expressions and non-verbal cues when evaluating testimony (Hunter *et al.* 2015: 212–14), especially where the witness is ethnically and racially different from the jury and not used to revealing her face in public, the courts have not been insensitive. Given the importance of cross-examination to the Common Law adversarial tradition, there can be little doubt the courts have attempted to accommodate Muslim women wanting to wear full face veils.

In relation to male dress codes, generally speaking, the wearing of 'sunnah clothes' has not been an issue because it has not conflicted with any right of due process. Even Muslim barristers in Australia have been permitted to don a turban in place of traditional robes and wigs.[20] Where a controversy has occurred, appeal courts have intervened on grounds of fairness. In Canada, a judge in an Ontario trial court refused to permit a Muslim wearing a 'kufi' to sit in the public gallery on the ground that it was an established court custom all men should enter the court 'bare-headed'. This was subsequently deemed an error by the Ontario Court of Appeal in that it gave the appearance of undermining a fair trial and a bias against minority religions (*Taylor* v. *Attorney-General of Canada* (2001) Fed.Ct. Trial LEXIS 1208.

Indeed, it appears the courts have been tolerant of even 'separatist' (see Chapter 2) positions which might be regarded 'disrespectful' of established court rules of etiquette or even a contempt of court. In *Mohamed Ali Elomar (and others)* (2007), in which the nine accused refused to stand when entering their pleas, Mr Justice Anthony Whealy replied: 'Judges are made of more robust material ... but a jury might take a different view' (Lamont 2007). Similarly, in the case of the Sydney Muslim rioters in 2013 (Mohammed Issai Issaka *et al.*), when the accused refused to stand and bow before the magistrate, Jacqueline Milledge, although she berated them for their 'disrespect' of the court, she nevertheless arranged a short adjournment to allow Issaka to leave the room and then reconvened the court while she remained seated. The former Attorney-General Greg Smith was later asked about the case and commented that while standing and bowing is expected court etiquette, it is up to the court how they run their courtroom. They might regard it is 'contempt in the face of court' and subject the accused to a criminal penalty; alternatively, they might let it pass, which is how both of the judges handled this particular case (Bodkin and Dale 2013). The current NSW Attorney-General, Gabrielle Upton, has recently announced the NSW Government now intend to pass new legislation to make it a criminal offence to refuse to stand up in court (ABC News 2015).

From an Islamic perspective, we suggest that the controversies over both the *niqāb* and refusing to stand in court were (and are) largely unnecessary. There is enough interpretative space within the texts to navigate this difficulty.[21] In respect of refusals to stand in court, sayings of the Prophet such as 'Whoever likes the people to stand up for him, let him take his place in Hell',[22] upon which the accused appeared to have relied, stand as authorities that it is '*ḥarām*' (unlawful) to ask others, out of arrogance or conceit, to stand up for you when you walk in (Ibn Athir n.d., vol. 4: 294). The accused appears to have taken a blanket ruling and applied it literally, whatever the circumstances. Again, we would suggest this reflects a separatist position. In the Prophetic sayings collected by at-Tirmidhi, it is reported that when the Prophet would enter a room and his daughter Fatimah was present, she would stand up for him and take his hand. It is also mentioned in the same saying she would enter a room in which he was present, would take her hand and make her sit in his place. Local religious leaders in Sydney have also questioned the stance and interpretation when applied to neutral and customary court processes (Lamont 2007). It appears even so-called 'Salafists', to whom these accused would have deferred, would exempt them from the ruling if to apply would cause 'rancour and hatred' (al-Munajjid n.d.).

Fair trial rights

As the above cases suggest, our 'puritanical separatists' (see further, Chapter 2) are not interested in engaging in the legal process. Common Law legal processes are deemed unfair a priori because they spring from a *kufr* (blasphemous) belief system and do not apply Sharī'ah. For them, the less they are seen to be applying Common Law rights of Due Process, the better. Participation rights, such as to present evidence, are less important than the right not to participate. The emphasis within the Common Law on the Prosecution and the State bearing the burden of proof in criminal cases, the privilege against self-incrimination and the right of silence accommodates even puritanical separatists. While there has been a trend over the past twenty years in Common Law legislatures to erode these traditional Common Law rights,[23] such persons can still refuse to testify if they so wish and, other than in cases of statutory reversal, can insist on the Prosecution to present sufficient evidence to prove its case beyond a reasonable doubt.

This right not to participate also includes such fundamental Common Law rights such as to elect trial by jury. In all of our jurisdictions, an accused which fears community prejudice has the ability to 'opt out' of jury trial, depending on how a case is categorised. Even in the most serious cases, some jurisdictions permit 'bench only trial' so long as it is not contrary to the public interest. In *R* v. *Belghar* [2012] NSWCCA 86, for example, a New South Wales trial judge initially permitted a Muslim accused to waive his rights to trial by jury because of his fears of a biased jury. While this was overturned on appeal, the appellate court would have allowed bench trial to go ahead if the defence had submitted evidence of actual prejudice within the community and established that judicial directions would not have been sufficient to overcome that prejudice.

It is also true to say that a fear of jury trial is not synonymous with separatist perspectives. Muslims from all persuasions, including those who adopt integrative approaches, benefit from Common Law Courts protecting accused persons from the vagaries of the adversarial process and the effects of popular prejudice as the context of the above case indicates. In American jurisdictions, courts have also been alert to the dangers of the adversarial process and its potential for prejudicing a Muslim accused before a lay jury. Appellate courts have intervened to curb prosecutors pandering to the religious prejudices of juries and required judges to make use of curative directions. So in *State of Oregon* v. *Shahin Farokhrany* (2013), 259, Or.App. 132 where the Ohio Court of Appeal criticised the prosecution for referring to 'honor killings' in order to inflame the jury, in which a Muslim accused was charged with sexual offences, the appellate court held a Muslim's right to a fair trial had been violated after a prosecutor drew comparisons with rape laws applying Sharīʿah in Iran and Saudi Arabia.

In addition to trial by jury, the right to present evidence is essential to a fair trial and exercise of that right is indicative of intent by a Muslim accused to engage with the trial and the trial process. As a general rule, Common Law Courts do not interfere with decisions of a party or legal representative over what type of evidence should be submitted, other than it must be relevant and not fall foul of an exclusionary rule.[24] Once evidence is deemed admissible, it is up to the jury (or tribunal of fact) what to make of it.

For Muslim parties, however, the uncertainties of jury decision-making can make the presentation and submission of evidence in criminal cases problematic, especially where the circumstances of the offences touch upon cultural issues. On the one hand, there is a recognition the jury may be ignorant of Muslim cultural mores and Sharīʿah rules, an accurate understanding of which may be necessary to appreciate the context in which the offence took place. On the other, there is the fear of anti-Muslim sentiment which presentation of cultural evidence may serve only to exacerbate.

In some cases in the United States, courts have regarded decisions by defence counsel not to present cultural evidence, for fear of jury prejudice, as matters of defence strategy. Although lawyers made these decisions in defiance of their party's wishes, this did not undermine a party's right to a fair trial. It was not the State preventing such evidence from being admitted.[25] The principle of party control, it seems, extends only to one's legal representatives. In other cases, US courts have regarded defence cultural evidence as irrelevant or a matter not falling beyond the expertise of lay jurors and therefore inadmissible.[26]

Cultural evidence presented by the prosecution has not met with such restriction, though the court has accepted it has a gate-keeping role to maintain the rights of an accused to a fair trial. In *State of New Jersey* v. *K.E* (2009), unreported, (WL 4908298 N.J.Super.A.D.), a Muslim accused was charged with sexual assaults involving rape and anal intercourse against his Egyptian wife. At issue was why the wife had delayed her rape complaints (with the defence submitting the wife had made these up in order to get a permanent residence visa in the United States). In order to explain the reason for delay, the prosecution introduced a 'cultural expert' with expertise in Comparative Law, Egyptian culture and gender issues, who testified that very few women in Egypt report sexual assaults because of the dishonour and shame, (especially in cases of anal intercourse). In addition, she spoke as to social attitudes in Egypt on virginity and 'honour killings'.

All of this testimony was admitted by the trial judge, but objected to on appeal on grounds of prejudice and the right to a fair trial. In particular, it was argued there was no precedent for a cultural expert in this context and that the expert had stepped into the domain of the jury by evaluating the credibility of a witness (the wife). The appeal court noted these objections, but refused to rule on them other than agreeing that the court had a gate-keeping role to determine whether there was a need for this evidence and what the parameters ought to be. The court also acknowledged that should this cultural evidence be adduced at the re-trial (the conviction was reversed and a re-trial ordered on other grounds), the expert's evidence must remain within the confines of relevant evidence and not address 'honour killings or virginity'.

In Australia, defence witnesses have been able to lead cultural evidence in a variety of different contexts from a variety of sources. The main issue has been the weight to attach to such evidence rather than its admissibility.[27] In *R* v. *Abdul Haque Omarjee* [1995] VSC 94; [1995] VICSC 94 the defence was allowed to adduce evidence from an Imām on Islamic rules of cleanliness to rebut the credibility of the principal prosecution witness. In *Guven Abdul Yildiz* (1983) 11 A. Crim.R. 115, a Turkish interpreter, with no qualifications in sociology or anthropology, was allowed to testify as to the attitude of Turks – generally – and in Melbourne – to homosexuality and, in particular, to 'deliverers' (*kulambara*) and 'receivers' (*ibne*). In *Regina* v. *G M Khan* [2001] NSWSC 1356, a sociologist was permitted to adduce evidence of how serious adultery was viewed in Sydney's Muslim communities and as evidence to support provocation. Similarly, in *R* v. *MSK, MAK, and MMK* [2006] NSWSC 237, a sociologist was also permitted to testify as to 'cultural conditioning' in a case of sexual assault. It was suggested the presence of unaccompanied teenage girls in a mixed gender gathering in itself was 'sexually provocative' to an accused brought up in gender-segregated Pakistan and 'unthinkable' that a woman would say 'no'. While the court noted the over-generalisation and 'essentialised' nature of the evidence, that went only to the weight and not the admissibility of the evidence.

Canadian jurisdictions have appeared very open to receipt of cultural evidence, for both prosecution and defence, even where the evidence submitted would appear to be 'antithetical' to fundamental Charter values of equality between men and women (*R* v. *Humaid* [2006], CarswellOnt 2278, 37 C.R. [6th]). The focus in most recent cases (pertaining to so-called 'honour killings') however, has been to admit cultural evidence for the prosecution to enable the jury to understand the context (and motivations) of criminal acts, notwithstanding clear prejudicial effect against an accused.[28]

In summary, Common Law Courts have generally recognised the right of Muslims to present cultural evidence and this has been regarded as a neutral application of due process and the right to a fair trial. But, as with other procedural rights, there has been a tendency to use this procedure to facilitate prosecutorial arguments (and therefore state interests) which has worked against Muslim accused persons.

Sentencing

Perhaps more than the trial itself, the sentencing stage of proceedings provides a forum for symbolic recognition or non-recognition of different aspects of a person's identity. Depending on the nature of the case and the particular circumstances in which the offence was committed, this is where the court will balance considerations that are particular to an offender against the public interest. These interests are not mutually exclusive as a sentence which promotes rehabilitation of the offender will also be in the public interest as the offender may less likely return to crime. Nevertheless, in certain cases the interests of the offender will weigh less in the court's evaluation because of the perceived need to deter the offence, to match the seriousness of the crime or to make a public denunciation of the offender's conduct. Surrounding environmental and political factors may also impact on the choice of sentence and its particular severity. It is not the place here to discuss alternative theoretical approaches to sentencing apart from to note that in recent years, courts across our jurisdictions have shifted towards more punitive and retributivist paradigms. As a result, courts pay less attention to mitigating factors and more to popular perceptions of the seriousness of a crime.

As we will see, notwithstanding the Common Law notion that all are equal before the law, this shift may impact disproportionately on Muslim offenders who appear before the courts, first: because of disproportionate numbers of convictions per head of population, and second, because of the types of offences Muslims stand convicted. The latter is particularly relevant post-9/11 as legislatures have sought enhanced penalties for those convicted of terrorist offences (see further, Chapter 1) and gender-based crimes. It will be apparent that in cases of the former, Muslims perceived 'extreme' have received condign sentences. In cases of the latter, courts have focused on 'cultural factors' and a failure of those particular Muslims to 'integrate'. Religion has appeared rarely as a mitigating factor and only then in less serious cases.

Since 9/11 and the global response to Islamist terrorism, with the distinct exception of Canada, courts have tended to examine the extent of religious motivation in terrorist offenders. Legislatures and courts have also ensured that persons found guilty of terrorist offences are given exemplary sentences as a symbolic denunciation of their acts, if not a deterrent as such. Given that the majority of the convictions are for 'pre-crime' preparatory offences or conspiracies, community campaigners have argued the frequently 'life' sentences are disproportionate, unfair and reflect 'Islamophobia' more than the harm actually caused.[29]

In offences other than terrorism, the courts have generally regarded the adoption of conservative or 'strict' Muslim family values as aggravating factors because of the clashes with majority civic values.[30] This has been particularly prevalent in cases involving 'honour-related violence' (HRV) or 'violence against women' (VAW). In *Andrew Iskandar* [2012] NSWSC 149, the New South Wales Supreme Court viewed the motivation for the killing of a woman for suspected adultery as an 'honour killing' (although there was no express reference to Islām), and as such merited exemplary punishment. The trial court stated:

> No society or culture that regards itself as civilised can tolerate to any extent, or make any allowance for, the killing of another person for such an amorphous concept as honour ... Such a notion has no place in this country ... The motive for this murder means that general deterrence assumes some importance in the determination of the sentence.

The appellate courts in England and Wales, where HRV cases have been more prevalent, have taken a similar approach to denounce the behaviour and the values it stands for and pronounced exemplary sentences (Ballard 2011: 124). In *R* v. *Imran Khalil* (2004) 2 Cr App Rep (S) 24, the daughter of the accused had married a Muslim man in secret and against the wishes of her parents. The father subsequently organised a hit-man (an undercover police officer) to kill the husband. The father was convicted of conspiracy to murder and during the sentencing hearing explained that his daughter's decision had 'dishonoured' him. The trial court, with the appeal court confirming, held this was a 'serious aggravating circumstance', justifying a deterrent sentence of sixteen years.

In the earlier case of AG Reference Nos 8, 9 and 10 of 2002 (Naved Mohammad and others) (2003) 1 Cr App Rep (S) 57, in which there was no indication any violence had been used or threatened, the Court of Appeal also stressed the importance of values. Here, the father and uncles of a Muslim young woman were convicted of kidnapping her to persuade her to end a relationship with a non-Muslim (and to arrange another marriage). The kidnapping had lasted less than a day. At the trial, the court sentenced the accused to a custodial discharge rather than a prison sentence on the ground that the latter would 'do far more harm to community relations than good'. This was rejected and 'regretted' by the Appeal Court because the trial judge had failed to take into account, as an aggravating factor, that the accused had failed 'to respect the victim's right to make her own choice as to the way she should conduct her life and the relationships she should form'. Although the court acknowledged their lack of bad character and 'genuinely held religious belief in what they thought would be in the best interests of the victim', the discharge was substituted with a prison sentence of eighteen months for the father and twelve months for the other offenders.

Although the Sentencing Guidance Note of the Lord Chief Justice's Sentencing Group of England and Wales announced in 2011: 'There is no separate category of "honour-based" crimes' and that 'an offender who is convicted of a crime which he/she seeks to justify as "honour-based" will fall to be sentenced in accordance with normal sentencing principles.' English courts have continued to specifically identify circumstances of HRV as falling within aggravating factors. So in *R* v. *Ahmed and Ahmed* (2012) (the 'Shafilea case') in the Chester Crown Court, confirmed killing perpetrated in defence of cultural notions of 'honour' was an aggravating factor. In sentencing the parents to twenty-five years' imprisonment, Roderick Evans J felt impelled to condemn them for imposing 'social and cultural attitudes ... of rural Pakistan' rather than to adapt to and engage with the values of English society.[31]

The third situation in which religious identity has arisen in matters of sentencing has been in mitigation. Although it is a general right in all of our jurisdictions to submit evidence in support of mitigation, the extent to which religion, per se, can provide a basis, depends in part on the surrounding constitutional and legislative framework. In the American state of Pennsylvania, for example, state statutes on freedom of religion prevent witnesses from being asked about their religious belief. Nevertheless, the Supreme Court of Pennsylvania in *Commonwealth of Pennsylvania* v. *Reid* (2014, 99 A.3d 427 at 39–40) has held that 'catch-all mitigators' in sentencing statutes still enable defendants to refer to religious conversions and new found values in support of rehabilitation. Unless a defendant can point to specific prejudice caused, however, a trial court decision to prevent him naming that religion (in this case 'Islām') will not be a reversible error.[32]

Where courts have been prepared to look at religion in mitigation, it is clear they must be convinced that the belief is genuinely held and that it does not also constitute an aggravating factor. In the English case of *R* v. *Sajad Qureshi* (2007) 1 Cr App Rep (S) 85, the appellant appealed against a custodial sentence of fifteen months for being a party to the kidnapping of his wife. His wife had visited the local swimming pool with some of her female friends and her children. She entered the pool in a swimming costume and was visible in front of men. She was told to get out of the pool as this was against their culture and religion. Later, with other members of the family, the wife was taken, without her consent, to her own parents' home where she was physically assaulted by her father. In mitigation and again on appeal, it was submitted that there was no significant risk of serious harm and that by leaving the appellant and breaching religious and cultural taboos, the wife had shattered his sense of pride. This was rejected by the Appeal Court on the grounds of lack of remorse shown, and the family's belief that they had been 'dishonoured'. Given the appellant's drinking habits during the marriage, the court also noted it was hypocritical for him now to insist on compliance with such a code. It was simply a tool, to control the wife and force her back into the marriage.

Another matter affecting court willingness to consider a defendant's adherence to Islamic codes of behaviour in mitigation has been the objective seriousness of the offence and whether it trumps subjective factors relevant to exculpation or rehabilitation. In driving offences, for example, which tend to be viewed as objectively 'less serious', English courts have accepted previous law-abiding behaviour and religious adherence in mitigation (See *R* v. *Waheed Akhtar* [2004] 1 Cr App Rep [S] 78). In drugs cases, however, the courts have focused on offence seriousness. So in *Vagh* v. *The State of Western Australia* [2007] WASCA 17, the Supreme Court of Western Australia held that, although the Muslim defendant had no previous antecedents, had pleaded guilty, had come from a devout South African Muslim family and had acted 'out of character' after coming under the influence of his criminal employer, and had been reconciled with his family and community, the nature of the case (prohibited drugs) and the charges (possession of ecstasy with intent to supply) precluded the court from using cultural evidence in mitigation. He was sentenced to six years imprisonment. Similarly in homicide cases, the courts have looked less at subjective factors. In *R* v. *Mohammed* [2004] VSC 423, for example, the Australian Supreme Court of Victoria, in sentencing a Muslim abattoir worker to fifteen years, imprisonment for the manslaughter of a fellow worker, accepted in mitigation that the accused had been subjected to two weeks of religious 'vilification, taunts and goading', that he had been kicked and abused while praying and that he had lost control when he killed. But they concluded a deterrent sentence was more appropriate given the severity of the violence he had inflicted on his colleagues. In sexual assault cases, Australian courts have also objected to any form of cultural evidence from Muslims who migrated from countries with 'traditional views towards women' that purports to mitigate or excuse their behaviour.[33]

The earlier Canadian court decision in *R* v. *Ammar Nouasria*[34] appears out of kilter in this respect. This was a case from the Court of Quebec in which the accused was charged and found guilty of sexual touching of a person under the age of fourteen (s. 151 of the Criminal Code), invitation to sexual touching of a person under the age of fourteen (s. 152), engaging in anal intercourse (s. 159) and sexual assault (s. 265). The offences were committed against the accused's stepdaughter (both the accused and the stepdaughter were Muslim) when she was between the ages of nine and eleven. The accused did not have complete vaginal intercourse with the victim. Approximately twenty incidents took place over the two-year period, with the accused applying a mixture of psychological pressure and threats to force the victim into the activities.

At the sentencing stage, notwithstanding 'culture' was not listed among mitigating factors, the court noted:

> The mitigating factors are ... the fact that the accused did not have normal and complete sexual relations with the victim, that is to say, vaginal sexual relations, to be more precise, so that he could preserve her virginity, which seems to be a very important value in their religion. We can say that, in a certain way, the accused spared his victim.
>
> (per Judge Raymonde Verreault)

As a result, the trial judge imposed only a concurrent sentence of twenty-three months, imprisonment and a one-year probation for the sexual offences. The maximum term for these offences was ten years. The case went to appeal and the appeal court substituted forty-three months for the anal intercourse charge on the basis the original sentence was not a sufficient deterrent.

This case sparked a huge controversy at the time and an inquiry was ordered by the Quebec Judicial Council after nine complaints were lodged against the trial judge for the grounds upon which her judgement had been delivered (Fournier 2002: 111). The Muslim community of Montreal was also outraged by the stereotypes her comments perpetuated. It appears that no cultural evidence was called during the trial and that the judge 'tried to guide herself as to legal principles and to take into account the factors she deemed relevant' (Conseil de la Magistrature, S. Guillemette Le Barreau du Québec *et al.* [Plaignants] et Madame la juge Raymonde Verreault [Intime] No. 8–93–40, cited in Fournier 2002: 112). She had assumed that because the victim had been sodomised, she had been spared future embarrassment and ostracism as she could still say she was a virgin upon marriage.

We would add that while it is true to say that Islām and Muslims value chastity before marriage, it is a gross distortion of the tradition (no matter what variant), to partially excuse an abhorrent crime and imply that Islamic values condoned sexual violence and sodomy (*liwāṭ*), let alone against a child. It is also perversely ironic that the judge considered the sodomy a mitigating factor, when under the Sharīʿah, under its Ḥudūd laws, such conduct, if proven, would have merited severe punishment.[35] We submit that the court could have avoided this controversy simply by following established mitigating factors as no cultural evidence had in fact been submitted.

A contrasting case to *R* v. *Ammar Nouasria* is the English decision of AG's Reference No. 51 of 2001 (2002) 1 Cr App Rep (S) 80. In this case, the Crown appealed against a sentence of five years for the rape of a Muslim girl on the grounds that it was too lenient. The Court of Appeal referred to her victim impact statement and recognised that she was a young, devout Muslim girl who had lost respect in her community and whose marriage prospects had been damaged. The proper sentence should have been ten years because 'any sex, even consensual sex would have a particularly serious impact upon her'.

'Excusing' Muslims: protecting 'honour', performing ritual, 'educating' family and community

In the first half of this chapter, we have examined how Muslims are 'processed' both in and out of court, and explored the extent to which, in the frameworks of our four jurisdictions, Common Law successfully navigates questions of Muslim identity and values through an implicit (in some cases, an explicit) balancing of freedom of religion with civic values and the protection of the public interest. We have noted that in matters that touch upon core liberal values of due process, fair trials and participation rights, courts (especially at the appellate level) have been generally careful to ensure that a Muslim's freedom of religious belief is not prejudiced and have only limited expression where it would conflict with fundamental procedural values. However, where Muslims have appeared to challenge security interests or contemporary Western civic values, the expression of religious identity has triggered a punitive response, whether at the hands of the legislatures or the courts when sentencing. We also have noted the instances in which this has occurred have generally been where Muslims have adhered to unnecessarily rigid or puritanical and separatist versions of the Islamic tradition with little or no recognition of Islām's internal diversity and practical moderation.

In the second half of this chapter, we look at the substantive Criminal Law and examine how legislatures and the Common Law Courts have addressed issues of culpability and the space given to a 'cultural' or religious defence. We focus on three main areas: first, so-called 'Honour Related Violence' (HRV) and 'Violence against Women' (VAW) in the context of homicide cases and the defence of provocation; second, the responses to forceful measures by Muslims to educate their families and the broader community in 'Islamic ways' (the 'Sharī'ah vigilantes'); and third, specific religious rites and rituals – where Muslim defendants purport to act with innocent purposes. We examine the first and second issues in the context of an 'excuse' and whether the law can and should be framed to reduce culpability on grounds of perceived compliance with a religious culture. We examine the third issue within the conceptual frame of 'consent' and consider a residual role for a cultural defence where consent cannot apply.

Honour Related Violence (HRV) and Violence Against Women (VAW)

The area, perhaps, which most symbolises and captures the complexity and controversy of Muslim engagement with the Criminal Law is 'Honour Related Violence' (HRV). The term itself is controversial and is frequently gendered, denoting: 'a family-initiated, planned violent response to the perception that a woman, as wife or daughter, has violated the honour of her family by crossing a boundary of sexual appropriateness' (Korteweg 2011: 136). As we will see in some cases below, this would omit killings against men where the killer's express motivation was the defence of 'honour'. Law enforcement authorities in the UK employ a more neutral definition of HRV as 'a crime or incident, which has or may have been committed to protect or defend the honour of the family and/or community' (see UK, ACPO Honour Based Violence Strategy), implying men, as well as women, can be victims and that the motivation may have nothing to do with sexual behaviour. It appears to exclude individual motivations of shame and dishonour. Authorities in Australia, Canada and the United States are yet to offer any working definition, but there is a general understanding between academics, community activists and law enforcement authorities that HRV should be regarded as a special form of domestic violence and violence against women (Korteweg 2011).

The extent of the problem globally and in our focus countries is unclear because of possible underreporting ('dark figures' are a particular problem in matters of domestic violence) and no reliable sets of statistics exist (Korteweg 2011). According to Aisha Gill, following research by the British Crown Prosecution Service in 2007, about twelve honour killings are reported each year in the UK, though due to the secretive and hidden nature of the offence, the actual numbers are possibly a lot more (also this does not take into account the huge numbers of non-lethal 'honour-based' violence crimes against women). Research from Canada provides similar annual figures (Korteweg 2011). In comparison with the overall homicide rates, and even the rates of domestic violence, these numbers do not appear extensive. In 2012, however, all thirty-nine police forces in the UK reported nearly 3,000 cases of 'honour-related' violence, 234 of which were taken to court with half resulting in a guilty verdict.

Yet there is nothing exclusively 'Islamic' in the preservation of a code of honour. Most groups and cultures have notions of 'honour', with their own particular idiosyncrasies, often inferring respect, status and standing, and may take steps to preserve it. Historically, legal traditions from across the world and cultural divide, have also acknowledged defences of 'honour'. Islām-influenced legal systems in Jordan, Iraq, Pakistan, Syria, Turkey and Saudi Arabia have all, at different times, mitigated homicides on the basis of some claims to defence of 'honour'; but so too have systems within the Common Law tradition. As noted by Jeremy Horder, the Common Law doctrine of provocation originated in 'duelling', allowing killers a partial defence to murder if their 'gentleman's honour' had been impinged (Horder 1992).

Contemporary discussions of HRV are frequently divorced from this historical and comparative context, with HRV constructed as a largely 'Asian', more specifically 'Muslim' phenomenon, symptomatic of a broken value system out-of-tune with 'Western' society. It is true that honour (*'irḍ* in Arabic or *izzat* amongst South Asians) is an important part of the Islamic religion, an aspect of one of the five underlying purposes (*maqāṣid*) of Sharīʿah,[36] and reflected in a number of rules of *Fiqh* ranging from simple moral dictates not to disclose the faults of your fellow Muslim (without a justifiable reason) to strict requirements on sexual mores and maintaining one's modesty (*al-ḥayyā*). Although there is no sexual distinction in these rules (it is as prohibited and sinful for men to have sexual relations outside marriage as it is for women, for example), due to religious violence and the socio-economic contexts of Muslim communities, the degree to which women, rather than men, observe these rules is perceived as a particular source of cultural pride, or shame, as the case may be (Meetoo and Mirza 2011: 49; see also Abbas 2010: 24).

It does not necessarily follow from this analysis that being more protective of women leads to violence and that this is somehow given both cultural and religious legitimacy. The Prophet himself was never violent to any of his wives and is reported to have said (in the collection of at-Tirmidhi): 'The best of you is the one who is best towards his wife, and I am the best of you towards my wives.' Also in several *Ḥadīths*, he warned his companions against violence. Laqit ibn Sabirah narrated that he said to the Prophet:

> 'I have a wife who has something in her tongue (i.e. she was insolent).' He (the Prophet) said, 'Then divorce her.' I said, 'Messenger of God, she had company with me and I have children from her.' He (the Prophet) said, 'Then request her (to stop). If there is some good in her, she will do so; and do not beat your wife as you beat your slave-girl.'[37]

In another *Ḥadīth*, Muʿawiyah al-Qushairi, one of the Companions, said:

> I went to the Prophet and asked him: 'What do you say (command) about our wives?' He replied, 'Give them food what you have for yourself, and clothe them by which you clothe yourself, and do not beat them, and do not revile them.'[38]

However, in their attempts to give effect to Qur'ānic mandates of bidding the good and prohibiting the evil, the boundaries of which are necessarily contextual, some Muslim men (and families under their instruction) have gone to the extreme, buoyed by prevailing cultural dynamics and sometimes fed by literalist and puritanical readings of the religious texts (see Chapter 2). This can even include excommunicating (*takfīr*) their family members and legitimating their murder. In common translations of Ṣaḥīḥ Muslim, it is reported that the Prophet said, through the companion Abu Huraira,

> The fornicator who fornicates is not a believer so long as he commits it (Lā yazni al-zāni ḥina yazni wa huwa mu'min). and no thief who steals is a believer as long as he commits theft, and no drunkard who drinks wine is a believer as long as he drinks it. 'Abdul-Malik b. Abi Bakr' narrated this on the authority of Abu Bakr b. Abdur-Rahman b. Harith and then said: Abu Huraira made this addition: No plunderer who plunders a valuable thing that attracts the attention of people is a believer so long as he commits this act.
>
> (Ṣaḥīḥ Muslim n.d., book 1, Ch. 24, *ḥadith* 109)

The person who understands this *ḥadīth* in accordance with a surface meaning, and without further clarification, might mistakenly think that a person who fornicates or commits adultery, is not a Muslim (unless they no longer commit that sin). In the most famous explanation (Sharḥ Ṣaḥīḥ Muslim) of Ṣaḥīḥ Muslim by Imām An-Nawawi, the actual meaning of this ḥadith is that the one who commits those acts is an "imperfect believer" and not an apostate. He adds:

> By the consensus of 'the people of truth' [referring to the Sunni scholars], the fornicator, thief and killer are 'big sinners' (*aṣḥāb al-kabā'ir*) but not polytheists; by that they do not blaspheme. Indeed, they are believers but with an imperfect faith. If they repent, they are relieved of punishment (in the Hereafter); if they die (without repenting), they die as big sinners relying upon the Will of Allāh – whether to pardon and admit them to Paradise at the start – or to punish them and then admit them to Paradise.

Imām an-Nawawi is one of the most famous Sunni scholars and is referred to by Muslims up to the present day, especially by those who claim to follow the school of Ash-Shāfiʿī. This interpretation, however, departs from the literal meaning of the *Ḥadīth*. As we mentioned in earlier chapters, puritanical separatists almost exclusively favour literal readings (see Chapter 2).

If we combine this religious understanding with cultural notions of honour, the potential effects are not only toxic but catastrophic, with fathers and brothers conferring upon themselves the right to end the lives of their wives, daughters, sisters, aunts and nieces. Not only would this be a gross violation of Common Law standards and values, but also an ignorant violation of the Sharīʿah as well.

Court responses

As we have mentioned above, the principal channel through which HRV has been engaged in Common Law Courts has been the doctrine of provocation. Although there has been an American case in which the accused sought to justify the lethal battery of his wives simply upon the basis of his religious conviction and 'religious right' to inflict spousal discipline,[39] excuses within the doctrine of provocation have been the most prevalent. In recent years, however, the defence has undergone substantial reform and restriction. In some jurisdictions, the substantive defence has been abolished (such as Victoria, Tasmania and Western Australia in Australia, and Texas in the United States), leaving such extenuating circumstances, if any, to mitigation of sentence. In others (e.g. England and Wales and New South Wales), the defence requires 'qualifying triggers'[40] or 'extreme provocation' that is in itself an indictable offence.[41] The narrowing of the defence of provocation has been a response to claims the defence consistently discriminated against women and appeared to legitimate patriarchal forms of violence.

The cases discussed below, therefore, are part of the history of Common Law decisions in the law of provocation and should not be read as prescriptive of how judges might or would decide today. The cases remain relevant as illustrations of how judges working within the Common Law tradition individualise cases and respond to a 'cultural defence'. Similar to our analysis of sentencing cases, while there are a few differences between the jurisdictions and shifts over time, we note that post-9/11, courts have perceived Muslim behaviour as 'counter-cultural' or threats to fundamental civic values. In doctrinal terms, this has meant a shift from 'subjective' to 'objective' tests of culpability.

The basis of the law of provocation, as it existed under Common Law in England and Wales, as modified by Part 3 of the Homicide Act 1957 prior to 2009, was that if an accused produced evidence of a possibility that he was provoked to lose self-control and that a 'reasonable person' would have done as he did in those circumstances (*R* v. *Duffy* [1949]), he should be found guilty of manslaughter rather than murder. The test comprised both a subjective test (was the accused 'provoked') and an objective test whether the reaction of the accused was the 'likely reaction of a person of ordinary stability and temperament' (Simester and Sullivan 2010: 396). Prior to the decision in *Morgan Smith*, subjective considerations, including any explanation for the accused's behaviour on grounds of religion or culture, were relevant only in considering the gravity of the provocation under the first limb of the test. After *Morgan Smith*, however, the English courts invested the reasonable person with 'all the characteristics of the accused' and enabled the jury to consider a 'culture defence' to determine whether, in Lord Hoffmann's words, his behaviour was 'excusable'.

In *Mohammed* [2005] EWCA Crim 1880, the appellant, a devout Muslim, had been charged with the murder of his daughter, stabbing her nineteen times after finding her alone with her boyfriend. At his trial, the appellant raised the defence of provocation, claiming his reaction had been triggered by devout religious beliefs surrounding sex before marriage. The prosecution countered the appellant was a man of violent disposition and had lost his temper rather than his self-control. The accused was convicted of murder, but appealed on the basis the trial judge had misdirected the jury to consider his violent disposition together with his religious beliefs in determining whether his behaviour was excusable. The Court of Appeal upheld the direction, holding it was unrealistic to divide the appellant's personality or character.

The Court of Appeal also considered the effect of the change in the law of provocation in AG of *Jersey* v. *Holley* (which had occurred while the case was still pending) and said that the outcome would not have been any different. Indeed, the law had been tightened, reinstating the objective test prior to *Morgan Smith.* While culture and religious beliefs remained relevant to the gravity of the provocation and whether the accused had lost self-control, the 'reasonable man' of the objective test was now a 'fixed rather than a variable creature', with the 'age and sex of the appellant having and exercising ordinary powers of self-control.'

We suggest that this case does not exhibit a failure to accommodate Muslim religious culture and identity. The trial and appellate courts both directed the jury to consider subjective considerations of the accused, but ultimately it was the particular circumstances and attributes of the accused, namely evidence of his violent disposition (which had nothing to do with religion), that had resulted in his conviction for murder, rather than any failings in court directions.

We would further argue that his extreme, as opposed to mainstream, interpretation of his religious belief, should have precluded him from being able to rely upon any cultural defence. His beliefs were not those of a 'reasonable Muslim' similarly situated. In cross-examination, the following exchange took place between prosecution counsel and the accused:

> Q. Despite it being against your culture, do you think it is reasonable to kill somebody for what your daughter did?
> A. Absolutely. It is in our religion it's in our holy book, the Koran, without marriage, a man and women cannot sleep together on the same bed. If they sleep together, they can't call themselves Muslim. There is no alcohol allowed in our religion and there is no sex allowed before marriage. This not allowed in our religion. If it was disallowed in your religion, you would have done that.
> Q. Would your daughter not have been entitled to some sort of trial, under the Muslim religion, sir?
> A. No. You can speak to someone amongst the family or in the bazaar or market, but not in bed.

The cross-examination continued:

> Q. So, you believe that what you did to your daughter was reasonable, Mr Mohammed?
> A. I can't say that it was reasonable, or not, but at that time, I had lost my temper and I had killed her.

It can be seen that while the accused sought to distance his stabbings through a lack of consciousness at the time, he clearly legitimated the act 'in principle' to his religious belief and that he thought all religious people with similar proscriptions in their religious texts would have done likewise. Yet in Islamic terms, his 'belief' is problematic in a number of ways. While the Qur'ān, Sunnah and Consensus of Muslim scholars clearly prohibit *zinā* (adultery and fornication) and actions which lead to *zinā* (here '*khalwat*' or unlawful proximity), as we mentioned above, it is an extreme misinterpretation to say the parties 'can't call themselves Muslim' and that it is legitimate to kill them. None of the religious texts categorise *zinā* or *khalwat* [or even anger] as offences of apostasy.[42]

Australian cases on HRV and provocation have followed a similar, if not initially a more culturally sympathetic, trajectory to cases in England and Wales, possibly due to some judicial willingness to recognise indigenous cultures.[43] The issue has been to what extent the 'ordinary' (as opposed to 'reasonable') person should be clothed in the particular attributes of the accused when determining the objective part of the test.[44]

The early cases appear to suggest the courts were prepared to invest the 'ordinary person' with a Muslim identity. So in *R* v. *Dincer* (1983), 1 VR 460, Lush J told a Victorian jury they must consider:

> an ordinary man who has the same characteristics as the man in the dock. In this case … the fact that Dincer is Turkish by birth … Muslim by religion … traditionalist … a conservative Muslim …
>
> (*R* v. *Dincer* (1983), 1 VR 460 at 477)

In the 1990s, however, the Australian High Court stripped the ordinary person of subjective factors (*Stingel* v. *R* [1990] 171 312; *Masciantonio* v. *R* [1995] 183 CLR 58, and *Green* v. *R* [1997] 191 CLR 334, [1998] 2 VR 19), so that in *R* v. *Tuncay* [1998] 2 VR 19, a Turkish Muslim who had killed his wife when she threatened to leave him and take her children and insulted him with the word '*gebber*' (implying he would be better off dead) was judged by a purely objective test (and subsequently convicted of murder) rather than the attitudes of a Turkish Muslim.

The shift to a more objective standard, however, has not prevented Muslim accused from relying on cultural and religious factors in determining whether they were provoked and the gravity of the provocation (i.e. the first part of the test), though the courts may clothe such circumstances in more general terms. So in *R* v. *G M Khan* [2001] NSWSC 1356, a devout Muslim Fijian was convicted of the manslaughter of a fellow Muslim Fijian whom he had invited to stay in his home and whom, it was alleged, later had an adulterous relationship with his wife. At the trial, the court allowed expert evidence to be presented to the jury as to the gravity of the provocation – namely as to the Muslim community's attitude to adultery by one's wife, and the fact of adultery by a friend invited into one's home. The appellate court, however, did not view the religious context as especially important – persons of any religion, or no religion, might have acted similarly given these circumstances. Allen J. stated:

> For many men adultery committed with his wife is an intolerable insult to his manhood and an act of gross betrayal. Violent reaction to adultery is no new phenomenon. It has existed as long as men have been men and doubtless it will continue for as long as men are men.

A predominantly objective test, with limited reference to subjective factors also now obtains in Canada. In *R* v. *Humaid* (2006) Carswell Ont 2278, 37 C.R. (6th), a Muslim accused was charged with and found guilty of the murder of his wife whom he believed had committed adultery. The accused denied murder but admitted manslaughter on grounds of either he lacked the necessary intent for murder or because of provocation. At issue were the characteristics to be afforded the 'ordinary person' under the Canadian Criminal Code and whether the accused's Muslim culture and beliefs could be taken into account in the assessment of that objective test (as well as the subjective part of the test). At trial, the accused led evidence of an expert on Islamic religion and culture, who testified that Islamic cultures do not tolerate the infidelity of a woman. It was admitted for the subjective part of the defence, but was considered irrelevant to determine the 'ordinary person'. It was argued on appeal that the trial judge erred in telling the jury the latter, but this was not accepted on the grounds that there was no evidence that the appellant shared the religious and cultural beliefs attributed by the cultural expert to Muslims in general. Absent such evidence, the invitation to accept the cultural evidence was to assign group characteristics to the appellant by stereotyping, whereas free choice and individual responsibility for those choices were the basis of the Canadian notion of criminal responsibility.

While expressing reservations on the relevance of cultural evidence to the objective phase of the test (especially where it would conflict with fundamental Charter values), the Ontario Court of Appeal did not preclude the possibility of a cultural defence where there was evidence that the accused shared those values and that they had an impact on his loss of self-control.

'Educating' family and community

Disciplining the family

The Qur'ān stipulates: 'O you who believe! Save yourselves and your families from Hellfire which is fuelled by people and stones' (The Qur'ān, At-Taḥrīm, 66:6). One of the scholars from the Followers of the Companions (at-Tābiʿeen), ʿAṭā ibn Abī Rabāḥ, interpreted this verse to mean a person saves himself and his family from Hellfire by 'learning and teaching his family how to pray, how to fast, how to buy and sell, how to marry and how to divorce' (al-Baghdadi n.d., vol. 1: 13). Learning and teaching is first, and foremost, by instruction through scholars from texts, but it is also reinforced by example, admonition and, in the case of blatant disobedience (to the Islamic rules), lawful correction. The form such correction takes is contextual and proportionate to the religious violation but can never be in anger or so severe as to occasional physical harm or serious injury. Nevertheless, physically disciplining a child over the age of ten for failing to pray or to fast is deemed an obligation on the parents or guardians of the child because of their importance in the religion.[45]

Muslim families who 'discipline' their children and siblings in putative defence of Sharīʿah norms, however, are vulnerable to criminal sanction in all of our jurisdictions. As with the defence of provocation, accommodation of Islamic values have depended upon notions of 'reasonableness' and to what extent the court is prepared to invest the reasonable person with an understanding of Islām and Islamic values.

In the Canadian decision of *R* v. *H* (2014) ONSC 36, Ontario Supreme Court of Justice, a Muslim accused from impoverished Yemen was charged (*inter alia*) with harassment of his wife (a Canadian Muslim convert) over a twenty-four-year period and with assaulting his children while disciplining them. At issue was the interpretation of 'reasonable force' and 'reasonable in the circumstances' under Section 43 of Canada's Criminal Code which provides parents a defence of 'lawful correction'.[46]

At trial, the accused claimed that he would hit the children sometimes with a belt or with a toy bat for corrective purposes but it was only done with the children's best interests in mind. Despite the son's testimony that the father 'never sought to hurt us', the court upheld convictions for assault on the basis the accused's use of a plastic toy bat in disciplining his nine-year-old son (leaving a very painful, swollen red welt which lasted a week or two) for a perceived transgression, under Section 43, was not reasonable corrective force in the circumstances. The court did not interpret 'reasonable in the circumstances' in the context of a Muslim brought up from a traditional background in Yemen, nor was there any cultural evidence submitted.[47]

It is not clear from the facts of the case what the reasons were that were deemed to merit such punishment. But given the painful wounds inflicted, the tendency to lose his temper and that the child had not even reached ten years of age, there is an argument this form of correction might not have lawful under the Sharīʿah either.

Civic responsibility: 'bidding the good and forbidding the evil' – the Sharī'ah vigilantes

In the Qur'ān, it mentions that the nation of Prophet Muḥammad is the best of the nations of humanity in human history and are victorious in the Hereafter because they are 'guardians of each other', bidding the good and prohibiting the evil while believing in God (The Qur'ān, Al-ʿImran, 3:104, 110; at-Tawbah, 9:71). Over Islamic history and during periods of Islamic governance, largely from the time of the Abbasids onwards (from 750 CE) many Muslim jurisdictions, from a variety of different sects, established the specific institution of 'Hisbaḥ', sometimes called the 'Market Authority', and later the 'Shurṭah' (police) by which this function was performed.[48] Even in the absence of an institution, individual Muslims were still obliged to stop flagrant breaches of the religious law; with their hands, if necessary, such as taking a back-slider to perform the Friday Prayer, or removing from his possession a glass of alcohol. If that was not possible, then their job was to denounce the actions verbally or, if that failed or would have been futile, then to move away from the site of the commission of sin while hating the conduct in their heart.[49]

The purpose of this obligation was to prevent rather than provoke civil strife (*fitnah*), and applied between individuals, families and the community at large. This obligation, however, did not extend to administering '*ḥudūd*' punishments which remained firmly in the hands of those officially appointed according to very specific criteria;[50] for to do so would lead to more violence and discord. Moreover, the one who commanded the good and forbade the evil was to pursue it with wisdom. The scholar Ibn Daqiq al-'Id wrote: 'It is necessary that the one who commands the good and forbids the evil does so with gentleness (*bi-rifq*) so that he may more likely achieve the desired purpose.' He also quoted Imām al-Shāfiʿī, saying: 'The one who warned his brother in secret has advised and covered him; but the one who warned him in public has exposed and dishonoured him' (al-'Id n.d.: 169).

In contemporary times, whether in predominantly Muslim countries, or where Muslims are minorities in the West, the notion of *ḥisbah*, or the need for a group which enforces the lawful and prohibits the unlawful, has emerged in the context of 'Westernisation' of Muslim communities and adoption of Western lifestyles which has engendered fears of moral degeneration and displays of 'public sin'.[51] It has also figured prominently in Islamist discourse and movements who have dispensed with having recourse to established authority and promoted the responsibility of all Muslims, individually, to take active steps to eradicate 'public sin'.[52] Taking this view, Islamists have regarded physical prevention of vice and promotion of virtue as the very essence of 'responsible citizenship' (Pieri *et al.* 2014: 41). They have argued the absence of any Muslim authority, or any authority, to take effective action in their areas, has necessitated the formation of Muslim vigilantes (Pieri *et al.* 2014: 42). Anjam Choudary, a former member of the militant group Hizb ut-Tahrir, and spokesperson for its banned offshoot, 'Al-Muhajiroun', said of their group's attempts to set up Sharīʿah and 'Gay free' zones in London in 2011:

> The Prophet said, it is not allowed for you to live among the non-Muslims and not to distinguish yourselves. Therefore we have no choice, we cannot isolate ourselves and certainly we cannot integrate into the pornography, alcohol, drugs, prostitution, thug life, loutish behavior, that the cities of Britain have sadly become accustomed to. In light of this, our only option is to interact to change society.
>
> (Pieri *et al.* 2014: 45)

He advocated neighbourhood patrols in predominantly Muslim areas of London, reminiscent of the Black Panther movement and so-called 'Guardian Angels' from the United States in the 1960s and 1970s. He further stated: 'We'll police the streets ourselves, you see, and if need be we'll do our own arrests.'

In what might be construed as an extension of commonplace 'neighbourhood watch' schemes, there is nothing prohibited under Common Law or English statute in the formation of a group of citizens to make citizens' arrests' where there exists reasonable suspicion of indictable offences and, amongst other restrictions, it is not reasonably practicable to inform a police constable beforehand (Police and Criminal Evidence Act 1984, s. 24A) and the offenders are subsequently brought to a police station or magistrate (similar provisions on citizen's arrest exist in all of our jurisdictions). While they are also permitted to use force 'reasonable in the circumstances' to secure the arrest, they are not otherwise permitted to commit criminal offences nor to arrest persons who are not committing acts that are offences under English Law and which they are otherwise free to do.

In 2013, Jordan Homer, who had earlier spoken openly about implementing Sharīʿah on the streets of London, was brought before the Old Bailey and convicted on charges of assault and using threatening words and behaviour. In one incident, Homer (and two associates) had followed a couple holding hands in

Bethnal Green and yelled at them through a megaphone, shouting: 'Let go of each other's hands. This is a Muslim area.' In another, he had attacked a group of men drinking alcohol on the streets of Shoreditch, and had shouted: 'Kill the non-believers.' In sentencing Homer to seventeen months' imprisonment (at the higher end of the scale), the presiding Judge, Rebecca Poulet, stated, while Islām was a peaceful religion, his behaviour was 'anything but'. She continued:

> One of the many good things about living in Great Britain is the tolerance and respect members of the public generally show to one another's religious beliefs, his dress or his chosen way of life. When, on occasions, a person shows their intolerance of another individual, whether by aggression or violence and in such a way as to cause real fear to the individual, then the law can be invoked to protect that individual.
>
> (Jones and agency 2013)

In *R* v. *Fayad* and others (2013),[53] in New South Wales, the accused went a step further than Homer and purported to administer a '*ḥadd*' punishment. The accused had whipped a Muslim convert with a drugs and alcohol problem forty times (one of the prescribed Sharīʿah punishments for illicit drinking of alcohol) with an electric cord.[54] In sentencing the main accused to sixteen months in jail for assault occasioning actual bodily harm, the Magistrate, Brian Maloney, stated the accused had 'brought much shame upon the Islamic faith' and had a 'contorted' belief in Sharīʿah.

If there had been evidence that their victim had consented to the punishment, it is possible a Brown-like argument (see below) might have been submitted. But even in the presence of consent, as we have clarified above, the Sharīʿah does not permit lay Muslims to administer ḥadd punishments, particularly in non-Muslim countries. We suggest that should have precluded the availability of any 'cultural defence' or 'good reason' under Common Law.

Performing religious rites and rituals

Mortification

As a general rule, any act which causes physical self-harm or harm to others is prohibited in Islām. This is inferred from explicit Qur'ānic prohibitions on suicide (The Qur'ān, An-Nisā', 4:27), consuming alcohol and gambling (The Qur'ān, Al-Mā'idah, 5:90), as well as, amongst others, the Prophetic proclamation: 'There is neither harm nor reciprocation of harm (in the religion).'[55] Religious mortification, or self-harming for a perceived Islamic purpose might appear contradictory in this context, but a number of groups from across the different sects have purported to justify it though they would contest that amounts to 'harm' due to the controlled situations in which they take place.[56] Shīʿah communities, in particular, are known to flagellate themselves ('*matam*') in commemoration of ʿĀshūrā and to 'revisit' the horrific slaughter of Hussein, the

Prophet's grandson, in accordance with their religious tradition (Kazmi 2008). It would appear there are different levels of matam – which include beating the chest with the bare hand to using chains with razors attached in public displays of their emotional grief. Certain India Shīʿah Muslims also inflict small incisions on the heads of their young children (a practice which has recently caught the attention of the Indian High Court, and was much criticised; see further, TNN 2014).

The case for permission of ritual harming and organised self-flagellation in English Common Law has rested on the Common Law of consent and the liberal notion that it is not the job of the law to intervene unless harm to 'others' is caused. Nevertheless, historically, the Common Law in all of our jurisdictions has generally resisted justifying inflictions of harm on grounds of consent where the harm inflicted is not 'transient or trifling' (*R* v. *Donovan*) and amounts to 'Actual Bodily Harm'. The courts have variably justified this intervention on public interest grounds, such as fearing public disorder,[57] corruption of the youth,[58] spread of disease[59] and, most famously, 'cults of torture'.[60]

The courts have only permitted greater harms as an exception, where the parties were able to show 'good reason'. The concept of 'good reason' has been typically amorphous and developed on a case by case basis rather than because of any principle. The courts have exempted recognised sports (such as boxing under the Queensbury Rules), 'rough horseplay',[61] informal tattooing (*R* v. *Wilson*), cosmetic surgery and male circumcision. In Brown, the English House of Lords also appeared to endorse 'religious mortification',[62] though were not called upon to decide the matter.

Where ritual harming involves only adults either beating their own chests or inflicting injuries on themselves, there is nothing that appears to conflict with English Common Law (or the law of any Western Common Law jurisdiction). The problem, however, is when adults introduce children to the practices. In *R* v. *Syed Mustafa* (2009) 2 Cr App Rep (S) 32, the only reported case of ritual self-harming to come before the English courts, the accused was charged (and convicted) under child protection legislation for allowing his two sons, aged thirteen and fifteen, to take part in self-flagellation in commemoration of ʿĀshūrā (there were no prosecutions of any adults). Although consent was irrelevant as to liability, lack of coercion, the fact no permanent or excessive injuries were caused and that this was done to fulfil a 'fervent religious belief' were relevant as to sentence. Nevertheless, the Court of Appeal upheld custodial sentences for the father on the grounds he had allowed 'impressionable youngsters' to take part and had ignored the advice of senior officers of the mosque they should not participate as they were under the age of sixteen.

There are no reported cases in Australia, Canada or the United States, though it is known that authorities have permitted '*matam*' through 'zoning' in American jurisdictions.

Circumcision

In contrast to ritual 'harming' and *matam*, the ritual of *khitān* or circumcision, is much more prevalent amongst Muslims and therefore has many potential conflicts with the Criminal Law. Male circumcision is not a peculiarly 'Islamic' practice, as baby boys are circumcised as a matter of course in the United States (for health and, for Jews, religious reasons). In Islamic terms, it involves the cutting (*qaṭ'u*), by which is understood the removal, of the foreskin and can be performed any time before puberty, but is encouraged on the seventh day after birth (An-Nawawi 2010, vol. 1: 366–67). The case of female circumcision, female genital cutting (FGC) or female genital mutilation (FGM), as it has become known, is much more complex. Like male circumcision, female circumcision is not found only in Muslim communities. In Ethiopia (a predominantly non-Muslim country), high rates of FGM or FGC are found in Christian, Jewish and Muslim women (Lavin 2013). It is both a cultural and religious tradition. According to Islamic texts within the Sunni tradition, it involves the cutting (*qaṭ'u*) of the clitoris (*al-laḥmatu fi 'alā al-faraji tushbihu 'urfa ad-deek*, which means 'the flesh on the external genitalia which resembles a cockerel's comb') on the seventh day after birth (as for boys), but it is unclear the precise extent of that cutting.

All of the Sunni schools of Islamic jurisprudence regard circumcision for boys and girls as a legitimate practice, and were part of the pre-Qur'ānic customs absorbed into the religion through different cultural pathways.[63] They disagree, however, whether or not it amounts to an obligation (*wājib*). According to the school of Imām Mālik, neither male nor female circumcision is an obligation. This means a person would not be sinful if he or she delayed their circumcision until after puberty or even until death; and a parent would not be negligent in fulfilling their parental responsibilities as a guardian for failing to ensure it was carried out. The Ḥanafis, and some of the scholars from the Ḥanbali School also agree that the practice is optional in the case of female circumcision (Al-Bar 1964: 63).

The Shāfi'ī school regards both male and female circumcision as an obligation,[64] but in accordance with general principles of *fiqh* (see above) it should not be done so as to cause harm to the girl. Moreover, the Prophet is reported (in the Sunan of Abu Dawūd, through the Companion, 'Ammār ibn Yāsir) to have addressed one of the women who used to carry out the procedure in Medinah, Umm 'Aṭiyyah, and told her: '*Lā tanhaki*' which means '*Lā tubālighi*', or 'Do not exaggerate' (An-Nawawi 2002: 350). This perhaps explains the prevalence of 'clitoral nicks' (classified as 'type four' female genital cutting [FGC] by the WHO) amongst Muslim women in South East Asia (Brunei, Indonesia, Malaysia and Singapore).

This contrasts with the more extreme forms of cutting as practiced in Somalia, North Sudan and Djibouti in which part or all of the external genitalia is removed and the remaining orifice repositioned (known as 'type III' FGC by the WHO); a practice which clearly does not comply with the sunnah, though might be justified by communities on grounds of controlling a woman's sexuality and preserving her chastity (some even argue it protects a woman's 'dignity', Lewis 1995: 1). It is the latter practice which has become the focus of international health campaigns and known to give rise to serious health complications (Queensland Law Reform Commission 1993).

As far as female circumcision is concerned, our jurisdictions have almost uniformly prohibited the practice, either by amending their Criminal Code (as in Canada) or by specific legislation,[65] without distinguishing between the different types of cutting we outlined earlier, nor allowing for a defence of consent. In some of our jurisdictions, there is no defence of consent even for persons aged over eighteen (this applies to all Australian jurisdictions, the UK, Canada, and some jurisdictions in the United States). The only statutory exceptions relate to medical procedures for 'genuine therapeutic purposes' or for 'sexual reassignment procedures'. In terms of criminalisation, the only ambiguities relate to 'removal' of persons overseas to have the procedure (which most jurisdictions have now prohibited under recent amendments to their legislation) and whether the prohibition would also apply to female genital 'cosmetic procedures' or hymenoplasties to hide loss of virginity and prevent domestic (and possibly lethal) family violence (O'Connor 2008: 164–66). It appears doctors in the UK (NHS Choices 2014)[66] have carried out thousands of these procedures legally, but the only difference between these and FGM would be the absence of a religious motivation and the existence of full consent; yet full consent is not a defence for FGM whether the person is above or below the age of eighteen in the majority of our jurisdictions.

In respect of enforcement, notwithstanding the alleged prevalence of the practice, there have been very few prosecutions in any of our jurisdictions. At the time of writing, there had been no prosecutions in Canada and only one arrest, in 2010, in the United States.[67] In the UK, a case was brought controversially in 2012 against a non-Muslim junior doctor 're-infibulating' a patient who had FGM immediately after childbirth in order to stem blood flow. The jury acquitted the accused after thirty minutes' deliberation. The failed prosecution followed a frenzied media campaign at the end of 2012 and pressure placed upon the Crown Prosecution Service for their inability to prosecute any cases since the passing of legislation banning the practice in 1985 (see further, Laville 2015a).

In the Australian state of New South Wales, an elderly woman belonging to the Dāwūdi branch of the Ismā'īlī faction of the Shīʿah was found guilty, along with the mother and a Shīʿah cleric, of mutilating the clitoris of two young girls and assault occasioning actual bodily harm in company in November 2015 (Jabour 2015b). The case is troubling for a number of reasons. First, according to reports of the trial, there was no physical evidence that any FGM had occurred. Medical evidence submitted could not confirm the existence of Type 1, Type 4 or any other form of FGM. While some procedure had clearly taken place and the girls had testified to some pain, there seems at least reasonable doubt whether this legally constituted 'FGM' under the NSW Crimes Act 1900 (Hall 2014).[68] Second, given the lack of physical evidence, and a clearly ongoing loving relationship between children and parents, it seemed an inappropriate exercise of prosecutorial discretion to bring the case. Third, we would suggest the daughters were wrongly compelled to testify against their mother. Under section 18(6) of the Evidence Act 1998 (NSW), the rules on compellability provide a person must not be required to give the evidence if the court finds that:

a there is a likelihood that harm would or might be caused (whether directly or indirectly) to the person, or to the relationship between the person and the defendant, if the person gives the evidence, and
b the nature and extent of that harm outweighs the desirability of having the evidence given.

In making that determination, among the matters under sub-section (7) the court must take into account include: the nature and gravity of the offence, the substance and importance of any evidence the witness will give, and the nature of the relationship between the defendant and the person. If we first examine the nature and extent of the harm alleged, while FGM is regarded as a very serious offence with liability of imprisonment up to twenty-one years (Crimes Act 1900 [NSW], Section 45 [1]), the extent of the harm, if we deem the medical evidence credible, was minimal. Of the four types of FGM defined by the WHO, this could only have fallen, if at all, within the least serious of those categories: Types 1 and 4 (World Health Organization 2000). While we cannot discount possible psychological trauma, there was little evidence available to the police the girls were suffering from any lingering psychological effects as a result of the procedure. On the other hand, the possible psychological harm caused to the children as a result of testifying against their mother, the social stigma caused to the family, and the likelihood of feeling to blame for their mother's incarceration is potentially very significant. Indeed, those who observed court proceedings and listened to their testimonies noted as such (Jabour 2015b).

Given the nature of the practice, the resistance and anger of some of the alleged victims who might not support the prosecution[69] and the possible break-up of Muslim families as a result of care proceedings (Press Association 2015), prosecutions for FGM[70] are likely to remain problematic irrespective of how the courts eventually define it in future appeals.

In summary, in the performance of religious rituals, such as mortification and circumcision, none of the participants believe they are inflicting harm to others (or themselves). But it has not prevented their 'symbolic' criminalisation in the category of violent assaults through legislative intervention and restrictions on the defence of consent. American jurisdictions, on the other hand, have permitted an accused to raise the defence of innocent purpose in matters of sexual assault. In *Kargar* 679 A2d 81 (Me 1996), the Maine Supreme Court reversed the conviction of an Afghani (Muslim) refugee for gross sexual assault. The accused had been charged for kissing his nine-month-old son's penis. The accused submitted that he did not know he was doing anything wrong as it was common in Afghani Muslim culture, considered neither wrong nor sexual.

He was convicted on the basis Maine's gross sexual assault statute prohibited any contact between an adult's mouth and a child's penis and did not require intent or sexual gratification. The Maine Supreme Court took a purposive approach to the interpretation of the statute and vacating the conviction, held unanimously that it was not intended to apply to innocent conduct that lacked any sexual component. A similar approach was taken in the Texas case of Krasniqi[71] in which an Albanian Muslim father touched his four-year-old daughter in a public gymnasium. The accused was prosecuted with indecent assault but was subsequently acquitted after an expert witness testified it was simply an Albanian way of showing affection.

Conclusion: towards a more 'nuanced approach'?

This chapter has examined Common Law's engagement with Muslims in the contexts of criminal justice across procedural and doctrinal terrain. We have argued that in the 'processing' of Muslims, Common Law has generally facilitated Muslim participation, so long as in doing so the law does not undermine fundamental values. In their different but complementary ways, our four jurisdictions have each acknowledged a right to manifest religious identity. As witnesses, accused, or as lawyers, Muslims have been permitted to wear clothing (*ḥijāb*, kufi, turban) which identifies them as Muslim and enabled them to avoid sin. They have been allowed to remain seated, on the basis of religious objection, when others have been required to stand up. Muslim accused have been protected from the inflammatory comments of over-zealous prosecutors and the arbitrary religious prejudice of jurors through fair trial principles and obligatory court directions. In exercise of their rights to be heard, Muslim accused, and Muslim complainants, have been able to present religious and cultural evidence, so long as it is relevant, through Imāms, academic experts, language interpreters and anyone else demonstrating cultural 'expertise'. They have also been permitted not to testify even where they refuse to recognise the legitimacy of the court.

However, they have not been permitted, through an insistence of religious right, to interfere with 'communication' and the exercise of police powers and the effectiveness of the trial process. Full face veils must be removed upon request, whether in front of a police officer, or before a judge and jury when testifying. Moreover, where found guilty of transgressing Western values, for example in gender equality, or violating national security, courts have clearly communicated their denunciation of 'traditional' or conservative Muslim values when sentencing, dispensing exemplary sentences and announcing aggravating factors, even when the written law does not explicitly demand it.

In similar fashion, the doctrinal law has also been fashioned to whittle away 'excuses' for commission of serious violent crimes and homicides, whether on cultural or religious grounds. Where, for example, at one time, multicultural sensitivities had allowed subjective factors to intrude into objective tests of provocation, Common Law and statute is increasingly turning a cultural screw to ensure majoritarian values prevail and that no Muslim can claim he was 'culturally conditioned' or religiously justified to kill, especially on putative grounds of honour, even where genuinely provoked. While judicial formulations technically permit cultural defences in assessing the gravity of provocation, new statutory requirements for 'qualifying triggers' and 'extreme provocation' render such minimal concessions nugatory.

The doctrinal Criminal Law has also intervened in devotional matters, delimiting how one is to worship God. Though Common Law notions of adult 'consent' and constitutional protections of freedom of religion, privacy and rights to family life can still permit even the most extreme expressions of religious exultation, legislators and judges have acted to protect and 'save' women and children. Whether one regards restrictions on '*matam*' and '*khitān*' as the benevolent hand of paternalism or a sinister shadow of cultural imperialism (Abu Lughod 2002), neither practising Muslim children approaching maturity nor practising Muslim women have been accorded individual moral agency. The law says 'no' irrespective of consent.

The Common Law also says 'no' to Muslim vigilantes, as it prohibits any vigilantes. The law cannot be left to the common person to define and enforce as it would lose its legitimacy, become arbitrary and ultimately lead to chaos. Nor can a unitary 'common' law allow an alternative conceptualisation of a public law, through Muslim policed 'Sharīʿah zones' or privately administered Sharīʿah penalties, whether the subject of its enforcement is Muslim or non-Muslim. The current construction of Common Law has little space for Sharīʿah defences, even where it purports to foster civic responsibility.

The 'moral communication' that represents the Criminal Law thus engages with Muslims in form (process), rather than substance. It announces that we will treat you equally and fairly, but not that we will share in defining communal values and norms. Given the marginalisation and social exclusion of Muslims across our four jurisdictions, we suggest renders the quality of Common Law justice morally problematic and diminishes the legitimacy of the system, certainly in the eyes of Muslims.[72] It fosters further grievances and develops momentum towards a downward spiral.

If the justice equation is already imbalanced in favour of procedure, is accommodation of Muslims within the Criminal Law context best achieved by looking for 'more nuanced legal procedures'? Responses to this question must be holistic and incorporate both substance and process. They must address Muslim cultural and religious identities within the broader multicultural context along with the need for civic integration. Ultimately, this may entail recognition of a general 'cultural defence' or a defence of 'innocent purpose' and require statutory intervention (though 'de minimis' provisions in American statutes and 'public interest' provisions arguably already provide sufficient flexibility). Given the hostile climate across our jurisdictions, however, and current political dynamics, statutory intervention ostensibly 'in favour' of Muslims is unlikely to eventuate. It might also be counter-productive and facilitate exculpation and mitigation of extreme behaviours, such as in the case of HRV, which the majority of Muslims would find abhorrent.

Rather, we suggest enhancing the Common Law and adapting liberal principles that already exist to the multicultural realities of our societies so that they recognise (and protect) the individual moral agency of Muslim men, women and (adolescent) children, while addressing the common good and protecting community welfare. We suggest reforms to the principle of consent, changes to objective tests of liability, and reforms of expert evidence are the most appropriate. While 'informed consent' plays a pivotal role in allowing invasive medical procedures, courts have been reluctant to expand its remit beyond this and other already well-established categories (even if they have little logical basis). We argue that where parties freely consent, are fully informed of the nature of the activities, are of an age where they can reason for themselves and where no permanent or serious harm (of a level equivalent to grievous bodily harm) is caused, those acts should be deemed lawful, irrespective of the context. This means that unless acts are committed against minors without the actual capacity to consent, the Criminal Law should refrain from intervening where a woman, a man, an adolescent male or female, are consensually performing what they regard as religious rites and especially where it has an innocent purpose. If the Common Law already permits cosmetic surgery to modify body parts on grounds of 'self-image', it appears inconsistent in terms of principle to deny the same to those concerned with their 'religious' self. But as a corollary, where acts are performed on children, Muslims should expect the intervention of the Criminal Law and to pay the consequences. Such acts where little harm is caused, though technically assaults, may be dealt with through prosecution guidelines. It may be that male circumcision on seven-day-old boys and 'clitoral nicks' on seven-day-old girls should be managed under the latter. From a Muslim perspective, their integration and acceptance as equal participants in society, depends on their ability to perform obligations (*wājibāt*) and avoid sins (*'muḥarramāt'*). These indicators of religious accountability are not triggered until a person is pubescent and has the capacity of conscious wrongdoing (*'tamyiz'*). So long as the law does not force Muslims into a corner and to make invidious choices, behavioural boundaries are negotiable.

Objective tests of liability, though contrary to the historical canons of a liberal Common Law tradition (as a person is judged on the basis of what he ought to have known, thought or believed as opposed to what was actually in his mind), are now an accepted method of drawing lines on acceptable social conduct and thresholds of tolerance. The problem, however, as Professor Stanley Yeo (1987) once argued, is that the 'reasonable' or 'ordinary' person is generally white, male and with the cultural assumptions and beliefs of majority communities. It discriminates against minorities from alternative cultural and religious backgrounds. Yeo's later move against investing the reasonable person with the subjective characteristics of the accused was that it tended to perpetuate stereotypes and to essentialise behaviour (Yeo 1996). It enabled an accused to point to an alleged cultural practice and that, as he enjoyed membership of the same cultural community, he should therefore be excused.

We argue the problem of stereotyping can be overcome through the appropriate use of expert cultural evidence and emphasising an objective cultural test. Where the issue is peculiarly religious, we could ask: how would a 'reasonable' or 'ordinary' Muslim, from his particular religious background, have reacted in those circumstances? There is no reason, other than available resources, why prosecutors and defence lawyers cannot ask a combination of community and academic experts, to enable juries to determine that question. While Muslim communities are fragmented and divided into Schools, there still exists the important notion of ' *'ijmā'* or consensus which can operate across communities. If a Muslim's conduct contravened a consensus (which might be contested), or where he made up his own belief for which he cannot find an expert to support (see *State of Illinois* v. *Edwin Jones*), it is prima facie 'unreasonable' or 'extraordinary' and should not go before a jury. Where there is no consensus, the 'reasonableness' of the accused's behaviour should go to the jury. Whether the accused acted in fact as a result of a purported belief is also, and always has been, a question for the jury.

That leaves us with the question of the jury and its composition. Ideally, accused persons should be tried by juries consisting of their peers, and that should include ethnic minorities and other Muslims.[73] In the absence of representative juries, we suggest trial court judges need to make appropriate directions to better ensure that jurors are able to divorce their decision-making from the broader prejudices of the surrounding society and to better guarantee that justice is not only done, but must also be seen to be done.

Notes

1 See further, A. Norrie, *Crime, Reason and History: A Critical Introduction to Criminal Law* (Cambridge: Cambridge University Press, 2014).

2 In the Australian context, see the recent comments of Samier Dandan, LMA President: Lebanese Muslim Association 2015.

3 In the Australian context, see D. Brown. 2013, 'Criminalisation and normative theory', *Current Issues in Criminal Justice*, (2013) 25 (2): 605, and 'securitisation' (cf. Zedner 2007).

4 On 'racial profiling' in the context of ethnic Middle Eastern populations in New South Wales, see Collins *et al.* 2000; Poynting *et al.* 2004.

5 See also, F. Ansari, 'British anti-terrorism: A modern day witch-hunt', Islamic Human Rights Commission, (2005) at: www.ihrc.org; D. Cole, 'Are we safer?', *The New York Review of Books*, 2006; E. Hagopian, *Civil Rights in Peril: The Targeting of Arabs and Muslims* (London: Pluto Press, 2004); D. Harris, *Profiles in Injustice: Why Racial Profiling Cannot Work* (New York: The New Press, 2002); T. Abbas, 'Muslim minorities in Britain: Integration, multiculturalism and radicalisation in the post 7/7 period', *Journal of Intercultural Studies*, (2007) 28 (3): 287–300.

6 For UK, see the reviews of Schedule 7 of the *Terrorism Act 2000*, in particular: Cage-Prisoners 2012 and Mythen, Walklate and Khan 2009. For the USA, see Patel 2013.

7 When having a driver's licence photograph taken, for example; see *Freeman* v. *State of Florida* [2003] WL 21338619 (Fla. Cir.Ct).

8 For New South Wales, see *Law Enforcement (Powers and Responsibilities) Act 2002*, Section 19A.

9 The amendment was prompted by the case of Sydney Muslim woman, Carnita Mathews. See further, AAP 2011. She was later acquitted of making a false allegation on the ground that the identification of the person making the complaint had not been confirmed because the person was wearing a 'burka' at the time. See further, Fife-Yeomans and Kent 2011.

10 There are different narrations of this *Ḥadīth*. See further, *Sunan* Abu Dawud, Book 21, Ḥadīth no. 119 (at: http://sunnah.com/abudawud/21/119, accessed 5 September 2015); *Sunan* Ibn Mājah, Book 6, *Ḥadīth* no. 1684 (at: http://sunnah.com/urn/1289660, accessed 5 September 2015). It is also narrated from the Companions, see Mālik ibn Anas, *Al-Muwaṭṭa*, Book 16, *Ḥadīth* no. 567 (at: http://sunnah.com/urn/405640, accessed 5 September 2015).

11 This is clarified in the narration of Ibn Mājah (above) and the explanation of Abu Zakaryiyyah al-Ansari of this *Ḥadith* (al-Ansari n.d.: 310).

12 The alternative reasoning of necessity would work in traditionalist thought as a '*rukhṣah*' (exception).

13 'Cause of death', in the traditional Islamic jurisprudence, was not dependent on scientific explanations or on the prognoses of experienced doctors. If unaccounted bodies were found in a particular locality, under the procedure of *qasamāh*, fifty residents closest to the location of the body would be asked to make repeated oaths that they did not kill the person or know who might have. If no one admitted to the crime or pointed to its perpetrator, the community as a whole would be asked to make reparation (*diyyah*) to the family of the deceased. While it might be thought that the perpetrator would escape, religious faith clung to a belief the latter would receive his or her just deserts in the Hereafter.

It was not until after scientific developments in the nineteenth century and increased urbanisation, that some Muftis saw benefits in autopsy. Then Chief Mufti of Egypt, Ḥassanyn Muḥammad Makhlūf, passed a *fatwa* in 1952 permitting an autopsy in cases of necessity (cf. Makhluf, cited in Rispler-Chaim 1993: 72). In cases of suspicious deaths, nearly all Muslims countries in the contemporary Muslim world permit invasive autopsies without the consent of the relatives. While in most cases, an external viewing of the body will be sufficient, even Saudi Arabia permits use of body dissection in cases of necessity (*ḍarūrah*) in criminal investigation (cf. Mohammad and Kharoshah 2014: 81, para. 6.1).

14 See the *Model Postmortem Examinations Act 1954* (Fed). This is a federal act, but has been implemented to varying degrees at state level. There are similarities, therefore, across American states, but the position is not uniform because they have different 'systems'. In particular, some states have medical examiners whereas others (28) have a coroner. The latter are a historical legacy of the colonial period and are generally not medically qualified, in contrast with the former who are usually pathologists or forensic pathologists. See further, Hanzlick and Combs 1998; Hanzlick 2007.

15 See the *Coroners Act 2009* (NSW), *Coroners Act 2008* (Victoria), *Coroners Act 2003* (Queensland), *Coroners Act 1996* (Western Australia), *Coroners Act* (Northern Territories), *Coroners Act 2003* (South Australia) and the *Coroners Act 1997* (ACT).

16 Like America, Canada also has a state-based death investigation system which follows a coronial inquiry in some territories and a medical examiner system in others. For the system and relevant rules in British Columbia, see the *Coroners Act* (SBC 2007), Chapter 15.

17 Unreported, but abstracted in WL 4529494. See also Gallagher 2015.

18 The authors noted suspicion of Police where Muslims objected to autopsy, but their requests were recognised nevertheless.

19 The case of *Anwar* Saeed, and a *niqāb*-wearing Muslim witness, named 'Tasneem'. See Styles 2010. See also the discussion by Hunter, Hunter *et al.* (2015: 214).

20 In England and Wales, the dispensation to discard wigs has been given to Sikhs and Muslim women since 2006.

21 There are texts which state a woman is obliged to cover all of her body *apart from* her face and hands. The Qur'ān directs women to draw their veils over their chests and not to display their beauty '*other than* that which is apparent' (An-Nur, 24:31). Most Qur'ānic exegetists agreed 'apparent' referred to the face and hands (Aṭ-Ṭabari n.d.: 54). 'Abdullāh Ibn Aḥmad Al-Nasafi interpreted 'apparent' to also include the feet (An-Nasafi 2008, vol. 2: 159). This interpretation reflects opinions of the doctrinal school of Abu Hanifah.

There are other texts which encourage her to cover all of her body in front of male strangers in emulation of the Prophet's wives and to avoid sexual attraction. This is particularly true of the later Shāfi'ī scholars, such as: Zakariyya Al-Anṣāri, Shamsud-deen Al-Ramli and Imām Al-Nawawi. They do not define the woman's face as '*awrah*' but they say she should cover her face to prevent '*fitnah*' or sexual attraction (Al-Anṣāri 2001, vol. 3: 110).

There are also texts that order males to avert their eyes should they fear such desire. The Qur'ān, Al-Nūr, 24:40, directs men to lower their gazes. The Māliki scholar, Qaḍi 'Iyāḍ said in the context of men fearing sexual attraction: 'It is not an obligation for her to cover them (face and hands), but it is an obligation for him to lower his gaze' (Al-Māliki n.d., vol. 1: 222). This ruling is supported by a *Ḥadīth* in which the Prophet physically turned to one side the face of his cousin, Al-Faḍl, to prevent him looking at a beautiful woman – who was not ordered to cover her face (al-'Asqalāni n.d., vol. 9: 54). While we would not want to deter Muslim women from wearing *niqāb* should they so choose, and many women from the Gulf and from rural Pakistan and Afghanistan do so customarily, for them to insist that they have no religious choice but to wear it in all public spaces and in court neglects much of the Islamic juridical tradition. There is a consensus of the *Mujtahid* Sunni scholars that the face of the woman is not '*awrah*' and need not be covered (al-Haytami n.d., vol. 1: 199). The '*awrah*' refers to that part of the body which must be covered in front of members of the opposite sex whom one is permitted to marry and which must be covered in prayer (Al-Rāzi n.d., vol. 23: 206–07). It is, therefore, a question of her *choice*. Covering the face out of modesty, while a 'sunnah' (something 'good'), is not required (*wājib*). She would not be committing a sin, therefore, if she complied with a request to remove her niqab as opposed to a request to remove her *ḥijāb* (head-covering). Indeed, in court proceedings, scholars specifically approved it to assist giving testimony.

Further, in respect of those scholars who urged women to cover their faces, they maintained it was to protect the public interest and prevent illicit sexual liaisons. We suggest such an eventuality is unlikely to materialise while giving evidence in a court room. Also it is questionable that it would be in the public interest for a Muslim to appear to want to hide her face from a jury. We would argue that to still insist on wearing the niqab, *in such circumstances*, is a separatist and puritanical perspective (because it ignores religious scholarship) but, in light of our argument in the final chapter, whether it is 'unreasonable' would depend on her actual reasons for wearing it (rather than what the Islamic texts say) and the choices available before the court.

22 This is narrated by al-Bayhaqi, Abu Dawud, At-Tirmidhi and others.

23 Curtailment of rights of silence by English and Australian legislatures provide but one example. See the *Uniform Evidence Act 1998* (NSW), s. 89A; ss 34–37 *Criminal Justice and Public Order Act 1996* (UK).

24 Although our four countries have multiple jurisdictions and a mixture of Federal and State rules, Evidence Codes (such as the US Federal Rules of Evidence and the Uniform Evidence Acts in Australia), supplementary statutes and Common Law, principles of party control, threshold questions of relevance, and exclusionary rules are generally the same. For US federal and state rules, see the Legal Information Institute n.d.. For Canadian Evidence Law, see Paciocco and Stuesser 2015. For authoritative accounts of English Evidence Law (but with international comparison), see Tapper 2010; and Roberts and Zuckerman 2010. On Australian laws, see Hunter *et al.* 2015.

25 See *Ahmad Fawzi Issa* v. *Margaret Bradshaw* (2008, 2008 WL 8582098 (S.D. Ohio).

26 *State of Maine* v. *Nadim Haque* (1999) 726 A.2d 205 (Me. 1999). See also Caughey (2009: 322).

27 This is due in part to the refusal of Australian courts to follow the US decision of *Daubert* v. *Merrell* and evaluate reliability of expert evidence. There is no express provision in the various versions of the Uniform Evidence Act which mandates the court to address reliability when determining admissibility of expert evidence under Section 79. The assumption is that this is a matter best left to juries or the tribunal of fact.

28 See *R* v. *Sadiqi* (2013 ONCA 250), on appeal from the decision of the 2009 Ontario Superior Court of Justice; *R* v. *Mohammad Shafia (and others)* (2012, ONSC 1538).

29 For the discussion in the UK where the problem appears the most acute, see Stuart 2015. There is also concern at the over-use of custody for Muslim youth more generally (The Young Review 2014).

30 There are cases in which the American courts have sought to distance associating religion with the actions of the accused. See *State of Arizona* v. *Faleh Almaleki* (2011) (reported in Rubin 2011) in which an Iraqi Muslim was convicted of second degree murder for an 'honour' killing of his 20-year-old daughter because of her adoption of Western lifestyles (and her living with her boyfriend). The judge, when sentencing, could not imagine this was anything to do with religion, referring to sayings from Prophet Muḥammad and Sufi saints, that religion was about love, compassion and patience. He said the father's response was more to do with the accused regarding his daughter as his property than with any religious belief.

31 For another illustration of exemplary punishment for 'honour killing', see *R* v. *Ibrahim and Iqbal* ([2011] EWCA Crim 3244).

32 *Commonwealth of Pennsylvania* v. *Reid* (2014, 99 A.3d 427), at 39–40. Other US jurisdictions have permitted religious values in mitigation. For an example, see *State of Arizona* v. *Yusra Farhan, Mohammed Altameemi and Tabarak Altameemi* (2012) in which the County court judge, in exchange for a guilty plea, sentenced an Iraqi to two years' probation for the unlawful imprisonment of her daughter, after she and her husband had padlocked her to a bed because the daughter had been seen chatting to males and had violated traditional Iraqi values (Reuters 2012).

33 See *R* v. *MSK, MAK, MRK and MMK* [2004] NSWSC 319 and the judgments of Sully, J and McClellan CJ at para. 62.

34 On 13 Jan 1994, from the Court of Quebec, referred to by Maneesha Deckha (2009: 269). See also Donald Brown (2007: 537), both relying upon the report and analysis of Pascal Fournier (2002: 103).

35 For further details on *ḥudūd*, the 'fixed' system of penalties in Sharīʿah, see Farrar (2003: 594).

36 Abu Ḥāmid al-Ghazali (a Shāfiʿī scholar), and the majority of scholars in *uṣūl al-fiqh*, listed the following five essential values: protection of faith, life, intellect, property and lineage. They incorporated *ʿirḍ* (honour) within the protection of *nasl* (lineage) (al-Ghazzali 1937, vol. 1: 287). Later Maliki jurists, such as Shihāb Al-Din Al-Qarāfi, added the preservation of *ʿirḍ* as a sixth essential value. See al-Qarāfi (2000 vol. 4).

37 The Prophet also forbade striking slaves on the face and ordered one companion to set her free after he had done so out of anger.

38 These *ḥadīth*s were both reported by Abu Dawūd, nos 142 and 2139, respectively.

39 *State of Illinois* v. *Edwin Jones* (1994) no. 5-94-0813, Appellate Court of Illinois, Fifth District. The accused was married to three women under Islamic law and believed that the teachings of the Qur'ān empowered him to beat his wives. He beat all three of them, but two of them died as a result of the brutality of the beatings. The accused was charged and found guilty of first degree murder and informed by the judge that if he thought he had religious sanction, then he could talk to God from prison. It is of note that the accused could not find any 'Sheikh' that would endorse his interpretation of Qur'ānic scripture.

40 See Sections 54 and 55 of the *Coroners and Justice Act 2009*.

41 For NSW, see Sections 23(1) and 23(2) *Crimes Act 1900*. Queensland has also restricted the defence of provocation notwithstanding the retention of the mandatory life sentence for murder.

42 Without further examination, it is difficult to construe what he actually meant – but it is quite common amongst communities to disavow their children and to exaggerate when they see them committing base acts (as they would see them) in the same religious language.

The former offence, though it is defined as a very serious offence which attracts the *ḥadd* punishment of one hundred lashes (to be carried out by a Caliph or his deputy in a Muslim country – not by members of the public or family, and not in a non-Muslim country), does not carry a death sentence for someone who has never been married, and certainly not where the offence has not been proved by confession or witnesses. Even if the person died in the course of punishment, s/he would be buried as a Muslim.

43 See *R* v. *Mudarubba* [1951–76] NTJ 317, and the discussion of Amirthalingam (2009: 51–52).

44 See *La Cava* (unreported, South Australian Supreme Court, 1976); *Moffa* ([1977] 13 A.L.R. 225 at 227 per Barwick CJ); *Webb* ([19760 16 SASR 309 at 314 per Bray CJ); and *Dutton* [1979] 21 SASR 356 at 377 per Cox J.

45 This is in compliance with both the literal and construed meaning of the following Prophetic *ḥadīth*: 'Order your children to pray when they reach seven lunar years of age, and hit them for leaving it when they reach ten.' This is narrated by Abu Dawud (and others) in his *Sunan*. Note the *ḥadīth* does not mandate physical correction for other than leaving out the prayer. The obligations upon the parents and guardians are confirmed in *fiqh* literature across the different schools. For a well-known example from the Shāfiʿī school, see Al-Siyūṭī (n.d.: 89–90).

46 The test under Canadian law is purely objective but has been further clarified by the Canadian Supreme Court to exclude corporal punishment for children below the age of two and for teenagers. Between those ages, courts will permit only corrective force (rather than out of anger or frustration) 'of a transitory and trifling nature', and even then should avoid blows or slaps to the head; see further, the *Canadian Foundation for Children, Youth and the Law v. Canada*, 2004. For the Australian position, see *W & DL* [2014] SASC 102 which held a parent has a lawful right to inflict reasonable and moderate corporal punishment on his or her child, appropriate to the age, physique and mentality of the child, and to use a reasonable means or instrument. See also s. 61AA, Defence of lawful correction, under the *NSW Crimes Act 1900*.

47 This may have been due to the accused not engaging any legal defence (he had been held in custody prior to trial for more than two years, largely because he had refused all legal assistance).

48 For a comprehensive account of the history of the Hisbah and the different approaches, see Cook 2010.

49 This procedure derives from a *Ḥadīth* of the Prophet narrated in the authenticated collections ('*Saḥīḥ*') of Imām Muslim, *Ḥadīth* no. 49.

50 The famous 'Abbāsid judge and Shāfiʿī scholar, Al-Māwārdi, dedicated a whole book – '*Al-Aḥkām al-Sulṭāniyyah*' – for that purpose.

51 See Jacobsen *et al.* (2012: Appendix 1: 15). They surveyed Muslim attitudes and found more than 63 per cent of respondents agreed western countries were lowering standards of morality in the Muslim world.

52 See Keppel (2009) and his discussion of Sayyid Qutb.

53 Magistrates Court, Sydney; reported in the *Sydney Morning Herald* (Davies 2013).

54 The magistrate doubted, on the evidence, whether there had been any religious motivation and that the assault had, in fact, a criminal purpose to secure a debt.

55 This *ḥadīth* is reported by Ibn Majah in his *Sunan* (*Ḥadīth* no. 2341) and by Malik ibn Anas in his Al-Muwaṭṭa (n.d., vol. 2: 846).

56 Some Sufi spiritual orders practice body piercing as 'tests of faith'. See further: Trimingham 1972; De Jong (1983: 149–58, 167–74); and Favazza (1996: 285–86).
57 See *Coney* and *AG's Ref no 3(?) of 1983*, per judgment of Lane LJ.
58 *Brown* [1994] 1 AC 212; see also *R* v. *Donovan.*
59 *Brown* [1994] 1 AC 212.
60 Ibid.
61 See *R* v. *Jones*, in which the victim suffered second degree burns.
62 See the judgment of Mustill LJ.
63 There is evidence of circumcision from Egypt going back 2000 years (El Dareer 1983).
64 See Al-Siyūṭī (n.d., 1: 48); al-Baghawi (1997, 1: 218); and al'Umrani (2002, 1: 193).
65 In Australia all States and Territories have passed legislation which applies domestically and extra-territorially to protect Australian citizens both at home and overseas (Attorney-General's Department 2013).
66 For examples from Australia, see *Sunday Life* 2013.
67 There are no details whether this led to a prosecution and/or a conviction. See further, Lalla-Maharajh 2010.
68 See also, Jabour 2015b. The trial is ongoing at the time of writing. The medical evidence would indicate that only a 'clitoral knick', if anything, was inflicted.
69 See the Dharmasena and Hassan Muhammad case, 2015 (Laville 2015b).
70 At the time of writing, in the first case of its kind, prosecutors in Brisbane (Australia) had charged parents with attempting to take their children back to Africa to have FGM performed (Robertson 2015).
71 (1995), see Foblets and Renteln, above, at 65 unreported.
72 For the results of a survey of current British attitudes, see Nawaz 2015.
73 Possibly on lines of affirmative action policies; see further, Fukurai and Davies 1997.

5 Muslims, business transactions and the Common Law

> Residence in the cash economy, beyond necessities of daily living, comes at a price for altruism, no less than avarice: exposure to theft, active or passive, is one element of that price. Moderation in all things remains a virtue worthy of notice, even in the accumulation of cash, lest our property, or that of somebody else, comes to possess us.
>
> (Lindsey, J, *Helou* v. *Nguyen*)

Introduction

In our previous two chapters, we have examined the extent to which the Common Law State legislatures and courts have accommodated Muslims in the contexts of family relations and crime. The picture is a mixed one, but there are clear instances across our jurisdictions of Muslims provided with sufficient legal space to manifest their belief and to practice a religious way of life. This is particularly true for Muslims who follow integrationist approaches and understandings of their religious texts (see Chapter 2). On the other hand, we have also witnessed an increasing narrowing of that space, especially in areas that raise issues of crime and security and which are perceived to touch upon foundational values of the Common Law. This has impacted on Muslims of all types of persuasions and influences as courts and legislatures have sought to lay down indicative value markers. Family, and even criminal laws,[1] once categorised as 'personal laws', are now both firmly in the public domain and seen as a channel for communicating 'acceptable' societal values.

Anne Black and Kerrie Sadiq (2011: 384) have argued this shift has occurred, in part, because the general public, legislatures and courts (in Australia at least) perceive Muslim family laws and their 'excuses' for crime as 'bad Sharīʿah'. On the other hand, the perception of Islamic transactional law (*al-mu'āmalāt*), according to them, is different and deemed 'good Sharīʿah'. They attribute this alternative view to the alacrity of financial markets and governments to search for new revenue streams in tightening international markets (Black and Sadiq 2011: 389). Perhaps it might also be due to the emphasis of Islamic transactional law on ethical values, transparency and freedom from exploitation, which has struck a chord with legislators and ordinary citizens alike; tired, angered and frustrated at the apparent amorality of the conventional banking system and its financial apparatus.[2] In this chapter, we examine to what extent Common Law jurisdictions, especially the courts, view Islamic transactional law in the same light and as 'good Sharīʿah'.

Much of Black and Sadiq's discussion has focused on the Islamic and Banking Finance (IBF) industry and the willingness of many Common Law legislatures to 'level the playing field' by removing tax and regulatory obstacles. We take an alternative approach with a focus more on IBF dispute resolution and case analysis than on legislative and administrative responses. We regard the latter as reflecting current political priorities more than the values underpinning the Common Law legal system and the ability of Muslims to navigate the systems. We also include within our analysis non-IBF cases which touch upon choices of law in a variety of commercial situations and forums where questions of Sharīʿah, particularly in civil law, evidence and procedural matters, have arisen directly or indirectly, and well before the current interest in IBF. These cases involve consideration of state legal systems: Saudi Arabia, the United Arab Emirates and Afghanistan. Though a state legal system is not Sharīʿah (see Chapter 2), a Muslim country's laws reflect interpretations of Sharīʿah and their consideration by Common Law Courts necessarily will also have a bearing on their approaches to Sharīʿah questions.

As will become evident, the analysis as a whole is heavily focused on England and the United States because of the limited number of cases reported in Canada and Australia. There is also an imbalance of choice of law cases from America and IBF cases from England and Wales. While this might not facilitate direct comparison between jurisdictions, and clearly qualifies our particular comments regarding Australia and Canada, it is inevitable reflecting each country's policy initiatives and emphasis. Given our focus is on the context of business as a whole, and the capacity of Common Law frameworks, as opposed to one particular country, to accommodate Sharīʿah-inspired approaches to business, we believe that this does not undermine the strength of the overall analysis and argument.

Just as in the family and Criminal Law contexts, we will argue there is evidence of disdain for Sharīʿah law in commercial spheres, although it assumes different forms and emphasis from one jurisdiction to another. That disdain is reflected in the preference for English and American jurisdictions in 'choice of law' clauses in international contracts and in tort cases. It is also reflected in judicial treatment of IBF contracts, particularly in England. The English courts have refused to engage with the substantive content of Sharīʿah, regarding it as either too contested or lacking in 'legal' content to be determinable or determined by a court. Instead, they have subjected purported IBF contracts to English law concepts irrespective of the actual wishes of the parties. This approach clearly has not recognised Sharīʿah. But equally, it has not prejudiced Muslims to any great extent either. Rather, it has afforded a degree of autonomy to Muslim communities to draft their contracts better and more clearly in line with their normative concepts. The current availability of arbitration, under

English Law, also enables Muslims to choose their own regulations, decision makers and forums to resolve their commercial disputes although that is yet to happen in any significant numbers. Whether this is a good or a bad thing, we discuss further in the conclusion to this chapter where we will revisit our typologies from Chapter 2.

In contrast to the English courts, American courts have been more willing not only to engage with Sharīʿah, but also to define its content for themselves. While this approach appears to recognise Sharīʿah explicitly, judicial recognition of Sharīʿah has been contrary to the understandings of Muslim experts and at the expense of Muslim participants to those disputes. Far from freeing space for Muslims to do business in accordance with Islamic norms and standards, it has in fact circumscribed the parameters of the 'Islamic' and limited the autonomy of Muslims to operate within their own particular normative and cultural contexts.

The few disputes that have come to court in Canada and Australia relate to ordinary, though 'conservative', Muslim communities rather than major Muslim corporate entities. There are insufficient cases to come to any general conclusion about judicial approaches in these cases, but their factual contexts usefully demonstrate the troubles of a marginalised and vulnerable minority attempting to apply Islamic transactional rules in everyday life. More positively, they also demonstrate amongst the judiciary an awareness of the broader socio-cultural context of Muslims and that Islamic values are not so alien or foreign to the values of Common Law after all.

The chapter is divided into three sections, though there are unavoidable overlaps. The first provides a preliminary and brief discussion of relevant Islamic transactional rules and principles: *al-mu'āmalāt*. This includes contemporary manifestations in Muslim countries and a summary of Islamic Banking and Finance. The second looks at choices of law, in contracts and tort, to understand the legal framework in which accommodation of Islamic commercial law arises. The third examines case law across the jurisdictions. This is divided into three sub-sections. The first deals with choices of law cases simpliciter, and explores Muslim commercial entities in the context of an 'Islamic' or partially Islamic legal system. Examination of such cases, we suggest, illustrates the extent of judicial understanding of and engagement with Sharīʿah in commercial and corporate contexts. The second sub-section examines the approaches of the courts to IBF contracts and IBF entities specifically. The third examines arbitration and its potential for Islamic dispute resolution within the framework of the Common Law system.

Islamic commercial law

Basic principles

Business and trade is explicitly permitted and encouraged in Islām (The Qur'ān, An-Nisā', 4:29) so long as that trade is consensual, contractual and complies with the limitations that Allāh has imposed. Illegal contracts would include anything the substance of which is ḥarām (unlawful) such as 'non-ḥalāl' slaughtered meat, pork, alcohol and gambling. Muslims are bound by their promises and should implement in good faith their agreements, whether with other Muslims or non-Muslims (The Qur'ān, Al-Mā'idah, 5:1).[3] The verses from the Qur'ān and the sayings from the Prophetic Sunnah apply in both contexts equally.

The Sharīʿah recognises freedom of contract in the sense that, according to the Islamic maxim, 'all that which is not prohibited is permitted'. But that freedom is not unlimited. Contracting parties only have a range of choices within particular contractual forms or nominate contracts.[4] Parties can only trade permissible items that exist. They cannot draft contracts for items that are speculative, deceptive, unobtainable or otherwise uncertain (*gharar*). Nor are any contracts permitted to contain interest (*ribā*).[5] This position obtains whether one is paying or receiving interest, and irrespective of whether it is with consent of the parties. The majority of the Islamic juridical Schools hold this is a universal prohibition and applies irrespective of the jurisdiction, whether in a Muslim country or a non-Muslim country, between Muslims or otherwise, because of a clear verse in the Qur'ān (The Qur'ān, Al-Baqarah, 2:275).

Given the contemporary world banking system is based upon interest and the difficulty of purchasing a property without a mortgage, this would appear to put Muslims at a severe financial disadvantage and hardship in non-Muslim countries (Ramadan 2004: 176). Yet, as we mentioned in previous chapters, the Sharīʿah can be interpreted in different ways, even from within its traditional Schools that enable Muslims to integrate and navigate within existing frameworks (see Chapter 2). In the school of Abu Hanifah, scholars confined the ruling between Muslims, and exempted interest-bearing dealings between Muslims and non-Muslims in non-Muslim countries. This is because of a *ḥadīth* of the Prophet narrated through their School[6] and the permission for a Muslim to trade with a non-Muslim through whatever manner he chooses so long as it is without any deception (*idhā lam yakun fīhi ghadrun*) (Al-Maidani 2001, vol. 1: 224; Al-Marghinani n.d.)[7] and with the consent of the non-Muslim.[8] Rather than fall back on this '*rukhṣah*' or exception, some contemporary writers have permitted Muslims to use banks and modern financing on the basis of '*ḍarūrah*' (necessity) or '*ḥājah*' (need) (Ramadan 2004: 176). There is also a small minority, including a former Sheikh of the Azhar,[9] who have claimed *ribā* applies only to excessive interest rates or usury, and so would not apply to customary bank interest rates.[10] In the terms of our typologies set out in Chapter 2, then, we find evidence of all three of our approaches: separatist, integrationist and assimilationist.

Sayings of the Prophet also forbid bundling multiple agreements into a single contract, so as to ensure transparency and reduce uncertainty, and attaching conditions to contracts (*shurūṭ*) which either amount to questioning whether an agreement was ever made or which result in benefiting only one of the parties (thereby amounting to *ribā*). Under the traditional law, any contracts which contain *gharar* or *ribā* are void and cannot be enforced before an Islamic judge (*Qāḍī*).

If the contracts do not contain prohibited elements or violate procedural forms, they are enforceable. In case of breach, parties can seek damages for losses actually sustained; but not for loss of future profits or intangible losses (such as emotional trauma). Both of the latter are indeterminable and fall foul of the prohibition on '*gharar*' (Vogel 2000). If circumstances change, however, liability for future performance is lifted, with the exception of some minority opinions within the Māliki School (Coulson, cited in Ballantyne 2000: 240).

While there are differences between Islamic commercial law and Common Law principles of Contract and Tort, there are also many similarities. Identifying the equivalent concept, however, can be difficult because of language and terminology. Take, for example, the Common Law tort of tortious interference with contracts (which is raised in the case law below). It is unclear whether it exists in the Sharīʿah. The closest equivalent might be *ghaṣb*, which the juridical schools define as the unjust usurpation of the rights or property of another (*al-istīlā' 'alā māl-l-ghair 'udwānan'* (An-Nawawi 2010, vol. 15: 54). It also requires force (*quwwah*; *qahr*)[11] and that it is committed openly (*mujāharatan*[12]). Indeed, it is more akin to the crime of robbery than to a civil wrong, and is distinguishable from *sariqah* (theft) which is committed secretly. Moreover, given such requirements, it would need to be carried out intentionally (*'amdan*). This might suggest that the money would not be recoverable, but it does not preclude alternative tortious interference claims and court sanctions based on cheating or deliberate misrepresentation (*ghishsh* or *tadlees*).

Dispute resolution

In terms of dispute resolution, where parties are claiming loss, they are encouraged to first go to mediation (*ṣulḥ*), failing which arbitration (*taḥkīm*) and ultimately judicial adjudication (*qaḍā*) (Othman 2007: 69–70). In practice, however, parties have preferred to mediate against the backdrop of judicial adjudication rather than to go to arbitration.

Adjudication prefers admissions over testimony, direct testimony over circumstantial and documentary evidence, male evidence over female (depending on the precise subject matter of the claim), and Muslim over non-Muslim. The burden of proof is on the party who asserts a claim. In the absence of any proof,[13] the party who denies the claim makes an oath where he swears by Allāh that the claim is untrue (this procedure is the same for all monetary claims). As in Sharīʿah generally, the parameters and boundaries of rights and liabilities are subject to scholarly interpretation in the absence of clear textual mandates, and differences manifest across the juridical schools (*al-madhāhib*). Judges (*Quḍā*) are not bound by the previous decisions of other judges (no *stare decisis*), deciding each case on its particular facts, but rather are bound by the terms of their appointment and the extent to which they can exercise particular powers.

Differences between countries

The national legislated commercial laws of some contemporary Muslim states do not reflect these rules or the doctrinal positions of any School. They exhibit characteristics more in keeping with contemporary Western legal systems (Saleh 2001: 349). Even what might be regarded as the clear-cut Sharīʿah prohibitions of *ribā* and *gharar* have been given license in some Arab states, under the guise of a 'civil'/'commercial' law distinction, with the latter permitting merchants and traders to make contracts with (mostly) overseas companies notwithstanding elements of *ribā* or *gharar* (Saleh 2001: 349). The UAE and Qatar even have Common Law carve-outs, or micro jurisdictions that apply Common Law precedents from across the Commonwealth and have judges drawn from all over the Common law world (see further, Dubai International Financial Centre 2015). Others reflect one juridical School more than others. The Jordanian Civil Code, and Afghani Civil Law, for example, are adaptations of the Ottoman (and Ḥanafi) Majallat al-Aḥkām al-ʿAdliyyah – the first attempt to codify Islamic civil laws (*mu'āmalāt*) – and the United Arab Emirates Civil Code largely expresses Māliki doctrine. However, many modern Muslims states, and the intellectuals/jurists (such as 'Abd al-Razzāq al-Sanhūri) who helped draft their laws or guidelines, did not feel bound to one school. They chose eclectically between them (a process called *takhayyur*), 'patching' one opinion (often less well-known) on another, using a practice termed *talfīq*, to legitimise a practice that might otherwise be prohibited by one or more of the schools (Hallaq 2009: 448–49).

Saudi Arabia is the one country in the Middle East region that appears to follow Sharīʿah rules more closely, affirming in its constitution that its sources of law are the Qur'ān and the Sunnah, as interpreted by the Ḥanbali School. The Saudi government is only given a residual area in which to pass regulations (*nidzāmāt*) and is not permitted to contradict those primary sources. Contracts containing *gharar* and *ribā*, therefore, are theoretically and legally prohibited. In practice, however, they have been widely tolerated as necessities to participate in international business (Saleh 1986: 5; see also, Vogel 2000).

Islamic banking and finance

The Islamic banking and finance industry (IBF) is a contemporary example of Islamic commercial law which has grown up in response to Muslim popular demand to comply with Sharīʿah dictates. Although its biggest operators are in the Muslim world, where countries such as the UAE, Bahrain and Malaysia, have legal structures and regulations suited and adapted specifically for its products and services, IBF is also present in countries where Muslims are a minority, including Australia, Canada, the UK and the USA. IBF takes a variety of forms, but it includes both wholesale corporate providers, merchant banks and financiers as well as retail. The former are engaged in capital financing and investing, and offer Islamic bonds (see below), joint-ventures and corporate 'interest-free' loans through commodity sales. The latter provide services to the general public, such as mortgages (see below), bank accounts, funds and pensions and even, in some countries, credit cards on purported Islamic bases. All products and services are offered on an 'interest-free' basis, but have their own particular profit or fee structures (Mirakhor and Zaidi 2007: 49, 52). Most are commercial operators, not charitable institutions, though they do pay *zakāh* (an Islamic levy, mandated in the Qur'ān and Sunnah, and distributed to specific categories of recipients, notably the poor) which they often use as a mechanism to 'purify' funds tainted from contact with the conventional banking and finance industry.

Given that the case law makes extensive reference to these products, and the lack of familiarity about terminologies and concepts amongst Muslims and non-Muslims alike, we will now briefly explain some of these products.[14]

The most popular transaction, accounting for approximately 80 per cent of all transactions in IBF, traditionally has been the *murābaḥah*[15] or cost-plus sale. Typically, this involves the banker or financier purchasing an item at the request of a customer who promises to purchase the asset from the bank at cost price plus a mutually agreed premium. Rarely is full payment made immediately, so Islamic bankers and financiers combine the *murābaḥah* with a payment deferral (permitted by consensus) to produce the Islamic financial instrument known as *bay' bi thaman 'ajil* or *bay' mu'ajjal*. The result is a transaction which is similar to a fixed interest loan.

In order to give liquidity to their markets and for short-term financing, some Islamic Financial Service Providers also make use of same item sale-repurchase with or without an intermediary. In South-East Asia, Islamic financiers use the latter (*bay' al-'inah*) and in the countries of the Gulf Cooperation Council (GCC), the former (*tawarruq*), though even this has recently fallen out of favour with regional regulator and *fatwa*-making bodies (e.g. AAOIFI and the Fiqh Academy of the OIC). Both practices entail a client selling a permissible item to a financier at cash price who then sells it back to the client on credit for a sum equivalent to the principal amount plus a profit margin, as in a classical form of *murābaḥah*.

Another common IBF instrument is the *mushārakah* (*shirkah*, in the classical literature). This refers to a contractual partnership in which joint capital is exploited and any ensuing profits and losses shared between the partners. The modern IBF industry tends to allow unlimited partnerships in which the partners contractually determine their precise share of the profits in excess of or below their actual proportionate financial contribution, with the losses fixed according to that proportionate share (Iqbal and Molyneux 2005; Mirakhor and Zaidi 2007). There is a general expectation that each partner will and can contribute in the management and operation of the scheme, but sleeping partners can only receive a proportionate return on their investment (Iqbal and Molyneux 2005).

Ṣukūk (plural of *ṣakk*, meaning a deed or cheque) are normally referred to as 'Islamic bonds', but are better described as trust or investment certificates representing proportionate or undivided shares in the profits or revenues of large enterprises (Uthmani 2007). Unlike conventional bonds, certificate holders are (or should be) true owners[16] of a portion of the underlying asset and share in the actual success or failure of the enterprise. There is a wide variety of legal structures for *ṣukūk* and they can be based on *ijārah* (leasing), *murābaḥah, mushārakah* or *muḍārabah* (joint venture) concepts. Where, however, the underlying contract is a *murābaḥah,* the *ṣukūk* cannot be sold on the secondary market because of the Sharī'ah prohibitions surrounding debt sales.

Controversies arising from these products are discussed in Part 3.

Conflicts and choices of law

Matters of Islamic commercial law arise in Common Law Courts within the framework of 'conflict of laws' or 'private international law'. Each country has its own conflict of laws case law as adapted by international conventions and constitutional articles. Particular rules and 'connecting factors' apply to different subject matter depending, for example, on whether the dispute is in contract, tort (or both), or whether it is merely a matter of enforcement (and therefore a procedural question) and whether a defence to enforcement exists.

Although the UK, USA, Australia and Canada all have their own laws pertaining to conflicts of laws, the underlying principles are similar and there has also been increasing convergence in recent years as a result of legislative intervention.[17] In contractual matters, liberal theory of freedom of contract and the 'party autonomy rule' predominates in which parties may express in their agreement their own choice that the law of a specified jurisdiction shall apply to their agreement. The only limitations on party autonomy in US Federal Law and in some American states[18] is that they cannot require that their contract be governed by the law of a jurisdiction which has no relation whatever to them or their agreement,[19] and that the laws of the foreign jurisdiction do not otherwise offend public policy.[20] In the absence of an express choice, the court can imply a choice either from the form of the contract, from an arbitration clause or from a jurisdiction agreement.[21] If no express or inferred choice is evident, then the courts can look at objective factors to determine the proper law of the contract.

In tort cases, the presumptive choice of law rule is the 'proper law' doctrine which states that the law with the greatest relevance to the issues applies. In a tort case that would mean there would be a presumption the law of the state in which the wrong occurred would be applied. That presumption can be displaced where a party has submitted to the jurisdiction for reasons of practicality (matters of domicile or enforcement) or public policy.

In both contract and tort cases, once the choice of law has been determined, the court must still prove that law in order to apply it. As a result of statutory changes to the federal civil procedural rules in 1966, in American jurisdictions proof of foreign law must be proved as a matter of law rather than fact. Identifying the relevant legal rule rests with the court, as in all 'passive' Common Law systems (Lalani 2013: 79) it remains with the parties to plead matters of foreign law (Michalski 2011: 1210). American civil procedure is still adversarial, allowing parties to prove foreign law with their particular expert witnesses, but the court can have recourse to its own independent witness and state the law for itself. In English, Australian and Canadian courts (see *The Ship 'Mercury Bell'* v. *Amoisin* [1986] 27 DLR 4th 461 [CA]), on the other hand, proof of foreign law is a question of fact, not law, leaving the court only to assess the reliability and credibility of the expert witnesses the parties call in the event of any conflict of testimony (Clarkson and Hill 2011: 46).

Sharīʿah and Common Law as choice of law – case law

Contracts

In *CPS* v. *Dresser* (1995) (Clarkson and Hill 2011: 46), the Texas Appeal Court was asked to determine choice of law to resolve an alleged breach of contract following the dissolution of a joint venture in Saudi Arabia between an American corporation and Saudi Arabian businesses. Reversing the decision of the District Court, which had held the law of Saudi Arabia applied, the Appeal Court ruled the governing law was the Law of Texas. Notwithstanding the parties had agreed to choose the Law of Saudi Arabia and arbitration forums in Saudi Arabia to resolve any disputes arising under their agreements, and references to the application of Saudi Arabian Law in two other contracts, the Appeal Court preferred a holistic textual analysis of the totality of the agreement. It noted an inconsistent choice of law provision in one other contractual document, the Technical Assistance Agreement (TAA) – the only document which appeared originally in English. Rather than separate the contracts and analyse their purposes, and consider whether some aspects of their contractual relationships were meant to be determined in the United States under US law and the remaining contractual issues under Saudi Arabian law, the court determined the contract could not have two separate governing laws.

Through an analysis of the clauses of the TAA, the court commented on its 'range of clarity and quality' and determined that this must have been the agreement which determined the 'choice of law' for all contractual disputes (rather than those specifically related to the TAA). By contrast, in its construction of the first 'Kriol' agreement (arguably, the governing and overarching agreement), and the second agreement, the court mentions only the religious preamble: 'In the Name of God the Merciful, the Compassionate', and the relevant article of the agreement referring (arguably) to the choice of law provision (here Saudi laws and regulations). For the purposes of interpretation, it was unnecessary for the courts to refer to the religious preamble, but it seems it was included so as to indicate these particular documents were not purely 'law', and so could not have been intended to indicate a choice of 'law' for ultimate determination of contractual disputes.[22]

A few observations can be drawn from this decision of the Texas Appeal Court. First, there is their construction of 'law' within the Common Law context. They dismiss as 'law' the Arabic documents on grounds of their religious content which indicates, in this court's view, that US law is singularly secular and cannot accommodate religion. The assertion that only one law can govern the agreement also implies they have a unitary notion of 'law' which cannot encompass legal hybrids or legal pluralism. Second, the courts are inferring the parties chose Texan law to govern the entire agreement notwithstanding an express choice made by the parties that Saudi Arabian law should govern any disputes. This prioritises the subjective preferences of the courts over the subjective intentions of the parties. It also appears inconsistent with the principle of party autonomy.

In cases where there is no hybrid choice of law clauses, however, the American courts have given effect to the party autonomy rule and not utilised any argument on public policy to thwart application of the law from an Islamic jurisdiction, even where it states the Sharīʿah explicitly.[23]

In *National Group for Communications and Computers (NGCC)* v. *Lucent Technologies* (2004) 331 FSupp 2d 290, a decision of the US District Court of New Jersey, proof of the relevant Islamic law was in issue. In this case, a subcontractor sued a telecommunications contractor for breach of contract and consequential damages stemming from termination of its construction projects in Saudi Arabia. A preliminary issue brought before the New Jersey court was the quantum of damages available under the law of Saudi Arabia if the plaintiff were to succeed in its substantive claim. It was agreed that the American court would apply the law of Saudi Arabia to resolve the contractual dispute. In determining the applicable Saudi law, the court referred to Rule 44 of the Federal Rules of Civil Procedure (Fed R Civ P 44) and held that the determination of foreign law was a question of law upon which the court had broad authority to conduct their own independent research, along with any submissions from the parties aided by expert witnesses. The court also pronounced that it had the authority to reject even uncontradicted conclusions of an expert witness on that law and reach their own decisions.

The complexity of the task facing the court was well appreciated by Linares J who stated:

> The legal system in Saudi Arabia is fundamentally different from that of the United States. Western conceptions of the role that law plays in society, the legal process, and methods of legal interpretation, often mistakenly assumed to be universal in nature, are in many ways poles apart from those concepts in Islamic countries such as Saudi Arabia. The difficulties in understanding Islamic law are multiplied by the fact that there is a paucity of literature specifically targeted at those who, like this Court, are steeped in other legal mindsets and seek guidance as to Islamic law's interpretation. Confronted with this formidable and difficult responsibility, this Court has examined various texts and treatises dealing with Saudi Arabian law and carefully considered the testimony of the experts presented and the submissions of the parties which included testimony and submissions from Saudi Arabian lawyers, Islamic scholars, and former Saudi Arabian judges.

Without questioning the appropriateness (constitutionally or otherwise) of a secular court second-guessing, or even trumping, the determination of those grounded in the religious law, the court went on to identify the relevant Islamic rule and then offered its own particular interpretation of that rule. The court presented itself as a 'strict' and literal 'follower' of Ḥanbali doctrine: the 'law was the law'. Opining and analogising (so utilising *qiyās*), it stated:

> Plaintiff attempts to sidestep the dictates of Shari'a by characterizing its claim as one for the loss in the 'present actual value' of the Projects Department rather than one for lost future gains. However, Plaintiff's expert himself admitted that 'trying to recover lost gains by reproducing them or representing them as a direct reduction in value … would be improper under Islamic law.' (Vogel Tr. 197: 4–7). The loss in a company's value is directly dependent on, and intertwined with, the loss of its future earnings. If a Saudi court would deny damages based on the latter because of its inconsistency with Islamic law, it would certainly also deny damages based on the former. Permitting Plaintiff to evade the ban on gharar by reframing its claim as a loss in present value would produce an exception that would soon swallow the rule, as most future claims have some present element to them. The Board of Grievances has not and would not permit this back-door approach to obtaining damages that is effectively identical to a forbidden claim for lost future earnings.
>
> (Fed R Civ P 44 at 11)

The court held that the relevant Ḥanbali doctrine precluded any expectation losses and future profits because of the Sharī'ah concept of gharar or inherent uncertainty. The plaintiffs would only be able to recover for the actual value of their assets (as determined by fair market rates; not their book value) and out-of-pocket losses.

We note that such a construction of Sharī'ah would appear to impact adversely on most forms of complex modern business transactions and representatives of the Board of Grievances were never called as expert witnesses to determine what they would permit. The construction was based on an assumption.

Unlike both the American and the English courts, Canada's courts have not yet had to deal with any large Sharī'ah commercial cases. This is indicative of the marginal role that Canada (as Australia) plays in the global financial markets compared with America and England. But the cases that have been determined would suggest similar approaches as adopted in the USA. So in *Khalij Commercial Bank Ltd* v. *Woods* (1985) 50 OR (2d) 446 the Court of Ontario affirmed that it had jurisdiction to determine the case as there was no clause which explicitly ousted Canadian jurisdiction or asserted 'exclusive' jurisdiction for Dubai (at 3–4). It would apply the law of Dubai, however, rather than the law of Ontario as that was an explicit term of the parties' agreement (at 5) and not contrary to fundamental public policy or Canada's conception of natural justice (at 6). The court recognised that enforcing payment for a fixed sum was not against the law of Ontario. They noted traditional Sharīʿah law was part of the law of Dubai, but commercial matters were determined in a civil court which could refer to a variety of sources and ascertainable commercial legal principles. The fact that a separate enforcement court in Dubai could reduce the amount payable in certain circumstances (in line with the Sharīʿah) was irrelevant given enforcement was a matter of procedure and determined according to the court forum (i.e. in accordance with the law of Ontario).

This case indicates that a Canadian court will apply the law of a Muslim country in a commercial case subject to the law being ascertainable and verifiable through expert witnesses, and subject to it not being contrary to Canadian conceptions of public policy and natural justice.

Torts

In *Rhodes* v. *ITT Sheraton* (1999) WL 26874, Massachusetts Superior, the plaintiff was a British citizen staying with her parents at a hotel complex in Jeddah, Saudi Arabia, when she seriously injured her spinal cord after diving off one of the jetties linked to the hotel's beach, and hitting a coral reef below the surface of the water. The plaintiff brought the case in the courts of Massachussetts, the corporate defendant's home forum, rather than in the courts of Saudi Arabia. The defendant sought a dismissal on the Common Law grounds that Massachussetts was not the most appropriate court forum. In refusing to dismiss the action, Hinkle J held that it would not be equitable if the plaintiff were forced to pursue her claim in Saudi Arabia. Evidential and procedural rules put her at a great disadvantage to explain her claim and she would also be very limited as to the amount of damages.[24]

According to Roark, 'the court, in reviewing the law of Saudi Arabia, made a character judgement that Saudi Arabian law was inadequate for the court's conception of justice' (Roark 2008: 234). That may or may not be true, though given the location of where the events occurred and possible witnesses to the incident there was a case for Saudi Arabia to be the appropriate forum in which to hear the dispute. But in weighing appropriateness, the court prioritised protection of a vulnerable claimant (a tetraplegic) who would have been placed at a procedural disadvantage in Saudi Arabia.[25]

In non-personal injury tort cases, American courts have also assumed jurisdiction but have accepted the chosen law of an Islamic country as the 'proper law'. The key issue, as in contract cases, has been how to prove that law and the precise role of the court. In the first of these cases, *Bridas Corp.* v. *Unocal Corp* (2000) 16 SW3d 893 (Tex App 2000), in which tortious interference with a contractual relationship was alleged, the plaintiff needed to prove Afghani civil law and the position of the Ḥanafi School (the predominant school of thought across South Asia, including Afghanistan) in respect of tortious interference. Both parties submitted the opinions of experts, drawn from professional practice as well as from academia, Muslim and non-Muslim. Notwithstanding the differences in opinion, the court found that Afghani Ḥanafi law could be ascertained not just from the Ḥanafi handbooks, but also from specific articles in the Ottoman Mejelle (the Ottoman Civil Code) which Afghanistan had continued to apply (at 906).

Five years later, the Delaware Supreme Court also held that the Shariʿah was determinable. In *Saudi Basic Industries Corp (SABIC)* v. *Mobil Yanbu Petrochemical Co (Saudi Basic III)* (2005) 866 A2d 1 (Del 2005), the quantum of damages awarded to American companies by a civil jury against a Saudi Arabian partner was in issue and whether it was recoverable under the Islamic tort of *ghaṣb* under Saudi Arabian law.

The trial court approached this task using the same approach as would a Saudi judge, with the mandate to exercise *ijtihād* (independent reasoning). Noting conflicting expert opinion, and the variety of 'shades of meaning' within the religious law, the court opined that it was as qualified as any other to determine the applicable law. There was no published case law to guide and Saudi judges would not have felt bound by any precedent in any event. Where Linares J in *Lucent* had regarded such a judicial task as 'formidable and difficult', (*Saudi Basic Industries Corp [SABIC]* v. *Mobil Yanbu Petrochemical Co [Saudi Basic III]* [2005] at 12) the Appeal Court in SABIC praised the trial judge's 'exceptional efforts' for even attempting such a 'daunting' task and rebuked the appellant's Saudi Arabian law expert, Dr Frank Vogel, for suggesting the court was not able to interpret the Sharīʿah. The appellant's argument 'that the trial judge "was simply not qualified to practice ijtihad"' was summarily dismissed. The Appeal Court added acerbically,

> If Dr. Vogel is correct, then why did SABIC choose to file this dispute in a United States Court? If Dr. Vogel is correct in that neither he nor Dr. Hallaq possess the qualifications to engage in the ijtihad process, then what Saudi law 'expert' would be able to assist this United States Court in determining the applicable Saudi law?
>
> (*Saudi Basic Industries Corp* [SABIC] v. *Mobil Yanbu Petrochemical Co* [Saudi Basic III] [2005] at 31)

The court proceeded to define *ghaṣb* as the wrongful exercise of ownership or possessory rights over the property of another without consent, which need not be intentional.[26] In coming to this determination, the court preferred the opinion of its own 'independent' expert, criticising the appellant's expert for being more an 'advocate' rather than an 'objective scholar' of Islamic law. The appellant's experts (Dr Frank Vogel and some Saudi lawyers) maintained that Saudi courts were conservative and would have adhered to a very narrow line of Ḥanbali authorities. They maintained *ghaṣb* would not apply as the appellants had not acted openly or notoriously. On the contrary, they had acted surreptitiously (!) and therefore could not be held liable for this particular tort.[27] The court also dismissed SABIC's claim that 'enhanced damages' were 'unprecedented'. Upholding the trial judge's comments, the Appeal Court asserted:

> [S]imply because SABIC's expert is unable to name a case in which a Saudi judge awarded damages for usurpation is of little import to this Court considering that Saudi law does not recognize stare decisis and Saudi law opinions are not published. To say that usurpation damages are 'highly unusual' presumes that there are Saudi law cases where judges refuse to award damages for usurpation even when the elements have been clearly established. No such case law was provided to the Court, nor could it be, given the nuances of the Saudi law system. Moreover, whether a form of damages is 'unprecedented' is also irrelevant if such damages are available according to the authoritative Hanbali texts which are the primary works consulted by Saudi judges to determine the law applicable to the type of dispute raised in this case.
>
> (*Saudi Basic Industries Corp [SABIC]* v. *Mobil Yanbu Petrochemical Co* [Saudi Basic III] [2005] at 34)

Noting that there is no system of precedent in Saudi Arabia, the Delaware Supreme Court also arrogated to itself the right of *ijtihād* to determine quantum in Sharīʿah law.

On the facts of the case and given the deception that was practised by the appellants, the desire of the court to re-work Sharīʿah and produce an acceptable result was understandable. In so doing, the court applied its own 'purposive' conception of 'Sharīʿah' justice in contrast to the 'strict' and 'literalist' stance adopted by the court in *Lucent*. We would argue, however, that it is inappropriate for a non-Muslim court to adopt either a 'purposive' or a 'literal' interpretation of Sharīʿah. It should be left to the Muslim experts themselves. Even the most qualified Muslim *mujtahid* jurists (see Chapter 2) would question their own judgement and check it many times before announcing their *ijtihād*. Indeed, some of the scholars deliberately 'washed' the ink from their parchments where they had doubt in the correctness of their judgements to avoid misguiding the people (al-Siyūṭī n.d.: 15).

Banking and finance

From the inception of modern international Islamic banking and finance contracts, it has been common practice to insert English or an American law as the law governing the contract to ensure its enforceability (see Moghul and Ahmed 2003: 190). This has tested the capacity of those jurisdictions to apply Sharīʿah transactional law within their respective Common Law legal frameworks. In some cases, it has also strained the very 'Islamicity' of those contracts themselves. Let us first look at the English cases.

The English case law

The first IBF case to come before the English court, indeed any Western Court, was *Islamic Investment Company of the Gulf (Bahamas) Ltd* v. *Symphony Gems N.V. & Ors* (2002) WL 346969. This concerned the validity and enforceability of a rolling Islamic financing facility based on a *murābaḥah* contract. It involved the plaintiffs agreeing to purchase gems from a third party (at the request of the defendants) at a stated price and the defendants agreeing to purchase the gems from the plaintiffs at a higher price incorporating an agreed profit margin. The total amount owed was to be repaid in instalments. The parties had agreed the 'choice of law' was English contract law and the agreement subject to the jurisdiction of an English court.

The plaintiffs purchased the gems and claimed that they had delivered them to the defendants, but the latter refused to pay any sums owing and to honour the agreement. The plaintiffs sought summary judgment in the English courts for the outstanding balance and for liquidated damages. The defendants challenged the agreement on three principal grounds: first, that the gems were never delivered and so the sale price was never payable (at 10). Second, as part of the contract was performed in Saudi Arabia, the validity of the contract should also be examined in light of Sharīʿah transactional law (*al-mu'āmalāt*). Under Sharīʿah law, the purported agreement was invalid as the plaintiffs had purported to sell the gems before they had ownership or possession of them. Third, as the charter of the plaintiff's company required all of its transactions to be Shariʿah-compliant, the invalid *murābaḥah* was ultra vires and therefore inconsistent with its own charter. The defendants argued that any demand for liquidated damages would be inappropriate for a company based in Saudi Arabia as it would constitute *ribā*. Before coming to his judgment, Tomlinson J noted: '...it is important to note – indeed, in my judgment, it is absolutely critical to note – that the contract with which I am concerned is governed not by Shariah law but by English law' (at 6).

Accepting, at face value, the expert evidence of a Saudi professional lawyer that the contract would not have been deemed a valid *murābaḥah* in Saudi Arabia, the court determined the parties' could only have intended for English law to apply (at 7). The court did not consider the possibility the parties had intended for two laws to operate at the same time: namely, that the contract would be consistent with both *al-mu'āmalāt* and English contract law.

As for the first argument, the court decided that the agreement stipulated payments were payable whether or not the seller had breached its obligations and that payment was not conditional upon delivery, the outstanding sums remained payable.[28] As to the second argument, the obligations of the contract were to be performed in Zurich, New York and Hong Kong rather than Saudi Arabia. The offer was sent to the plaintiffs in Saudi Arabia and accepted there by them, but this was held insufficient for the contract to be 'performed' in Saudi Arabia. The court also dismissed the third argument, as the plaintiff's company was registered under Bahamian law which provided that companies were no longer subject to the ultra vires doctrine. Further, as the company was a 'Bahamian' company and not Saudi Arabian, English contract law applied and so liquidated damages were recoverable.

This first case on IBF in a Western jurisdiction represented, for some, the 'irrelevance of Islamic jurisprudence to Islamic finance', involving 'an ostensibly Islamic contract (a *murabahah*) made by an Islamic financial institution (which) by its own terms invoked the coverage of a non-Islamic legal system and the jurisdiction of a non-Muslim court' (Moghul and Ahmed 2003: 183).

In *Beximco (et al.)* v. *Shamil Bank* (2004) [2004] EWCA Civ 19, the English Court of Appeal, heard an appeal against summary judgment pertaining to various financing agreements again based on a *murābahaḥ*. The Court of Appeal went further, however, than the High Court in *Symphony Gems* by refusing to apply Sharīʿah law even where the parties had expressly provided for it in the terms of the contract. According to the Court of Appeal, the terms 'Glorious Sharīʿah' were too broad in expression, indeterminable and necessarily uncertain. Potter L.J. stated:

> The general reference to principles of Sharia in this case affords no reference to, or identification of, those aspects of Sharia law which are intended to be incorporated into the contract, let alone the terms in which they are framed. It is plainly insufficient for the defendants to contend that the basic rules of the Sharia applicable in this case are not controversial. Such 'basic rules' are neither referred to nor identified. Thus the reference to the 'Glorious Shari'ah' stands unqualified as a reference to the body of Sharia law generally. As such, they are inevitably repugnant to the choice of English law as the law of the contract and render the clause self-contradictory and therefore meaningless.
>
> (at 52)

The parties had not identified the relevant principles to incorporate, and therefore in contractual terms, it was unlikely they would have intended for a secular English court to decide the appropriate Islamic principles. The court continued:

> Finally, so far as the 'principles of ... Sharia' are concerned, it was the evidence of both experts that there are indeed areas of considerable controversy and difficulty arising not only from the need to translate into propositions of modern law texts which centuries ago were set out as religious and moral codes, but because of the existence of a variety of schools of thought with which the court may have to concern itself in any given case before reaching a conclusion upon the principle or rule in dispute. The fact that there may be general consensus upon the proscription of Riba and the essentials of a valid Morabaha agreement does no more than indicate that, if the Sharia law proviso were sufficient to incorporate the principles of Sharia law into the parties' agreements, the defendants would have been likely to succeed. However, since I would hold that the proviso is plainly inadequate for that purpose, the validity of the contract and the defendants' obligations thereunder fall to be decided according to English law.
>
> (at 55)

Just as in Symphony Gems, the principles of English contract law were applied, but not in accordance with the express intention of the parties. Also in contrast to the finding of Judge Tomlinson, the Court of Appeal viewed the principles of a *murābaḥah* as uncertain and indeterminable. The disagreement between the parties' experts (a former justice of the Pakistan Federal Shariʿat Court and a senior lecturer from the School of Oriental and African Studies in London) provided evidence of uncertainty in identifying the relevant Sharīʿah principles and rules in dispute. In the view of the court, it was not for them to suggest what they were as that was religious doctrine rather than law.

In this case, the English Court of Appeal refused in unequivocal terms to recognise Sharīʿah on two grounds. First, the court maintained that the very plurality of Sharīʿah meant Sharīʿah was necessarily uncertain and indeterminable. As we mentioned in Chapter 2, however, the mere fact a choice as to interpretation of a law exists does not necessarily imply that a choice cannot be made. If that logic were acceptable, it would cast a shadow over the entire doctrine of precedent in Common Law where an Appeal Court is often faced with conflicting decisions from courts of an equivalent status. Rather, the court evaluates those decisions in light of the particular facts of the case and provides a reasoned basis for preferring one over another. There is no reason, logically, why an English court could not do the same here.

The second ground, and arguably the main justification for not evaluating the witness' interpretations of Sharīʿah, is that it would necessarily involve the court in religious rather than legal questions. The court is asserting English law is secular and cannot accommodate religion. Yet, as we mentioned in Chapter 2, this is asserted rather than demonstrated. The history of the development of English law, as American law, is not entirely divorced from religious values as Judeo-Christian values have been encoded within the law's content. Further, we also argued the neutrality of secularism in a liberal state, which underpins the court's distancing itself from religion, has been overstated (see Chapter 2). Law in a liberal state requires the active promotion of values of personal autonomy. It therefore follows a court should look to favour those interpretations of Sharīʿah which value autonomy rather than refuse to evaluate them at all.

In *Investment Dār* v. *Blom Developments Bank Sal* (2009) [2009] EWHC 3545 (Ch), 2009 WL 5386898, the Chancery Division of the High Court appears to have reverted to the earlier approach of Symphony Gems.[29] The appellants were appealing against a summary judgment relating to a *wakālah* (contract of agency). The master *wakālah* contract provided that the agreement was expressly governed by English Law. The plaintiff company, however, was registered in Kuwait. Under its Memorandum of Association, its objectives were to be 'Sharīʿah compliant'. This meant that none of its objectives were to be construed or interpreted as permitting the company directly or indirectly to practice 'any usury or non-Sharīʿah compliant activities'. The appellants sought to avoid payment to Blom Bank on the basis the contract was not Sharīʿah-compliant and that the bank was taking deposits at interest.

The High Court overturned summary judgment (holding there was a triable issue) on the basis that a fixed rate of return irrespective of the success of the enterprise was in substance an interest charge and potentially ultra vires its

Memorandum of Association. The court reached this conclusion notwithstanding the relevant Sharīʿah committee determining the *wakālah* contract was Sharīʿah-compliant.[30] In determining a triable issue, the court noted contested expert evidence, but did not go on to suggest the principles of a *wakālah* contract were indeterminable and therefore Sharīʿah principles could not be applied.

According to Lawrence, Morton and Khan (2013), the net effect of *Symphony Gems* and *Shamil Bank* is that: 'so far as the English Courts are concerned (i) the governing law of a contract has to be either English law or the law of a country; therefore, Sharīʿah law cannot be the governing law of a contract; (ii) it may be possible to incorporate as a term of the contract certain principles of Sharīʿah law, provided there is certainty as to what is being incorporated. In our view, the position of the English courts is not as clear-cut as they suppose because the courts do not agree as what amounts to 'certainty'. The mere existence of interpretative plurality was enough for the Court of Appeal in *Shamil Bank* to hold Shariʿah law uncertain, and that would surely count also for 'principles of Sharīʿah law'. Both *Symphony Gems* and Investment Dār are inconsistent in this regard.

In terms of accommodation of Sharīʿah then, this line of cases (though not consistent) suggests that English courts will enforce the Sharīʿah content of IBF agreements through English Law but only where those agreements are clear, explicit and contain sufficient evidence the parties are not intending to operate in line with 'conventional' commercial principles.[31] The cases also suggest a tension between, on the one hand, wanting to give effect to the agreement the parties intended and, on the other, the role of an English court. The leading authority of Shamil Bank suggests that it is not for an English court to determine the governing Islamic content of a commercial dispute. High Court judges sitting alone, however, have not felt so constrained, even being prepared to second-guess the religious judgements of Sharīʿah Advisory Boards (see *Invesment Dar*).

The American case law

For the most part, the English case law has provided the international benchmark for law firms advising on IBF and the enforceability of IBF contracts. The American case law, on the other hand, indicates advantages to the IBF industry of using stable secular legal jurisdictions in times of economic crisis and protecting the rights of investors, whether Muslim or non-Muslim, in Muslim companies facing insolvency. While only a few IBF cases have been decided within the framework of US bankruptcy law, they indicate the American system has enough flexibility within its rules and principles to recognise distinctly Islamic concerns.

Unlike conflicts of law, bankruptcy law[32] is federal and contained in Title 11 of the United States Code. No particular state is allowed to regulate bankruptcy (US Constitution, Art. 1, Sect. 8), so it matters little in which particular jurisdiction our cases originate. Under Chapter 11, the party applying for bankruptcy has many options to reorganise their debt, allowing them to re-pay some, cancel others and restructure the rest. There have also been recent changes to filing for bankruptcy under Chapter 11, making it easier and potentially less expensive for businesses in the future (HG.org Legal Resources 2015). It is, therefore, 'debtor' as opposed to 'creditor' friendly, as English and European jurisdictions are sometimes described (Baird and Rasmussen 2002: 751). Although IBF organisations, who are based in the Middle East, could make use of the bankruptcy laws in those jurisdictions (such as Bahrain), which can often reduce the debt to be repaid and are 'debtor friendly', there remains uncertainty about the content of those laws and the effectiveness of their enforcement procedures (see further, Kuwait Financial Centre 'Markaz' 2013). This has meant IBF financiers have preferred Western jurisdictions, such as the United States, over Middle Eastern jurisdictions to structure their debts and remain in operation in the event of a financial crisis.

The first IBF Chapter 11 Bankruptcy case was *In re East Cameron Partners, L.P., Debtor* (2008) (Unreported, trial transcript, case no 08–51207, decision of the US Bankruptcy Court, WD Louisiana). In 2006, East Cameron became the first US entity to issue a *ṣukūk* using a two-tiered *mushārakah* structure. East Cameron was an American Oil and Gas company (without any Muslim shareholders) which needed capital injection. Following legal and financial advice, the company sought out a *ṣukūk* to secure necessary finance but without diluting their equity. The *ṣukūk* consisted of a transfer of oil and gas royalties to a Special Purpose Vehicle that would issue *ṣukūk* certificates to ṣukūk holders, representing their proportionate share in those royalties. Less than two years later, East Cameron filed for Chapter 11 bankruptcy and sought to re-characterise the *ṣukūk* as a secured loan so as to deny *ṣukūk* holder claims to the oil revenue. That the transaction was, in reality, a 'loan' in the eyes of ECLP clearly was evident from the original context of the transaction (compare with *Project Blue*). But it was not the understood characterisation of the transaction from the perspective of the *ṣukūk* holders many of whom would have invested because the transaction was purported to be Islamic. The assets had been transferred to the SPV so that they would proportionally share in the asset.

At issue, therefore, was whether the transfer of royalties of oil and gas to a Special Purpose Vehicle (SPV) effected a 'true sale' rather than a secured loan, and whether the court would give effect to the stated wording of the conveyance. Without any direct case law to guide it, the US Bankruptcy Judge, Robert Summerhays, examined whether it would be inequitable were the conveyance re-characterised as a secured loan. In granting the motion to dismiss, he held that the sale of the royalty interests could not be re-characterised as a loan, and regarded it as a 'simulation' as the language of the contractual documents unequivocally conveyed title. This, together with an absence of any documents indicating that the parties did not intend a true sale, and the absence of any evidence that the transaction was effected to perpetuate a fraud or produce an inequitable result resulting in an unfair windfall, indicated a genuine transfer and therefore that a 'true sale' had taken place. Moreover, this was a transaction whose stated purpose was to 'be compliant with Sharia or Islamic Holy Law and

... the structure of the securitization was an integral part' (at 15). It was held out as such to the *ṣukūk* certificate holders (who were interveners in this action), to re-characterise the transaction as a loan would adversely affect the latter's rights as they had acted in reliance on the transfer of the royalty interests as a 'true sale' (at 14).

In terms of accommodation, East Cameron, upheld the validity of a purported Islamic transaction through its application of general principles of American contract law and distinguishing of previous case law. It also protected the interests of Muslim and Islamic investors, notwithstanding the original purpose of the East Cameron Gas company when it sought the financing, through a consideration of principles of equity. The absence of religious motivation was not a relevant consideration for the American court (see *Project Blue*).

The potential flexibility of American Bankruptcy law and its capacity to incorporate Sharīʿah contracts and investor claims is also borne out in the latest and most important case to come before the American courts. *In Re: Arcapita Bank BSC et al.* (2013) Unreported, US Bankruptcy Court, Southern District of New York, No. 12–11076, was a case involving twenty-seven law firms with investments in the United States worth $7.4 billion dollars. Arcapita was a Bahrain-based Islamic investment firm, the world's first Islamic investment bank set up in 1996, which provided alternative investment opportunities for rich families, institutions and sovereign wealth funds in the Gulf region (Hals 2013).

The company filed for Chapter 11 Bankruptcy in the US Bankruptcy Court after it was unable to meet its $1.1 billion debt obligations in March 2012 due to the ongoing debt crisis, credit crunch and weakness in the global markets.[33]

Arcapita filed for voluntary bankruptcy in the USA because of the inadequate bankruptcy laws in Bahrain. Although there was some doubt whether the New York court had jurisdiction (as Arcapita was based in Bahrain), the court held the company could make use of US bankruptcy laws because it had some investments in the country. After extensive and extended negotiations, the New York South District Bank Bankruptcy Court agreed to a complex restructuring of Arcapita, taking into account the need for Sharīʿah-compliance of its predominant investors (including the Central Bank of Bahrain, the National Bank of Bahrain, Saudi Arabia's Riyad Bank and the UAE's Mashriq Bank, CIMB and Maybank) rather than authorising a fire-sale to liquidate all of the company's assets in satisfaction of US creditors.[34] However, this caused considerable losses to Muslim investors who only had residual claims on the assets of the company.

The court-approved bankruptcy plan was hailed as the first compliant with Sharīʿah law. Under the plan, a distinction was drawn between the secured (Standard Chartered Bank) and the unsecured creditors (largely the Muslim institutional and high net-worth individual investors). Arcapita would pay the secured creditor in full, with all of its assets transferred to a new holding company so that it could dispose of its assets over time and avoid a fire sale liquidation. The unsecured creditors would receive equity (equivalent to 7.7% of their amount invested) in the new holding company and a pro rata share in a new Sharīʿah-compliant loan. Arcapita also secured additional funding in the form of a $350 million *ṣukūk* issued to Goldman Sachs so the company could keep afloat, with the hedge funds compensated over time.

The proposed Refinancing Agreement through Goldman Sachs was stated to be a *murābaḥah* – but was challenged by one of the Gulf investors on the basis that it was not 'Sharīʿah compliant'.[35] At most, it constituted an *'ināh* (same item sell-back with deferred term), prohibited under Standard 30 of the AAOIFI and by the Islamic Fiqh Academy of the OIC. The US District Court refused to address these substantive appeals and dismissed the objections on grounds of 'equitable mootness' (*In re Arcapita Bank B.S.C.* [2014], 13 Civ.5755 [SAS]). As some time had passed since concluding the agreement, there had already occurred a 'comprehensive change in circumstances' that would have had a detrimental impact on multiple parties affected by the case. (*In re Arcapita Bank B.S.C.* at 2).

In this case, therefore, the court gave effect to an interpretation of Sharīʿah. This was on the basis that the court-approved bankruptcy plan formed the substance of an agreement between the parties. Whether the agreement was 'Sharīʿah-compliant' in fact was not a matter that the court was prepared to rule upon (this is consistent with Shamil Bank). The Sharīʿah defence was raised too late in the proceedings, which ultimately was the fault of the intervener.

In the words of Michael Rosenthal, co-chair of Gibson, Dunn & Crutcher, which represented Arcapita, the upshot of the court's decision is,

> Any restructuring that now takes place in the Middle East has to consider the possibility that if the parties don't reach a consensual deal, they may find themselves in a U.S. court, where U.S. principles can be applied to exert some leverage to get them to reach a deal. That threat will now be the backdrop for negotiations.
>
> (Johnson 2014)

The Canadian case law

More recent decisions of the Canadian courts have become involved in Sharīʿah-compliant mortgages and deal, not with big commercial enterprises (wholesale IBF), but with the financial and commercial rights of individual Muslims against 'boutique' Sharīʿah financial providers (retail IBF). These cases lay bare the vulnerability of individual Muslims to exploitation and fraud. Canadian courts have sought to resolve disputes surrounding Canada's nascent IBF industry, with four cases involving Canada's first, and troubled, Islamic finance institution and Sharīʿah home-finance provider, UM Financial.

In the first of these, *Alenezi* v. *UM Financial* (2008) [2008] ONSC 60160, the plaintiff sued UM Financial for increased costs incurred by having to seek alternative and more expensive funding for a house after UMF was unable to secure promised funding within the agreed time frame. Analysing the dispute within the frame of contract law, the court held the defendant liable in damages for the differences in the costs of the mortgage in relation to the entire contracted period (here two years). That the plaintiff arranged an alternative mortgage within one year of taking out the initial mortgage was deemed irrelevant to the question of damages. Ironically, the plaintiff had originally sought out a Sharīʿah-compliant, interest-free mortgage with UMF and ended up paying not only an interest-based mortgage, but also receiving interest on his court damages from UMF at the rate of 4.5 per cent from 5 June 2006 until the date of the judgment.

The second case, *Central 1 Credit Union* v. *UM Financial* (2011) ONSC 5612, concerned an application to intervene by UM Financial's Shariʿah Advisory Board (SAB) following the bankruptcy of UM Financial and the appointment of a receiver to take over its assets and undertakings. The SAB had sought to intervene on the basis that the Sharīʿah aspects of the contracts could not be properly articulated by the existing parties and because of possible litigation against Board members by the affected clients. The Superior Court of Ontario rejected the motion on the ground that the SAB had no substantial corporate interest that would be substantially affected by the action and that any possible reputational risk of its board members was purely speculative. Further, there was no evidence of any need for them to intervene even on Sharīʿah grounds. The receiver was bound to administer UM's assets, including its contracts, in accordance with the terms of those contracts, subject to the approval by a court to the contrary. The appointment of a receiver, therefore, would not radically transform the nature of the rights and parties under the Diminishing Mushārakah Agreement as the SAB had contended.[36]

In direct response to the SAB's counsel's closing submission to the court that a refusal to grant leave to intervene would amount to a symbolic rejection of religion and Islām within Canada's legal system, the court concluded:

> [32] I do wish to add one final comment. During the course of its written and oral argument MCC emphasized the religious dimension of its activities and its desire to participate in this proceeding. Freedom of religion is one of the most precious of our constitutional freedoms. I have written at great length, both as a lawyer and as a judge, about the cardinal position enjoyed by that freedom in our political and legal community – religious belief plays a central role in the lives of a very large number of Canadians. At the same time, arguments about religious freedom can assume a strong emotional dimension. I wish to say, with respect, that counsel who advance freedom of religion arguments must take great care about how they cast their arguments and should avoid the temptation to personalize or emotionalize their submissions. I raise this point somewhat reluctantly, but I think necessarily, given the dramatic closing submission by MCC's counsel who, picking up the copy of the Koran kept by the court registrar, suggested that if leave to intervene was not granted to his client, then the Koran would not have a place in Canadian culture or its court system. Such a style of argumentation is inflammatory, even before a judge alone, and, in my view, improper in a forensic submission to a Canadian court by professional counsel on such an important constitutional right as freedom of religion.
>
> (at 10)

The third instalment involving UM Financial is *Central 1 Credit Union* v. *UM Financial Inc* [2012] ONSC 889, a case concerning civil contempt of court following a remarkable turn of events in the UM Financial saga. For our purposes, the judgement (ordering six months' imprisonment for the Finance Manager of MCC, the newly incorporated Sharīʿah Advisory Board of UM Financial) is relevant only because of the facts it discloses about the operations of UM Financial, how it failed to look after (arguably misappropriated) the deposits and mortgage accounts of its 170 clients and the lack of genuine independent oversight. The court transcript discloses that shortly before a receiver was appointed, the head of the MCC (UM Financial's SAB) ordered the CEO of UM Financial to prepare an invoice for payment to the SAB of $2,790,000, representing back-pay for Sharīʿah consulting services between 2004–2011. The CEO subsequently used depositor funds to purchase thirty-two gold bars and silver as the SAB did not want to be paid in cash, claiming they did not have a bank account. In what still remains a mystery, the gold bars were then delivered to the Finance Manager of MCC who, in his examination before the court, claimed that he subsequently delivered them to his cousin in Egypt as payment for fatwas consisting of one page only to twenty Sharīʿah scholars who themselves, he claimed, did not wish to be identified because they were not licensed to give opinions in Egypt. The Finance Manager of MCC refused to disclose to the receiver or the court the names and addresses of the 'Sharīʿah consultants' in Egypt and was handed a six-month prison sentence (in absentia). Since this case, both the Finance Manager of MCC and the CEO of UM Financial have gone missing and remain the subject of a major fraud investigation (Ha 2014).

The fraud and bankruptcy left the 170 clients of UM Financial in a great state of uncertainty and eventually led to them having to rearrange their mortgages (with 'non-Sharīʿah compliant' providers) at higher rates. Notwithstanding the pent-up market of Sharīʿah mortgages in Canada, the case also dealt a severe blow to the credibility of the industry. It led some Muslim community representatives to warn against IBF in general and of its 'charlatans trying to squeeze money out of an already marginalized community' to whom you have to 'pay more but receive less' (Fatah, cited in Alini 2012).

For others, the UM Financial episode stands out as a lesson on the need for tighter regulation and oversight of IBF providers and for the banks to establish 'Islamic windows'. They would be able to offer Sharīʿah-compliant products to prevent 'conservative' Muslims from being further marginalised and becoming a perennial class of renters rather than home-owners (Hejazi, cited in Alini 2012). Having the major banks provide the service would also reduce the perceived need to seek out less well-known, less well-funded and possibly less well-managed financial institutions (Hejazi, cited in Alini 2012).

The final Canadian case, *Farzana* v. *Abdul Hamid* [2014] ONSC 4913, was the first resulting from the bankruptcy of UM Financial in 2011. Again, as with the 2012 decision, the judgment does not indicate one way or another a particular judicial approach to Sharīʿah-compliant mortgages, but rather explicates the opaque and ambiguous contractual arrangements entered into by UM Financial with its Muslim investors and Muslim home buyers.

The court transcript indicates that UM Financial provided its Sharīʿah-compliant mortgages at its early stages of business by way of *murābaḥah*, acting as both financier and intermediary. In later years, it changed over to diminishing *mushārakah*. It had a *muḍārabah*, or joint-venture agreement, with the Muslim investor, in which it would share an agreed ratio of the 'profits' of the sale of a house it would sell on to the purchaser, representing a proportionate share of regular deferred payments.

As part of the *muḍārabah* agreement, the investor would lend the home buyer a specified amount to purchase the house which would be secured by a Sharīʿah-compliant second mortgage. UMF's right to a share was founded upon its managing of the second mortgage. It is unclear whether those payments would represent full payment of principal and profit, or whether a balloon payment would be paid upon completion of the mortgage term.

UM Financial's relationship with the home purchaser would be in the form of a four-stage purchase and sale agreement (here termed the 'Borrower's Financing Agreement') in which the eventual purchaser, upon receiving the funds from the Muslim investor, would first purchase and acquire legal ownership of the property; second, assign his rights to ownership to UM Financial; and, third, 'resell' the house to the purchaser to be repaid in instalments. The resale value of the house would be higher than for the first purchase, the difference (in this case 25 per cent of the initial purchase price) in the two representing the profit. Each of the parties in this case had an agreement with UM Financial to which the other was not a party.

In an action to dismiss a summary judgment for the repayment of a loan, the defendant argued that first, he had not been given proper notice of the proceedings, and second that he had a defence to the claim. The court agreed with the defendant noting: the ambiguity of the Muslim investor's Lending Finance Agreement with UM Financial; the documents fail to explain why the defendant's payments were more than the profit amount provided for in the Borrower's Financing Agreement signed by his wife (allegedly on his behalf) and UM Financial, and whether they related to profit or principal; uncertainty about whether the mortgage agreement had to be renewed, and the Borrower's Financing Agreement not providing any clear terms that made out the fundamental elements of a mortgage agreement between the Muslim investor and the home-buyer (at 20). The court concluded tersely: 'The only facts that are certain are that Ms. Farzana advanced $24,600 to Mr. Abdul-Hamid, who used the proceeds to purchase the property, and that he gave a mortgage as security for the amount advanced' (at 20).

As this was merely a motion to dismiss summary judgment, the court did not decide on the substantive merits of the case. Nevertheless, the court questioned whether there was any contract (at 20) between the Muslim investor and the home purchaser and if there had been any 'true meeting of minds' (at 12). Such a query potentially unravels the validity of the documentation underpinning these types of Sharīʿah-compliant home financing packages under the law of contract. The case also exposes the problems arising in the retail context between Muslim investors, the IBF financier and Muslim home purchasers, and what potential remedies may be available, and against whom, in the event of bankruptcy.[37]

The case would suggest that parties to contracts with small IBF finance providers should secure legal assistance to check that their agreements with IBF providers are properly drafted. They should also determine their precise remedies to which they will be entitled in the event of any corporate default. It also points to the inadequate supervision of such operators and the need for tighter regulation to protect the rights of Muslim investors and Muslim home purchasers.

The Australian case law

To date, there have not been any cases decided in Australia concerning conflicts of law between Sharīʿah and Australian jurisdictions, or any retail IBF cases as a result of any bankruptcy of a local IBF provider. Nevertheless, the recent decision of *Helou* v. *Nguyen* [2014] NSWSC 22, points to the gap which IBF seeks to fill in the banking needs of conservative Muslims and indicates a measure of judicial understanding and accommodation of a seemingly 'foreign' and 'alien' approach to transactions and savings.

The plaintiff in this case brought an action in Common Law and Equity to recover property bought with $467,500 in cash allegedly stolen from the family home by the defendant. The cash had been stored in the roof cavity of their townhouse along with the family's gold jewellery. The court established that the whereabouts of the stored cash had been inadvertently made known to a local shopkeeper by an intellectually impaired member of the plaintiff's family whom he had befriended, and then subsequently exploited. The money and jewellery was stolen by the shopkeeper and then spent gradually over time, including in the purchase of three Sydney properties.

The trial transcript notes that the plaintiff's had stored all of this money in the house, rather than in a bank account, because of 'the family's strong commitment to their Muslim faith' (at 8). Mr Helou Senior believed that it was against the Muslim faith to receive income by way of interest earned on money and that, if any interest was earned, the faithful were under a religious obligation to contribute it to charity as 'Zakat' (at 20). The family had been saving and collectively pooling their money in order to buy a bigger family home without recourse to any interest-paying mortgage. After the father had returned from the Ḥājj (the pilgrimage to Mekkah), he become more strict and assertive, demanding that all of the family remove their money from bank accounts, even those that had been set up to donate to charity.

Although attributing this alleged aversion to interest and bank accounts to possible cultural influences and his Lebanese origin, Lindsey J, embarked on an historical analysis of the usury laws in Anglo-Australian law, remarking that the

British who colonised Australia had a 'mindset not unlike that of Mr Helou' and which 'is part of this nation's Anglo-Australian heritage' (at 26).

In framing the analysis of his decision in this way, the court not only bolstered the plaintiff's credibility, assisting a finding of the tort of conversion and the imposing of an equitable charge against the defendant's properties, on facts which had depended on one person's word against another. It also articulated, for the consumption of future legal audiences, the proximity of Islamic values and law to the values and legal tradition persisting in New South Wales and Australia generally. Justice Lindsey's approach, we suggest, offers hope and optimism of the potential for accommodation of Islamic banking and finance within the Australian legal system as it becomes more widespread, and difficult issues begin to emerge. It also suggests that even 'conservative' or what we term 'separatist' perspectives[38] can be accommodated within the law.

Sharīʿah, courts and arbitration

Historically, in the context of arbitration, there has been some disdain for Islamic law. In the 1950s, English arbitrators[39] refused to follow Islamic law even where they accepted it was the governing law. For Lord Asquith, Islamic law lacked a consistent body of principles and resembled more 'palm-tree justice'.[40]

Since the 1990s, however, English law has embraced arbitration and regarded it as an efficient and cost-effective method of case diversion. Moreover, as was mentioned in our chapter on Family law, under the English Arbitration Act 1996, there is no bar on a 'religious' law being applied in arbitration proceedings, whether in the family or business context. As clarified by the English Supreme Court in *Jivraj* v. *Hashwani* [2011] IRLR 827; [2011] UKSC 40, European employment regulations and Human Rights law do not prohibit the parties from specifying and restricting the religious denomination of the arbitrators, as arbitrators are not employees but rather independent contractors for services.

A Muslim Arbitration Tribunal (2015) has been established in various centres across the UK. Its awards are enforceable as if they were High Court judgments (though its decisions are still subject to judicial review). Though focusing on small-scale commercial disputes, the MAT has offered a cheap, flexible and Islamically-based forum for dispute resolution that has attracted both Muslims and non-Muslims.[41] Judging by the absence of any appeals against its arbitration awards by way of judicial review, it would seem to have been a success in its own spheres of influence.

In the United States, there is a general presumption in the validity of arbitration proceedings, whether they relate to an Islamic arbitration body or otherwise. Any allegations of fraud or impropriety are put to strict proof (see *Abd Alla* v. *Mourssi* [2004] 680 NW 2d 569). There also appears to be a protective constitutional perimeter around religious arbitration proceedings. In *El-Farra* v. *Sayyed (et al.)* (2006) 365 Ark 209, 226 SW 3d 792, an American court refused to assert secular jurisdiction on an ostensibly Islamic arbitral body. An Imām for an Islamic centre in Arkansas sought to bring an action against an Islamic arbitral body for breaches of contract and tortious interference with a contract after his dismissal from his post. The court refused subject-matter jurisdiction applying the First Amendment to the United States Constitution which protects the free exercise of religion. Even though the case had 'secular' aspects (the appellant had a contract of employment and was seeking damages), the nature of that employment was in the capacity of a religious minister. It was not for courts to interfere in the hiring and firing of religious ministers which related, directly or indirectly, to religious doctrine. A court would intervene only in the cases involving property rights or where religious authorities had specifically given jurisdiction (which was not the case here).

So long as the parties to the contract have clearly and explicitly selected an Islamic forum of arbitration, an American court will not intervene. In *Re Aramco Services Company* (2010) WL 1241525, the Court of Appeals of Texas overruled a decision of a Texas district court to appoint arbitrators through its construction of an arbitration agreement. The contract contained an arbitration agreement which provided the laws of Saudi Arabia as its choice of law; Arabic as the language of arbitration; and its arbitrators to be either Saudi nationals in origin or Muslims with a Chairman knowledgeable in Sharīʿah. In the absence of the parties agreeing to a choice of arbitrator(s), the 'Authority' competent to hear the dispute would appoint the arbitrators upon request of the party interested in expediting the arbitration.

When arbitration proceedings were raised, Aramco appointed a Muslim arbitrator, but none of the arbitrators proposed by the American corporate respondent were Saudi nationals or Muslims. Aramco rejected the appointment, but it was upheld by the Texas District Court. Aramco sought judicial review and an order for mandamus. The review court held, through a construction of the totality of the contractual agreements, that the 'Authority' referred to could not be a Texas court (especially as notices would have to be in Arabic) and so it did not have the authority to appoint any arbitrators. No reference was made to considerations of public policy.

Given the flexibility and opportunities for Islamic arbitration in both the American and English contexts, it is surprising the multi-billion dollar IBF industry has been reluctant to go to arbitration. Contractual parties have preferred either resolving their disputes through negotiation or, failing that, going to secular courts. Some have argued this may be a result of the demand by credit rating agencies to have legal certainty before they evaluate IBF deals and the perceptions of unpredictability, uncertainty and secrecy which go with arbitration. The fear is magnified where arbitration is located in the Middle East (McMillen 2001: 1195). Ratings agencies prefer the transparency and predictability of the Common Law and so only provide favourable ratings of IBF offerings if parties insert English or American law governing clauses. Others, such as Megat Hizaini Hassan, have argued it is also partly due to the reticence of Islamic jurists themselves who see *taḥkīm* – or arbitration – as naturally inferior to judicial decisions (*qaḍā'*), given that in classical Islamic law, an arbitration award would need the sanction of a court to be enforced in any event.[42] While arbitration would appear the natural solution for IBF financiers wanting to ensure that dispute resolutions are more rooted in Islamic principles, global financing structures and influences militate against its use.

Conclusion

At the beginning of this chapter, we referred to the claim that Islamic transactional law is regarded as 'good' Sharīʿah because of an apparent appreciation of the ethical values underpinning it. If that were true as a general statement, we would have expected to see facilitation of application of Sharīʿah rules in the business context unless there was an explicit constitutional, statutory or Common Law rule that prevented it. When examined comparatively through the conceptual prism of 'accommodation' and the case law, as one would expect, the reality is more nuanced and with a few (important) differences between the jurisdictions.

In terms of choice of law, our jurisdictions adopt different positions in the contexts of business contracts and torts. As far as contracts are concerned, both American and English courts have allowed parties to choose the laws of Muslim states to resolve their transactional disputes, so long as those agreements have been drafted explicitly and clearly. This approach is consistent with the fundamental principle of party autonomy and suggests a degree of accommodation.

Where, however, some contracts have not been drafted clearly or there have been 'hybrid' choice of law clauses denoting certain aspects of the contract to be interpreted by Islamic Law and others by American Law or English Law, the courts have applied the substantive law of their own jurisdiction to the entire contract, without exception. This has also been true of IBF cases where parties have written contracts to be governed by the 'Glorious Sharīʿah', a term which the English courts have deemed contractually void for uncertainty. English judicial perceptions of uncertainty have centred on perceived pluralism in the Sharīʿah and the inability of the courts (or the inappropriateness) in determining what is 'Islamic'.

Where, however, the Sharīʿah contractual terms have not been deemed void for uncertainty, and have linked to a country's posited laws, courts in both England and the United States have not shied away from identifying and applying the relevant Islamic rule through their use of expert evidence. In the case of the English courts, this has been limited to what the parties themselves have presented to the court. In the American context, the courts have clothed themselves with the garb of Islamic scholarship and offered their own interpretations. In each case, this has been due to the particular statutory rules of evidence law operating in that country and which guide the role of the court. In both cases, this would suggest a degree of recognition of 'contextualised' Sharīʿah by the courts, though it does not defer to how Muslims themselves define it.

The above approach is also true for tort cases involving tortious interference with contracts. As for tort personal injury cases, based on the few that have come before the courts, the Common Law judges are here much less accommodating of Sharīʿah or of the laws of Muslim states applying Sharīʿah rules. In these cases, courts have a broader discretion to incorporate considerations of Equity and public policy, and have assumed jurisdiction under their respective laws to prevent Sharī'ah rules, in their eyes, from adversely affecting an individual's claim (which would be recognised under English or American laws).

Court approaches towards IBF cases have, in part, been shaped by the same considerations we have discussed above: certainty, clarity and 'one law for all'. So long as parties have specifically embedded their Islamic principles within contracts governed by English or American law, the courts will apply them because, in doing so, they are applying English law or American law. This is also true of bankruptcy cases in the United States. In the English context, however, the absence of a clearly articulated religious motivation may cause a court to default to a commercial reading of a contract, and refuse to immunise a party from state liabilities (notably in taxation). This is problematic as it seems to imply having a 'profit motive' is contrary to religious motivation when the entire IBF industry purports to be based on blending commerce with religious ethics and principles (see further, Istana Hotel Kuala Lumpar). Such an approach, in our view, clearly does not accommodate Sharī'ah as it financially handicaps IBF operators and indirectly discriminates against them. It also assumes that IBF operators would only transact with Muslims (as non-Muslims would not say they are 'obliged' to so transact), when the reality is that a large proportion of their clientele are non-Muslims who are increasingly seen as vital towards IBF's future growth and global expansion (Vizcaino 2014; see also Black and Sadiq 2011). IBF is for everyone; not just for Muslims.

None of the judges, in any of our jurisdictions, have refused to apply IBF contracts on grounds of public policy nor expressed any opposition in terms of principle or sentiment to its underlying value premises. Indeed, in the one case heard in Australia, the court went out of its way to articulate the commonalities and historical meeting points between Sharī'ah transactional law, local cultures and the principles of Common Law. Any criticisms from the Canadian courts have related to the practical operations of retail entities and the behaviour of the people running them and not to the Sharī'ah itself. This, in turn, points to issues within the Muslim communities themselves. It raises the question of the viability of IBF organisations when operating as a small minority in a non-Muslim state and whether governments ought to encourage more initiatives that embrace integrationist perspectives (see Chapter 2), such as through 'Islamic windows'.

Further, while some resistance to religious arbitration still obtains in Canada – on political rather than legal grounds – in Australia, England and the United States, laws appear to provide sufficient flexibility for all business disputes to be resolved through Islamic arbitration methods. In the case of IBF, the reason parties have not made much use of religious arbitration may be a result of the commercial market's historical preference for the supposed certainties of the Common Law, and the 'unknowns' of religious arbitration. In part, it may also flow from the extensive involvement of lawyers in the industry who necessarily gravitate towards court-based negotiation rather than arbitration.

All of the above discussion, we suggest, points to a high degree of accommodation, though not universal acceptance, of Sharīʿah transactional law. In choice of law cases, the problems that arise can be addressed through reforms in the laws of evidence. We discuss this further in our final chapter. In the case of IBF, the problems that have arisen have been due largely to poor drafting of contracts or, perhaps, to limited understanding of Sharīʿah in courts due to lack of exposure. If Muslims want to have specific Islamic interpretations of their agreements, they need to state exactly what they are (as in *Re Arcapita*), or to counter that contingency through 'Sharīʿah waivers'. The effect of the latter, in practice, would be to defer all Sharīʿah questions to the relevant Sharīʿah Advisory Boards. The other alternative is to opt out of the judicial procedure altogether and use arbitration, for which the current system generally provides. This requires a reorientation of the players and stake-holders within the global financial industry – of which IBF is a part – rather than any fundamental reforms to the systems of Common Law.

The proposal for Sharīʿah waivers and greater use of arbitration might indicate to some we advocate a 'separatist' perspective, as Muslims who do business will slip further and further away from public view. But this is not the case as the public interest will be preserved through availability of judicial review. In reality, the proposal is 'integrationist' as it represents an attempt to navigate the existing system, not to work against it.

Notes

1 In English Criminal Law, it was not until the mid-nineteenth century that the Police assumed responsibility for prosecutions. Even after that, a fiction was maintained a police officer prosecuted 'in the shoes' of the victim. It gradually became part of 'public law' through the expansion and greater powers handed to the 'state' through modernisation (Hay and Snyder 1989). During colonial times, Family laws across the Common Law world were also categorised as a species of 'Personal laws'. While the enforcement of criminal laws by that time had become the responsibility of colonial government and part of the public law, Muslims in different parts of the Empire were allowed to follow their own 'personal laws', predominantly family laws, under colonial administration. Family law was not construed as 'public law'.

2 In the last eighteen months, Islamic banking has become very popular in the UK amongst both Muslims and non-Muslims. According to Tim Sinclair, chief of marketing and sales at Al-Rayyan Bank (formerly the Islamic Bank of Great Britain), in 2014, approximately 84 per cent of fixed term deposits and 47 per cent of ISA new customers were non-Muslims (Hanna 2015).

3 The verse includes covenants made between Man and God as well as agreements between people (An-Nasafi 2008: 303).

4 See discussion of IBF below and Saleh (2001: 347).

5 Linguistically, *ribā* means 'excess'. There are a number of definitions of *ribā*, but in the context of loans, the Sunnah defined it as anything lent which draws a commercial benefit to the lender. This would necessarily include 'interest'. See further, Farrar 2011: 417. Some modernist opinions have permitted fixed interest rates (Black and Sadiq 2011: 391).

6 The Prophet is reported to have said: 'There is no *ribā* between the Muslim and the Non-Muslim in *dār al-ḥarb*' (Al-Marghinani n.d., vol. 3: 67). This hadith is

controversial for a number of reasons and is not deemed reliable by the majority of the Sunni Schools of Fiqh. Nevertheless, it was accepted by Abu Hanifah, the eponym of the School, and by one of his most famous disciples, Muḥammad Al-Shaybāni.

7 See in particular, ibn 'Ābidīn (1994, vol. 7: 423). This judgement is reliant on a distinction between *Dār al-Islām* (the Land of Islām) and *Dār Al-Ḥarb*. There is an intense discussion on the meaning of both terms within both the traditional schools of thought (*al-madhāhib*) and contemporary writers but there is insufficient space to refer to the discussion in any detail here. We interpret the latter term, *Dār al-Ḥarb* in its general meaning, as a country whose 'legal system as well as the government are non-Islamic' (Ramadan 2004: 65).

8 Consent is a necessary requirement of all valid contracts (The Qur'ān, *An-Nisā'*, 4:29).

9 Based in Cairo, this is one of the leading and most famous academic institutions in the Muslim world.

10 An Analysis. See also Mallat (1988: 69).

11 For the Shāfi'ī School, see al-Harari (2012, vol. 2: 184). For the Māliki school, see al-Dusuqi (2011, vol. 5: 157).

12 As in the Ḥanafi school, see al-Marghinani n.d., vol. 4, n. 1, p. 293. For the Ḥanbali position, see the case law discussion below.

13 'Proof' is generally synonymous with testimony or *shahādah*. According to juridical schools (with the exception of the Ḥanbali school), circumstantial evidence is ancillary to testimony (Al-Husari 1977, vol. 1: 8).

14 This section draws on Farrar (2011: 413, 418–21).

15 In recent years, there has been a shift towards profit-and-loss products and a move away from debt-based products, such as the *murābaḥah*.

16 Ideally, this means *ṣukūk* holders should be both the legal and equitable owners, rather than simply holders of equity. This means *ṣukūks* should be 'asset-backed' rather than 'asset-based'. However, this does not reflect the majority of contemporary sukuk structures. See further, Kumpf (2014: 23).

17 This has been to deter forum shopping. See further, Ruhl 2007.

18 Texas, California, Illinois and New York now allow for a free choice as a result of recent legislative interventions (Ruhl 2007: 15).

19 There is no requirement for a connection to the parties under English law because of the operation of the Rome Treaty (Ruhl 2007: 11; and Clarkson and Hill 2011: 204). A connection to the parties is not required under Australian law either (Davies *et al.* 2013: part III). In Canada, a connection to the parties is only required if the parties fail to state explicitly their choice of law (*Imperial Life Assurance Co. of Canada* v. *Segundo Casteleiro Y Colmenares*, [1967] SCR 443 at 448 and *Lilydale Cooperative Limited* v. *Meyn Canada Inc.*, 2015 0NCA 281).

20 R. Weintraub, *Commentary on the Conflicts of Laws*, cited in *CPS* v. *Dresser* 911 SW 2d 18 – Tex: Court of Appeals, 8th Dist., 1995.

21 Ibid.

22 The fact that these documents were in Arabic and that all official laws in the Saudi state would include honouring God by naming Him (The Saudi Network n.d.), appears not to have been considered.

23 Contrary to the assertion of Mark E. Hanshaw (2010: 13), the earlier case of *Nakhleh* v. *Chemical Construction Corporation* (1973) 359 F.Supp. 357 did not decide that public policy would deprive a plaintiff of rights he may have acquired under the law of Saudi Arabia. Rather, it held there was a 'triable issue' as to whether Saudi Arabian or New York Law applied and no public policy issue prevented such a consideration.

24 Although not a commercial case, a similar decision and rationale was provided by the Californian Court of Appeal in *Karson* v. *Soleimani* (2010 WL 2992071 (Cal App 2 Dist)) in its dismissal of an order of the Superior Court of Los Angeles on the ground of *forum non conveniens*. In this case, in consideration of its equitable jurisdiction, the

court had to consider the legal system of Iran and determined California, rather than Iran, was the most suitable location to decide an action for damages arising out of the probate in Iran of the appellant's father. A unanimous court decided Iran did not respect due process of law, as an American court would understand it. The respondent had failed to show that Iran had an independent judiciary and that that judiciary, at the practical level, was not under the influence of executive and religious authorities. The court also noted that the testimony of two women were worth the testimony of one man and that inheritance laws favoured Muslims over non-Muslims (the appellants were Baha'i in this instance), and mention even 'Baha'i blood is considered "mobah", meaning Baha'is may be killed with impunity.' (at 8–9). As the respondent had the burden of proving California was not the appropriate forum and that Iran was more suitable, and had failed to adduce any evidence to rebut the above, the Appeal Court upheld the appeal.

25 For a recent confirmation of the explicit distinctions being drawn between contract and tortious disputes, and choice of law, see *Teece* v. *Kuwait Finance House (Bahrain)* (2014 WL 2186887 (ND Cal)). Although the contractual agreement had stated its terms were subject to the law of Bahrain (and therefore to principles of Islamic Law), the plaintiffs contended the law of California applied, and the defendants that the Law of Bahrain or California could apply. The court determined (at 2) that as this action was not based in contract but on tort, and that as the plaintiff was a resident of California, the laws of California would apply. No other justification for choice of law was provided.

26 None of the established authorities determined *ghaṣb* could be constituted without intention, though the court assumes 'intention' here means the same as they would understand it in American law.

27 The position of the Ḥanbali School corresponds, in its terms, to the Shāfiʿī, Hanafi and Maliki positions outlined above.

28 This was because it was not an 'orthodox contract of sale', but rather an engineered financing agreement; see p. 12.

29 The court does not mention *Beximco v Shamil Bank.*

30 Ibid., at para. 17.

31 In a decision involving tax treatment rather than choice of law, the First-Tier Tribunal Tax Chamber also required clear evidence of religious motivation to avoid an IBF contract being construed in the same way as a conventional finance agreement. See *Project Blue Ltd* .v. *The Commissioners for Her Majesty's Review and Customs* [2013] UKFTT (TC) (Official Transcript 2013 WL 3550423).

32 For a summary of American Bankruptcy law, see Skeel 1998.

33 Though analysts argued it had grown too fast and purchased huge assets in the USA for which it did not have the relevant market knowledge; in effect, the company had over-extended. See further, Kureshi 2013.

34 Comprising an aggressive US hedge company who had acquired the debt at a discount following debt sales by one of the bank's original partners: European Islamic Investment Bank (Kureshi 2013).

35 It was argued first, that the proposed deal had only received a *fatwa* from one scholar on the Sharīʿah Advisory Board when, under AAOIFI Rules applicable in Bahrain, you needed three. Second, the refinancing was not a *murābaḥah* but an organised *tawarruq* (or monetisation), amounting to a 'disguised loan with interest (riba)' [para. 30]. This was supported by the fact neither one of the parties physically delivered any metals to the other (so no actual transfer took place as required under Sharīʿah). This is a similar objection to the murābaḥah in *Symphony Gems*; namely, that the 'seller' never had actual or constructive ownership of the sale item.

36 So their entire claim was based on misunderstanding of the powers and duties of a court-appointed receiver – see p. 9.

37 This says nothing of any potential challenges under consumer protection legislation and whether the mortgages are, in fact, Sharīʿah-compliant and have all of the necessary procedures in place to ensure their operations remain so.

38 Mr Helou would be approximate to our first kind of separatist. See further, Chapter 2.

39 Also there are banking cases before the Saudi Arabian Board of Grievances in which parties have sought to have enforced judgments of the English courts, but have been turned down on the basis of the absence of any evidence of reciprocal recognition of Saudi Arabian judgments in English courts (McMillen 2001: 1200).

40 See *Petroleum Development (Trucial Coasts) Ltd.* v. *Sheikh of Abu Dhabi* (1951); *Ruler of Qatar v. International Marine Oil Co. Ltd.* (1953). Both are cited by Colon (2011: 413–14).

41 See Hirsch 2010; and confirmed in interview with Shaykh Siddiqui in November 2013, in Nuneaton, Coventry, UK.

42 'Legal Framework and Cross Border Transactions for Islamic Financing', 22 May 2007, Istana Hotel Kuala Lumpur.

Conclusion

> The distinction between religious belief and its manifestation may be an artificial one, and unacceptable to much religion. That admission does not solve the problem of whether some genuine religious practices should be constrained, or even banned altogether, even in a free and democratic society. However much religion should be protected from the arbitrary power of the state, it has to be recognized that some forms of religion are pathological, and cause great harm, by any normal human standard ... The problem is what criteria it can draw on to distinguish between acceptable and unacceptable behaviour.
>
> Roger Trigg, *Equality, Freedom and Religion* (2012a: 111)

In this book we have sought to explore two matters: first, the extent to which Western Common Law States have been able to and should accommodate Muslims and their religious practices; and second, whether Muslims, as informed by their practice and understanding of Sharīʿah, have the capacity to participate in a liberal democratic society and want accommodation in the first place. These two questions, as all matters of conscience, are intensely personal. They pose dilemmas for the authors who, as practising Muslims, are in effect crafting justifications for how they would like to be treated by the state in which they live as well as for others who share (at least in part) the same religious and civilisational motivations. This does not fit the neutral traditions of the liberal academic establishment and we can stand charged as biased.

Yet it is our bias and religious voices which a secular political and legal establishment needs to hear if it is to truly comprehend the seriousness of the issues which are at stake. The willingness of the State to include and recognise the specificities and particularities of religious identity, to provide the space in which they can manifest their religious identity, as we are increasingly seeing with the unfolding refugee crisis in Europe, can promote a sense of fidelity and loyalty to the State which provides that sanctuary. This is the same for Muslims as it is for Christians and others who are fleeing persecution. By the same token, a reluctance or refusal of the State to provide space, to recognise the particularities and importance of religion in the formation of personal identity, sends out a signal of exclusion and rejection to those who see their religious belief and its manifestation as the most important part of who they are. They regard their religious identity as no more susceptible to change as their gender or race which is increasingly seen (at least in the West) as socially constructed. If the West can accommodate different racial and ethnic groups, then why can it not accommodate Muslims? If the moral underpinning of Common Law is respect for individual autonomy, then surely the individual autonomy of Muslims needs to be respected as equally as those of racial or ethnic groups? Acceptance of the latter but refusal of the former smacks not only of duplicitous standards, but also fuels the propaganda machines of religious extremists seeking recruits in increasingly marginalised Muslim communities.

But is it 'accommodation' that we all want? We discussed this problematic concept in our opening chapter and questioned whether the sense of 'unilateral favour' it sometimes implies is the most appropriate in our multicultural and pluralistic settings. The term sends out a signal that one's presence is merely tolerated as an 'other' rather than conveying a sense of belonging. It is particularly invidious, when articulated at the community level, if the 'favours' afforded to Muslims would appear to indicate a non-application of a rule that otherwise applies to all or that Muslims in some way would be receiving 'special treatment'. We argue that there is no evidence that Muslims want 'special treatment' – across our jurisdictions, and especially in the form of parallel laws. The political climate and growing sense of 'Islamophobia' also indicates that none of our State jurisdictions would be willing to provide 'special treatment' in any event.

If, on the other hand, accommodation means simply 'recognition', that would appear more compatible with a liberal democratic society's commitment to equality, multiculturalism and pluralism. It is important, however, that Muslims are recognised not as an ethnic or 'cultural group' but as a religious entity and for that recognition to be afforded potentially to all who claim a religious affiliation. As Roger Trigg has argued, 'religion, or at least the impulses that help to produce the characteristic features of so-called religious belief, is a basic component of humanity' (Trigg 2012a: 24). We would also reiterate that being able to practise or manifest a religious belief is a fundamental human right. Unless there are important and substantive countervailing considerations that should otherwise limit its expression, liberal theory would imply that Muslims, along with other religious groups, have a fundamental right to legal recognition of their religious practices.

'Recognition', however, does not necessitate 'establishment' or 'facilitation'. As our discussions of case law in the American context have shown, State support for or interference with religious institutions can be construed as 'establishing' religion and run counter to the First Amendment of the American Constitution[1] and contrary to similar provisions in Australia and the Canadian Charter of Rights and Freedoms. Rather, we suggest that 'recognition' entails only an acknowledgment through law of the *relevance* of a person's religious identity, be they Muslim or otherwise. It may be that a person's religious identity and needs to manifest that religious belief will be outweighed by other factors and broader community welfare considerations. But an acknowledgment that certain laws and administrative processes may impact disproportionately on persons because of their religious beliefs should be weighed as an important factor that needs substantive justification before any State interferences are deemed legally and constitutionally valid. This will go some way to conveying a message, to Muslims at least, that they 'matter' and are not just 'subjects' of an imperialist law.

It follows from this that Muslims should not expect all of their religious practices, even where they have a base, or an apparent justification in their religious texts, to be endorsed or excused by Common Law Courts or the legislatures. Roger Trigg has argued Western Common Law States should only provide '*reasonable* accommodation' (Trigg 2012a: 123–25) which, in our parlance, translates as legal recognition of religious practice but subject to reasonable *limitations*. But in constitutional terms, we argue these State actions should still be subject to 'strict scrutiny' and their actions not validated unless the means chosen are proportionate to legitimate ends. As political minorities unlikely to wield the necessary influence on political majorities in a democracy,[2] Muslims should expect judicial protection in the event of legislative 'overbite' and intrusion into their religious space.

This also implies that it should not be left to minorities to justify why their practices should be legalised or 'accommodated'. In evidential terms, the burden (and the legal resources necessary to establish it) should be on State authorities to justify why their religious practices should be curtailed. In a liberal democracy, power and resources are disproportionately held in the hands of the majority. To impose that burden not only on a minority, but also a peculiarly marginalised and, if public opinion polls are correct, increasingly disliked minority, would impose great hardship and injustice as they navigate the discretionary world of administration. In this sense, therefore, accommodation is part of the discourse of equality and non-discrimination. It advocates equality *in substance* as opposed to it being only *in form*.

While this approach to accommodation of religion and of Muslims under Common Law appeals to equality, it sits uncomfortably with secularism, that other integral component of liberal democracies. As we mentioned in the Introduction and chapter one, however, secularism does not necessarily entail absence of religion in the public space. Secularism can be 'strong', as in the laic democracies of France and Turkey, and exclude religion from the public sphere for fear it may 'contaminate' the neutrality of justice and the Rule of Law. But it can also be 'soft', permitting religious expression in the public space, though without favouring one version of it over another.[3] So long as all communities are equally able to shape that space, there is no reason for a liberal democratic state to exclude religious groups from it.

In order for Muslims to be able to make use of that space, some argue it necessitates embracing an 'overlapping consensus' and utilising Rawlsian 'public reason'[4] or 'civic reason'.[5] If they are to communicate in that public space Muslims require shared goals and to articulate a common language. They may have their own religious conceptions of 'rights' and 'freedom', for example, but they cannot come to terms without first agreeing there are such things as 'rights' and 'freedom'. Moreover, if they want to have any impact on policy and political decision-making, they cannot fall back on their religious texts and assert simply, 'Islām says this.. '. Arguments for legal recognition of Islamic rules and precepts, they argue, must be founded on independent rational arguments – in other words, 'public reason'.

The problem with this approach, as the thrust of our argument suggests, is that it stifles religious expression in its own right and smacks of the 'strong' secularism more evident in continental Europe. It may provide a mechanism for contributions by religious groups and Muslims in the civic arena, but ironically asks them to articulate them behind a secular veil. Why should Muslims, or any religious group, be invisible and forced to 'to leave behind their religious convictions when they enter the public square'?[6] This is especially true when their vision and understanding of the world can only be in religious terms. While it may not be impossible for a Muslim woman to make a non-religious reasoned argument which justifies her wish to wear *ḥijāb*, for example, *her* reason is that she believes it is a religious obligation which brings her closer to piety and an obedient servant of God. The 'public reason' claim is that wearing these head and facial coverings (in the case of *niqāb*) is an expression of modesty and avoids sexual objectification of women. But when it comes to the public square, these items of clothing are seen as symbols of male oppression and as protection for men from their own sexual desires. In the heat and majoritarian dynamics of contemporary political debate, her 'public reason' is almost certainly 'trumped' by the feminist 'public reason' discourse of equality. In short, religious expression is not given equal weighting to secular expression which, in our view, short changes the meaning of a *liberal* democracy and the value of individual autonomy.

Our argument, then, is that legal recognition of Islām is compatible with 'soft' secularism so long as that does not deprive other groups and individuals who may not have any religious view an equal right to shape the public space. Secularism in a liberal democracy must imply freedom of expression and that must include religious articulation. It may or may not convince others in the public space, but it is a voice that has an equal right to be heard and, to use Miroslav Volf's expression, should be able to be presented as a 'life worth living'.

To take the discussion back to Roger Trigg's main point, legal recognition of religion and of Islām does not mean the State should recognise *all* religious viewpoints or all interpretations of Islām. Trigg argues only those interpretations that pass a threshold of 'reasonableness' should be recognised. In the tradition of the Common Law, this is likely to be worked out on a case by case basis and may change over time. Worked out, in the words of Oliver Wendell Holmes, not through 'logic but experience' and 'the felt necessities of the time',[7] this must incorporate considerations of public policy and what interpretations of Islamic tradition are consistent with contemporary constitutional values and principles as well as international standards of human rights.

We argued in Chapter 2 that the Islamic legal tradition, the Sharī'ah, like the Common Law, is not a rigid edifice but has evolved over time, producing a multiplicity of opinion thereby providing flexibility to Muslim communities in different times and places. The Sharīʿah, the Islamic legal and moral code, is the well-spring drawn upon by Muslims whether they are in the majority or minority to help them live an 'Islamic' way of life. Knowledge of it enables the Muslim to define and distinguish the 'good' from the 'bad' as well as to plot a course in life which they believe will assist them in the Hereafter. While it does not define them as people, individually or culturally (personality and identity are complex composites), for a Muslim to be without Sharīʿah, is like a plant in a desert without access to water. Eventually, it will wither away and die. Although the Sharīʿah is perceived by many in the West as synonymous with incapacitating and corporal punishments, the legal and moral code normatively encompasses every aspect of a Muslim's life. The Sharīʿah is followed even in the absence of criminal punishments because it provides the framework for personal and family life. Culture also plays a role, certainly, but the precise role it plays is defined by Sharīʿah – however that might be interpreted. In a very real sense, therefore, to be *anti*-Sharīʿah is to be *anti*-Muslim and to prohibit Sharīʿah, in all its aspects, is to prohibit a Muslim's way of life.

The Sharīʿah, however, is capable of being interpreted in a variety of ways, some of which are quite clearly contrary to Western constitutional values, international Human Rights and Common Law notions of the Rule of Law. In Chapter 2, we grouped followers of these types of interpretations together as 'puritanical separatists'. None of these groups have an inclination to integrate and, where they exist in America, Australia, Canada and the UK, they promote separatism, hatred of non-Muslims, exclusive control of women and freedom from State interference. In addition, these are the groups that are the most active in rallying Islamist and violent opposition in Syria and Iraq, and attracting youth in the West to fight in these conflicts. They do not seek accommodation with or in the West; nor should governments in the Common Law jurisdictions of the West seek accommodation with them. We suggest, therefore, that it cannot be good public policy to provide legal recognition of any of these groups, or their affiliates, directly or indirectly. Their positions are also extreme interpretations in that they do not represent the beliefs and practices of the vast majority of Muslims, of whatever denomination. Necessarily, this would make such interpretations 'unreasonable'.

It follows, therefore, those litigants who appear in Common Law Courts and who make Sharīʿah claims which derive exclusively from the above sources, also should not receive legal recognition. This is especially true in the Criminal Law where defendants rely on so-called 'Sharīʿah defences'[8] or in family custody cases where one of the parents exposes the children to extremist influences (see Chapter 4 [30–31]). That does not mean that all their substantive claims should be ignored, as some of their rights and interests may already coincide with substantive elements of the relevant domestic laws. Where, however, their case rests upon 'freedom of religion', it should be rejected on grounds of public policy or 'unreasonableness'.

On the reverse side of this coin, we argue that the Sharīʿah can be interpreted in such a way which enables Muslims to engage positively with all communities in societies governed by the Common Law while still retaining a firm Islamic identity. We term these 'integrationist'. They may be rooted in conservative, *madhhab* or School-based opinions, or in the more reformist approaches of contemporary Islamist thinkers. It may be that particular Muslim communities will need to look beyond their 'traditional' school or the opinions they have customarily followed, and select the most suitable opinions to meet the exigencies of their situations from scholars belonging to other schools.[9] So long as these opinions are deemed legitimate by community leaders and local scholars (which requires a process of internal debate), there seems little to oppose this. But it is something for the Muslim communities themselves to determine and develop organically; it is not for governments to dictate, and that includes any particular formulation of 'an Islamic Law of Minorities'.

Similarly, it is not for any Common Law judge to determine the Islamic *canon* when matters of Sharīʿah law come before the Common Law Courts. Common Law judges do not share in the set of beliefs which underpin the Sharīʿah law, nor do they have the necessary expertise or training to make such a conclusive determination. For the most part, courts have stressed that they are secular and resisted the temptation to give 'certainty' to ambiguous Islamic positions or to provide a definitive Islamic interpretation. In commercial conflicts of law cases, however, the American courts have proved the exception to the rule and purported to define Islamic doctrine. Unlike in our other jurisdictions, matters of 'foreign law' are deemed questions of law rather than of fact and are matters for the court to determine. Federal Civil Procedural Rules have even empowered the courts to disregard expert testimony in favour of their own research and opinion (see Chapter 5 [10–13]). During colonial times, the efforts of colonial judges to interpret Islamic texts through the interpretive prisms of Equity, Natural Justice and Public Interest produced what became known as 'Anglo-Muhammadan Law'.[10] It was neither English Law nor Sharīʿah law, but a localised hybrid of the two. It seems American judges are now doing the same, producing their own 'Sharīʿa Americana'.

Other than in these commercial cases before the American courts, generally speaking Common Law judges[11] across our jurisdictions have reacted to Sharīʿah and Muslim claims with singular reference to domestic secular legal categories. In many instances, that has resulted in satisfactory solutions. As we observed in Chapter 3, judges have deemed valid unregistered religious legal marriages through notions of 'Common Law marriage', 'voidability', 'marriage ceremony' and an intention to comply with marriage statutory regulations. They have also upheld a Muslim woman's rights to her dowry (*mahr*) by applying principles of contract law (see Chapter 4 [16]); recognised an informal Islamic divorce (*ṭalāq*) not even registered overseas (Chapter 4 [27]) and put pressure on Muslim husbands to divorce their wives in Islamic law when already divorced in secular domestic law (Chapter 4 [38]). They have even implemented a devout Muslim mother's wishes for her daughter to go to an Islamic school on the basis it is in the 'best interests of the child', in direct opposition to a father's wish for the child to go to a secular school (Chapter 4 [31]).

Also in Chapter 4, we noted how the Common Law Courts across our jurisdictions have been sensitive to Islamic identity in criminal cases and adopted 'nuanced procedures' (Conclusion [2]). In terms of process, Muslim men and women have been able to wear clothing, such as the *ḥijāb*, *niqāb* and turban – signifying Islamic identity – so long as communication before the court is not obstructed. In criminal investigation, there is now authority for Muslims to object to invasive post-mortem procedures on religious grounds (Conclusion [5]). Courts have also been careful to accord Muslim accused persons due process, applying procedures that protect them from undue prejudice (Conclusion [8]) and allowing them to adduce cultural and religious evidence through experts where relevant in their defence (Conclusion [9–10]). This has included adducing cultural evidence to reduce culpability in murder cases, notwithstanding the evident shift from subjective to objective standards in provocation defences (Conclusion [18–22]). In respect of the rights of Muslim victims, the courts have also enhanced sentences by accepting the relevance of harm to a victim's religious reputation in the community through Victim Impact Statements (Conclusion [14]).

In Chapter 5, we have seen secular courts in commercial cases enforcing Islam*icate* contracts. In conflicts of law and choice of law clauses in contractual disputes, American Common Law Courts have applied principles of Freedom of Contract and party autonomy to enforce contracts even where they refer explicitly to Sharīʿah law (Chapter 5 [9]). They have also refused to intervene in religious arbitrations (Chapter 5 [27]) and upheld the Sharīʿah content of Islamic Banking and Finance contracts in application of bankruptcy laws (Chapter 5 [19–21]). Although their decisions have caused difficulties for the IBF industry, the English courts have also been prepared to uphold Sharīʿah-based agreements so long as they are clear, explicit and contain sufficient evidence the parties are not intending to operate in line with 'conventional' commercial principles (Chapter 5 [17, 29]).

It is also true, however, that there are numbers of cases across our jurisdictions in family, commercial and criminal cases, in which the outcomes do not accord with any known interpretations of Sharīʿah law and cannot be said to recognise positively an Islamic identity whether directly or indirectly. An English Court has construed a marriage between a consenting Muslim woman and an intellectually handicapped Muslim man as a 'forced' marriage even where its ostensible purpose was for the handicapped man's welfare (Chapter 4 [12]). American courts have also deprived Muslim women of their dowries, deeming the latter invalid 'pre-nuptial agreements' (Chapter 4 [18–19]). Courts across our four jurisdictions have also rarely recognised a Muslim man's unilateral right to divorce (*ṭalāq*), even where registered overseas (the case noted above representing an exception). In commercial contract cases, English courts have invalidated contracts requiring interpretation based on the 'Glorious Sharīʿah' on grounds of uncertainty (Chapter 5 [15–16]). They have also interpreted terms contrary to the express subjective intentions of both parties (Chapter 5 [16]). In tortious personal injury cases, American courts have refused to apply common Islamic laws and procedures on grounds of public policy (Chapter 5 [10]). Also, in criminal sentencing, where Islamic identity and belief has been deemed relevant, courts have been more ready to regard them relevant to aggravating factors than to mitigating ones (Conclusion [10–13]).

In some of these cases, the courts were being asked to interpret statutory legislation and so, to a certain extent, the options available to the court were limited. In others, the courts were confronted with traditional Common Law notions of needs for 'certainty' and the very understandable wish to avoid being seen pontificating an Islamic view. There are also, of course, evident examples of courts seeing conflicts in values between Islamic and Western 'world views', particularly in relation to women, notions of due process, parental discipline and the rights of the child. It is pure conjecture whether the courts in another era would have decided in the same way. But we should note that these decisions have taken place against the backdrop of the events post-9/11, 'Islamophobia' and increasing security fears (Chapter 2 [32–46]). The courts have provided a forum not just for Muslims to manifest their religious identities but also for the courts to reassert what it means to be American, Australian, British or Canadian and the civilian values which bind all together. In some cases, the courts have looked to find common ground;[12] in others they have chastised the Muslim parties for holding to 'traditional' cultural values akin to rural areas of their countries of origin (see Conclusion [11–12]).

There is no single, 'one-size-fits-all' solution to the problems faced by Muslims and their 'hosts' in Western Common Law countries, notwithstanding the proximity of cultures and the sharing of legal tradition. Each country has its own constitutional framework and sets of cultural values that will frame inevitably the 'cultural conversations' which take place in the contexts of legal problems and conflicts. In our analysis, however, the rules of evidence and procedural law can better manage this conflict and promote liberal democratic values of participation as well as greater sensitivity to Muslims and their Islamic traditions. Not only should Muslims have an unequivocal right to offer and respond to 'cultural/religious evidence' where relevant, but it should also be presented in such a manner that it promotes openness and is less tainted by bias.

The field of expert evidence is not without controversy and is looked at with some scepticism, particularly in the United States.[13] Further, fears of 'advocacy bias' and usurping the tribunal of fact (whether judge or jury) are as evident, if not more so, with cultural expert evidence than with other types of 'scientific' expert evidence. Across jurisdictions, there has been a move towards alleviating perceptions of bias by 'hot-tubbing' in which experts from both sides give evidence concurrently, have pre-trial meetings and even offer joint reports.[14] The emphasis is on consensus and on achieving a more well-rounded view of the events than the climate of adversarial Common Law Courts would normally permit. Rather than their testimony lasting several days, the tribunal of fact is able to observe responses and counter-responses by experts on matters where they disagree in real time. Also, where a problem may cut across many different subject disciplines, having a panel of experts with a variety of perspectives address the same problem facilitates juror/judge education and a more holistic understanding of the problem.[15]

In a context of conflicting Sharīʿah opinions, cultural variations and gender disparities, a panel of experts combining a variety of academic disciplines (including sociology, anthropology, law and theology) with local community expertise, would be both useful for the tribunal of fact and appropriate, given the frequently multi-layered nature of the problems. In the civil context, there are no obvious barriers in taking this approach where such evidence would be relevant. Even in the United States, where the spirit of adversarialism is strongest and has lawyers most resistant to change, there is nothing in the Federal Rules of Evidence which prohibits 'hot-tubbing'. In Australia, Canada and the UK, civil procedure rules already allow for and encourage, though do not dictate this approach. So far, however, 'hot-tubbing' has not been extended to criminal cases because of issues surrounding availability of experts, expense and implications for the burden of proof. We would argue that given the public interest dimensions of Criminal Law and the consequences for both accused persons and victims, government support and financial assistance to develop expert panels would be an important and valuable next step.

The above discussion suggests that recognition of Islām and Sharīʿah in Common Law jurisdictions does not require fundamental changes in terms of doctrine. Common Law is sufficiently robust and flexible to accommodate and adjust to 'reasonable' interpretations of Sharīʿah as it is to reasonable interpretations of other religious beliefs. The necessary changes we advocate are primarily evidential and procedural and, in our opinion, enhance rather than detract from Common Law processes. They will better enable judges to respond to particular fact situations where resolution to a dispute will depend on a proper and more complete understanding of Sharīʿah and Muslim behaviours.

Moreover, the substantive changes we advocate are more a reaffirmation of liberal principle than the incorporation of Shariʿah 'transplants'. At its heart, a liberal conception of law and justice respects a space for private ordering and not to intervene unless to protect others from harm. Unless there is clear evidence of harm or potential harm, this means that in the context of Family Law, we can see no mandate for the Liberal State to dictate how a couple are to marry, divorce and parent. This does not mean that a state cannot reserve a right to intervene, for that might imply parallel jurisdictions otherwise. Rather, it implies that Muslims and other religious communities, should be free to administer their own family relations through community structures, but under the loose supervision of the State. So long as bodies such as the Muslim Arbitration Tribunal in England remain subject to judicial review, and all of the parties genuinely consent to choose this form of conflict resolution, Muslims remain under the regime of the Common Law, and it is no more the business of the State. To assume such a regime will necessarily oppress women denies Muslim women individual agency and is an affront not only to their religion, but also to their gender. We leave to another forum whether such reaffirmation of liberal principle would also entail the repeal of state marriage laws.

In business matters, a Liberal State holds the principle of freedom of contract sacrosanct. If parties contract explicitly that the terms of their contract are subject to particular Sharīʿah laws, and Muslim expert witnesses can depose to their existence, content and limitation, the terms of that contract are no more uncertain than contracts governed by any other 'foreign law'. Whether the context is the Sharīʿah business law as contextualised in Saudi Arabia, or 'Sharīʿah principles' distilled into financing contracts by Muslim bankers and financiers, the principle of freedom of contract governs them both the same. The fact that the contracts appear 'hybrid' is merely an indication of legal pluralism at work within the Common Law and how both the parties have determined where one norm ends and another norm begins. In this case, the parties are choosing the *substance* of a Sharīʿah agreement, but the *form* of the Common Law to enforce it.

In matters related to Crime, a Liberal State protects civil liberties and places limitations on State Power. The problem is that the State legislatures have become too powerful and undermined individual rights under the guise of security and affirmation of 'Western' (please do not read 'liberal') values. There has been too much law and order legislation which has resulted in the criminalisation of the Muslim community with many of them feeling they are 'suspect communities'. There is a strong case for courts to recapture the high ground and to reassert the rule of law by protecting civil liberties, human rights, including the right to practice and manifest a religious faith. This is true in respect of religious groups as a whole. It is especially true of minority religious groups in the West, such as Muslims, who are unable to protect themselves through the democratic process. While not all of our judiciaries have the constitutional mandate to trump and strike down offending legislation, they can still subject it to principles of 'strict scrutiny', proportionality and equality. In this instance, it is not the form of Common Law that matters, but its substance, so that Muslims are able to lead as free a life as non-Muslims in Common Law jurisdictions. Outside of the legislative context, there are unresolved issues within Criminal Law as to the role of consent and the subjective/objective distinction, not to mention the public/private divide. As a matter of liberal principle, Muslims should be able to avail themselves of a general defence of 'consent' in the light of religious rites, where they have capacity. This preserves and promotes their moral and personal autonomy. Also in alleged violent assaults, the default standard of mental culpability should be subjective rather than objective. This would take into account any so-called 'cultural defence' as the tribunal of fact would be empowered to judge an accused in accordance with all of the circumstances, including the circumstances as s/he perceived them.

Common Law states, indeed all states, rarely act consistently in accordance with principle. The business of life is too messy for that. There will always be erosions of civil liberties and interference in the lives of individuals and families where public welfare dictates. Considerations of public welfare, however, should not be directed solely or predominantly at one group. Race, gender, ethnicity, religion – it does not matter. For the law that we have is a liberal 'Common Law' and a pluralist one at that.

Notes

1 See Michael W. McConnell (1992), 'Accommodation of Religion: An Update and a Response to the Critics', 60 *George Washington Law Review*, 685, at 686.
2 This follows the constitutional theory of John Hart Ely. See further, *Democracy and Distrust: A Theory of Judicial Review* (1980), Harvard University Press, 135–80.
3 See further, Lorenzo Zucca's discussion of András Sajó, in, 'A Secular Europe: Law and Religion in the European Constitutional Landscape' (2012), 23.
4 On John Rawls, see 'Political Liberalism' (New York: Columbia Press, 1993). For a discussion of Rawls in the context of multiculturalism, see G.F. Gaus, 'The place of religious belief in public reason liberalism', in M. Dimova-Cookson and P.M.R. Stirk (eds), *Multiculturalism and Moral Conflict* (Oxford: Routledge, 2010), pp. 19–37.
5 Abdullahi An-Na'im, 'Islam and the Secular State: Negotiation the Future of Shariʿa', (Cambridge, MA: Harvard University Press, 2008), pp. 6–8. It should be noted that An-Na'im's focus was on the Muslim world and the need for secular states in Muslim countries. His argument, and certainly that of John Rawls, however, applies equally in the countries of the Liberal West where Muslims are a minority.
6 Gustav Steinhardt, 'Rawls on Religion and Public Reason', *Colloquium*, 5 September 2013, at: https://lucian.uchicago.edu/blogs/colloquium/2013/09/05/rawls-on-religion-and-public-reason/ (accessed 30 September 2015).
7 Oliver Wendell Holmes Jr (2000), 'The Common Law,' Lecture 1, para 1, at: www.hourofthetime.com/1-LF/November2012/Hour_Of_The_Time_11132012-The%20Common%20Law_Holmes.pdf (accessed 30 September 2015).
8 See Chapter 6, 22–31, particularly the case of 'Muslim vigilantes' (at 28–31).
9 This applies to matters of family law, such as women securing a divorce (Chapter 4, [28–30]); commercial contracts incorporating interest (Chapter 5, [4–5]), and criminal assaults amounting to female genital mutilation (Conclusion, [23–24]).
10 For examples from the Indian subcontinent, see Asaf Ali Asghar Fyzee, 'Outlines of Muhammadan Law' (Oxford: Oxford University Press, 1964). For examples from South East Asia, see M.B. Hooker, 'Legal Pluralism: An Introduction to Colonial and New-Colonial laws' (Oxford: Oxford University Press, 1975). See generally, Strawson, J., 'Revisiting Islamic Law: Marginal Notes from Colonial History', *Griffith Law Review*, (2003) 12 (2): 362–83. 'Orientalism and Legal Education in the Middle East: Reading Frederic Goadby's Introduction to the Study of Law', *Legal Studies*, (2001) 21 (4): 664–78.
11 For an exception in the criminal context, see the Canadian decision of *R v Ammar Nouasria*, discussed in Conclusion, [13–14], where the Court plunged into deep waters after conducting its own 'research'.
12 See the Australian case of *Helou v Nguyen*, discussed in Chapter 5, [25–26].
13 See Elizabeth Reifert (2011), 'Getting into the Hot Tub: How the U.S. Could Benefit from Australia's Concept of "Hot Tubbing" ', *University of Det Mercy L.R.*, 89: 103.
14 See E. Arnold and E. Sorriano (2013), 'The Recent Revolution of Expert Evidence in Selected Common Law Jurisdictions Around the World', CVPL, at: https://cicbv.ca/wp-content/uploads/2010/10/2012-CICBV-Research-Paper-CVPL-FINAL.pdf (accessed on 8 October 2015).
15 On the general advantages (and problems) of 'hot-tubbing', see Gary Edmond, 'Merton and the Hot Tub: Scientific Conventions and Expert Evidence in Australian Civil Procedure', *Law and Contemporary Problems*, (2009) 72: 158–89.

Glossary

'adālah trustworthiness; justice

'aqīdah the rules of Islamic belief; the creed

bida' innovation

birr virtue

Dā'ish a belittling Arabic acronym for 'Islamic State of Iraq and the Levant'

ḍarūrah necessity

diyyah reparation; a specific payment paid to a victim, or the victim's family, for an injury, or killing, carried out intentionally or unintentionally

fatwa – al-fatāwā ruling/rulings given by a Mufti in response to a question pertaining to the religious law

fiqh the substantive law deduced by scholars from the religious sources, the Qur'ān and Sunnah

Fiqh al-'Aqallīyyāt the 'Law of Minorities'

fitnah civil strife

gharar uncertainty/hazard

ghishsh* or *tadlees deliberate misrepresentation

Ḥadīth sayings, actions and agreements of Prophet Muḥammad; the second source of the Sharī'ah

ḥājah need

ḥalāl the lawful

ḥarām the unlawful

al-ḥayyā modesty

ḥijāb an item of clothing covering all of the hair and the neck, but revealing the face

ḥisbah market authority or body for promoting virtue and preventing vice

al-ḥudūd non-discretionary criminal punishments mentioned specifically in the Qur'ān and Ḥadīth

ḥukm judgement/ religious ruling

iḥsān perfection

al-Ijmā' Juristic Consensus

ijtihād exercise of effort by a top religious scholar to deduce the ruling from the religious sources

'irḍ honour

al-istisḥāb presumption of continuity
'itizāl isolation/separation
izzat honour: South Asia
jāhiliyyah ignorance
kāfir non-Muslim
katb āl-kitāb Islamic marriage ceremony surrounding the formation of an Islamic marriage contract
khalwat unlawful proximity
khitān circumcision
khul' divorce (one sought solely by the wife)
kufr blasphemy
liwāṭ sodomy
madhāhib Schools of Islamic jurisprudence
madrasah institution of Islamic instruction
makrūhāt discouraged (pl., sing. ***makrūh***)
muḥarramāt a prohibited act (pl., sing. ***muḥarram***)
mahr dowry (paid by the husband to the wife)
mandūbāt encouraged (pl., sing. ***mandūb***)
maqāṣid purpose (pl., sing. ***maqṣūd***)
maṣlaḥah public benefit; public interest
matam flagellation
al-mu'āmalāt transactional rules and principles
mubāḥāt permitted (pl., sing. ***mubāḥ***)
mujaddid renewer
mujtahid muṭlaq complete ***ijtihad*** (highest rank accorded to a religious Islamic scholar)
munkar vice
murtaddūn apostate (pl., sing. ***murtadd***)
mustaftī the one asking for a ***fatwa***
mut'ah temporary marriage
muttaqī perfect believer
nafaqah maintenance payment given to the wife, or for child support, or to assist poor parents
nafs inner self
nikāḥ marriage
Qāḍī Islamic judge
al-Qā'idah the 'Base'; group formerly led by Usāmah bin Lāden
qaṭ'u cutting
quwwah; qahr force
Ramaḍān the fasting month
rasūl messenger
ra'y opinion
ribā unlawful gain
bi-rifq with gentleness
rukhṣah exception

ṣadaq marriage payment

sariqah theft

Shīʿah lit. the 'partisans'; the second largest historical sect, who claim to follow the teachings of the fourth Caliph, Imām 'Alī ibn Abi Ṭālib, and his blood descendants

Shāfi'īs followers of Imām Al-Shāfi'ī, the eponym of one of the main Four Schools of Sunnite jurisprudence

Sharī'ah the revealed religious law

shurūṭ prerequisite (pl., sing., ***sharṭ***)

ṣukūk a deed or cheque (pl., sing., ***ṣakk***)

ṣulḥ mediation

taḥkīm arbitration

tajdīd renewal

takfīr excommunication

ṭalāq unilateral divorce

ṭalāq at-tafwīḍ delegated divorce

tamyīz age of discernment

ṭarīqah a spiritual movement under the guidance of a Sheikh

'ulemā' religious scholar (pl., sing. '***ālim***)

al-'urf/al-'ādat custom (a secondary source of Sharī'ah Law)

wājib obligation (sing., pl. ***wājibāt***)

walīmah wedding celebration

zakāh an Islamic levy (mandated in the Qur'ān and Sunnah, and distributed to specific categories of recipients, notably the poor)

zinā adultery and fornication

Bibliography

Legislation

Anti-Social Behaviour, Crime and Policing Act 2014 (UK)
Arbitration Act, 1991 (Ontario)
Arbitration Act, 1996 (UK)
Children and Families Act 2014 (UK)
Coroners Act (Northern Territories)
Coroners Act (SBC 2007)
Coroners Act 1996 (Western Australia)
Coroners Act 1997 (ACT)
Coroners Act 2003 (Queensland)
Coroners Act 2003 (South Australia)
Coroners Act 2008 (Victoria)
Coroners Act 2009 (NSW)
Coroners and Justice Act 2009
Crimes Act 1900 (NSW)
Criminal Code (Canada)
Criminal Justice and Public Order Act 1996 (UK)
Family Law Act 1975 (Cth)
Law Enforcement (Powers and Responsibilities) Act 2002 (NSW)
Marriage Act 1961 (Cth)
Model Postmortem Examinations Act 1954 (Fed)
Offences Against the Person Act 1861 (UK)
Police and Criminal Evidence Act 1984
Terrorism Act 2000 (UK)
The Marriage Act 1949 (UK)
Uniform Evidence Act 1998 (NSW)
Zero Tolerance for Barbaric Cultural Practices Act 2015 (Canada)

Cases

A v. *A* [2013] Fam. 51
Abd Alla v. *Mourssi* (2004) 680 N.W.2d 569
Abdirashid Mohamed Isse v. *Linda A Said* 2012 ONSC 1829
Abney v. *Paris* [2013] FMCA fam 7

AG Reference Nos 8, 9 and 10 of 2002 (Naved Mohammad and others) (2003) 1 Cr App Rep (S) 57.
AG's Reference No 51 of 2001 (2002) 1 Cr App Rep (S) 80
Aghili v. *Saadatnejadi* 958 S.W.2d 784 (1997)
Ahmad Fawzi Issa v. *Margaret Bradshaw* (2008, 2008 WL 8582098 (S.D. Ohio)
Akileh v. *Elchahal* 666 So. 2d 246 (Fla. Dist. Ct. App. 1996)
Alenezi v. *UM Financial*(2008) [2008] ONSC 60160
Al-Saedy v. *Musawi* [2010] EWHC 3293
A-M (A Child) [2006] EWCA Civ 1068
Andrew Iskandar [2012] NSWSC 149
Arrowsmith v. *UK* [1978] 3 EHHR 218
Aubrey v. *Ellerby* [2011] FMCA fam 535
Aziz v. *Aziz* 488 N.Y.S.2d 123 (Sup. Ct. 1985)
Basma Sulaiman v. *Walid Ahmed Al Juffali* [2002] 2 FCR 427 (UK)
Beximco (et al.) v. *Shamil Bank* (2004) [2004] EWCA Civ 19
Bridas Corp. v. *Unocal Corp* (2000) 16 S.W.3d 893 (Tex. App. 2000)
Central 1 Credit Union v. *UM Financial* (2011) ONSC 5612
Commonwealth of Pennsylvania v. *Reid* (2014, 99 A.3d 427)
CPS v. *Dresser* 911 SW 2d 18 – Tex: Court of Appeals, 8th Dist., 1995
Dajani v. *Dajani* 204 Cal. App. 3d 1387; 251 Cal. Rptr. 871 (1988)
Daubert v. *Merrell* 509 U.S. 579 (1993)
Dinal v. *Tohim* [2009] FamCA 540
El-Farra v. *Sayyed (et al.)* (2006) 365 Ark 209, 226 S.W. 3d 792
Essey v. *Elia* [2013] FCCA 1525
Essey v. *Ella* [2013] FCCA 1523
Farzana v. *Abdul Hamid* (2014) [2014] ONSC 4913
Freeman v. *State of Florida* [2003] WL 21338619 (Fla. Cir.Ct)
Green v. *R* (1997) 191 CLR 334)
Guven Abdul Yildiz (1983) 11 A. Crim.R. 115
Habibi-Fahnrich v. *Fahnrich* No. 46186/93 1995 WL 507388 (N.Y. Sup. Ct. July 10, 1995)
Hammoud v. *Hammoud* 2012 Mich. App. LEXIS 417, 1, 2012 WL 752044
Heiden v. *Kaufman* [2011] FMCA fam 478
Helou v. *Nguyen* [2014] NSWSC 22
Imperial Life Assurance Co. of Canada v. *Segundo Casteleiro Y Colmenares* [1967] S.C.R. 443
Investment Dār v. *Blom Developments Bank Sal* (2009) [2009] EWHC 3545 (Ch), 2009 WL 5386898
Islamic Investment Company of the Gulf (Bahamas) Ltd v. *Symphony Gems N.V. & Ors* (2002) WL 346969
Jivraj v. *Hashwani* [2011] IRLR 827; [2011] UKSC 40
Juma Mussa v. *Nikki Palmer-Mussa* 722 S.E.2d 608 (N.C. 2012)
Kargar 679 A2d 81 (Me 1996)
Kasun-Stojanovic v. *Kasun* [2007] FamCA 877
Khaddoura v. *Hammoud* [1998] 168 D.L.R, 4th 503 (Ont. Ct of Justice, Gen. Div)
Khalij Commercial Bank Ltd v. *Woods* (1985) 50 OR (2d) 446
Lilydale Cooperative Limited v. *Meyn Canada Inc.*, 2015 0NCA 281
Lodhi v. *Regina* [2006] NSWCCA 121
Marriage of Nemer Osman [1989] FamCA 78

Masciantonio v. *R* (1995) 183 CLR 58
Mohamed v. *Mohamed* (2012) NSWSC 852
Mohammed [2005] EWCA Crim 1880
Momin Khawaja (2010)
Najjarin v. *Houlayce* (1991)104 FLR 403
Najmi v. *Najmi* [2008] – Ohio – 4405
National Group for Communications and Computers (NGCC) v. *Lucent Technologies* (2004) 331 F.Supp. 2d 290
Odatalla v. *Odatalla* 810 A.2d 93
Ohio v. *Phelps* (1995) 100 Ohio App 3d 187 (1995)
Oltman & Harper (no 2) [2009] FamCA 1360
Project Blue Ltd v. *The Commissioners for Her Majesty's Review and Customs* [2013] UKFTT (TC)
Quereshi v. *Quereshi* [1971] 1 All ER 325
R v. *Abdul Haque Omarjee* [1995] VSC 94; [1995] VICSC 94
R v. *Ammar Nouasria*
R v. *Belghar* [2012] NSWCCA 86
R v. *D* (R) [2013] Eq LR 1034
R v. *Dincer* (1983), 1 VR 460
R v. *Duffy* [1949] 1 All ER 932 (1949)
R v. *Elomar, K. Cheikho, M. Cheikho, Hasan and Jamal* (2009)
R v. *G M Khan* [2001] NSWSC 1356
R v. *H* (2014) ONSC 36
R v. *Humaid* (2006) Carswell Ont 2278, 37 C.R. (6th)
R v. *Ibrahim and Iqbal* ([2011] EWCA Crim 3244)
R v. *Imran Khalil* (2004) 2 Cr App Rep (S) 24
R v. *Khawaja* 2010 ONCA 862
R v. *Mohammad Shafia (and others)* (2012, ONSC 1538)
R v. *Mohammed* [2004] VSC 423
R v. *MSK, MAK, and MMK* [2006] NSWSC 237
R v. *MSK, MAK, MRK and MMK* [2004] NSWSC 319
R v. *Mudarubba* [1951–76] NTJ 317
R v. *N.S.* [2012] 3 S.C.R. 726
R v. *Sadiqi* (2013 ONCA 250)
R v. *Sajad Qureshi* (2007)1 Cr App Rep (S) 85
R v. *Syed Mustafa* (2009) 2 Cr App Rep (S) 32
R v. *Tuncay* [1998] 2 VR 19
R v. *Waheed Akhtar* (2004) 1 Cr App Rep (S) 78
Rahman v. *Hossain* No A-5191–08T3, 2010 WL 4075316 (N.J. Super. Ct. App. Div. June 17, 2010)
Re Aramco Services Company (2010) WL 1241525
Re: Arcapita Bank BSC *et al.* (2013) Unreported, U.S. Bankruptcy Court, Southern District of New York, No. 12–11076
Re East Cameron Partners, L.P., Debtor (2008) (Unreported, trial transcript, case no 08-51207, decision of the U.S. Bankruptcy Court, W.D. Louisiana)
Re the Marriage of Fereshteh R and Speros Vryonis 202 CAL.APP.3d 712 (1988)
Regina v. *G M Khan* [2001] NSWSC 1356
Rhodes v. *ITT Sheraton* (1999) WL 26874
Rotsztein v. *Her Majesty's Senior Coroner for Inner London* (2015)

S (Children) [2004] EWHC 1282 (fam)
Saudi Basic Industries Corp (SABIC) v. *Mobil Yanbu Petrochemical Co* (Saudi Basic III) (2005) 866 A.2d 1 (Del. 2005)
Shahnaz v. *Rizzan* [1965] 1 QB 390
Sohrab v. *Khan* [2002] S.C.L.R 663
State of Arizona v. *Faleh Almaleki* (2011)
State of Arizona v. *Yusra Farhan, Mohammed Altameemi and Tabarak Altameemi* (2012)
State of Illinois v. *Edwin Jones* (1994) no. 5-94-0813, Appellate Court of Illinois, Fifth District
State of Maine v. *Nadim Haque* (1999) 726 A.2d 205 (Me. 1999)
State of New Jersey v. *K.E* (2009), unreported, (WL 4908298 (N.J.Super.A.D.)
State of Oregon v. *Shahin Farokhrany* (2013), 259, Or.App. 132
State v. *Ahmed* (2006) WL 3849862 (Ohio App. 7 Dist.)
Stingel v. *R* [1990] HCA 61–171 CLR 312
Tarikonda v. *Pinjari* (2009) No. 287403, slip op. at 2 (Mich. Ct. App. Apr. 7, 2009)
Taylor v. *Attorney-General of Canada* (2001) Fed.Ct. Trial LEXIS 1208
Teece v. *Kuwait Finance House (Bahrain)* (2014) WL 2186887 (N.D. Cal.)
The Ship 'Mercury Bell' v. *Amoisin* [1986] 27 D.L.R. 4th 461 (C.A.)
Uddin v. *Choudhury* [2009] EWCA Civ 1205
UM Financial is Central 1 Credit Union v. *UM Financial Inc* [2012] ONSC 889
Vagh v. *The State of Western Australia* [2007] WASCA 17
Wafa v. *Faizi* (2014) CarswellBC 2788, 2014 BCSC 1760
Williamson and Others v. *The Secretary of State for Education and Employment* [2002] EWCA Civ 1926
Wold v. *Kleppir* [2009] FamCA 178
X v. *United Kingdom* [1984] 6 EHHR 558

References

AAP 2005, 'Muslim political party registers in ACT', *Sydney Morning Herald*, 5 September, at: www.smh.com.au/articles/2005/09/05/1125772447441.html (accessed July 2015).

AAP 2006, 'Some Muslims pose immigration problem: PM', *Sydney Morning Herald*, 20 February, at: www.smh.com.au/news/national/some-muslims-pose-immigration-problem-pm/2006/02/20/1140283975195.html (accessed July 2015).

AAP 2011, 'Burka laws ready for NSW', *The Australian*, 19 August, at: www.theaustralian.com.au/news/nation/burka-laws-ready-for-nsw/story-e6frg6nf-1226117944473 (accessed July 2015).

AAP 2014, 'Lambie stumbles over sharia explanation', *Sydney Morning Herald*, 21 September, at: www.smh.com.au//breaking-news-national/lambie-stumbles-over-sharia-explanation-20140921-3g8ra.html (accessed July 2015).

Abbas, T. 2007, 'Muslim minorities in Britain: Integration, multiculturalism and radicalisation in the post 7/7 period', *Journal of Intercultural Studies*, 28 (3): 287–300.

Abbas, T. 2010, 'Honour-related violence towards South Asian Muslim women in the UK: A crisis of masculinity and cultural relativism in the context of Islamophobia and the "war on terror" ', in M.M. Idriss and T. Abbas (eds), *Honour, Violence, Women and Islam*. London: Routledge.

ABC News 2015, 'Proposed NSW law change to make it a criminal offence to refuse to stand in court', ABC, 3 December, at: www.abc.net.au/news/2015-12-03/court-struggles-with-murder-accused-who-refuses-stand-in-court/6997092 (accessed 7 December 2015).

ABC News24 2014, 'PUP senator Jacqui Lambie stands by "ban the burka" Facebook post, says she knew background of Afghan policewoman killed by Taliban', ABC, 21 September, at: www.abc.net.au/news/2014-09-20/lambie-says-burka-photo-honours-policewoman-killed-by-taliban/5758324 (accessed July 2015).

'Abd al Aṭī, H. 1995, *The Family Structure in Islam*. Indianapolis, IN: American Trust Publications.

Abd al-Samee' Al-Ãbi Al-Azhari, S, 2009, Al-Thamar Al-Dāni Sharḥ Risālah Ibn Abi Zayd Al-Qayruwāni, Beirut, Maktabah Al-Thiqāfiyah.

Abdalla, M. 2013, 'Sacred law in a secular land: To what extent should sharī'a law be followed in Australia?', *Griffith Law Review*, 21: 567–679.

Abdul-Bari, M. 2007, *Marriage and Family Building In Islam*. London: Ta-Ha Publishers Ltd.

Abou El Fadl, K. 1994, 'Legal debates on Muslim minorities: Between rejection and accommodation', *The Journal of Religious Ethics*, 22 (1): 127–62.

Abou El Fadl, K. 2005, *The Great Theft: Wrestling Islam from the Extremists*. New York: HarperCollins.

Abu Lughod, L. 2002, 'Do Muslim women really need saving? Anthropological reflections on cultural relativism and its others', *American Anthropologist*, 104 (3): 783–90.

ACT for America 2015, Act for America, US, at: www.actforamerica.org/alac (accessed July 2015).

A Current Affair 2005, television programme, Nine Network, Sydney, 11 November.

Adam, N. 2011, 'Muslim voices in school: Narratives of identity and pluralism', *Race Ethnicity and Education*, 14 (4): 579–83.

Addis, A. 1991–92, 'Individualism, communitarianism, and the rights of ethnic minorities', *Notre Dame Law Review*, 67: 615–76.

Ahmad, I. 2015, 'Reclaiming Australia? Liberalism's role in Islamophobia', *The Conversation*, 17 July, at: http://theconversation.com/reclaiming-australia-liberalisms-role-in-islamophobia-44662 (accessed July 2015).

Ahmed, F. and Norton, J.C. 2012, 'Religious tribunals, religious freedom and concern for vulnerable women', *Child and Family Law Quarterly*, 24 (4): 363–88.

Ahmed, H. and Stuart, H. 2009, *Hizb ut-Tahrir: Ideology and Strategy*. London: Centre for Social Cohesion.

Ahsan, M. 1995, 'The Muslim family in Britain', in M. King (ed.), *God's Law Versus State Law: The Construction of an Islamic Identity in Western Europe*. London: Grey Seal Books.

Akbarzadeh, S. 2008, 'Muslim majority wants secular law', *The Australian*, 19 April, at: www.theaustralian.news.com.au/story/0,25197,23539447-7583,00.html (accessed April 2008).

Akbarzadeh, S. and Smith, B. 2005, *The Representation of Islam and Muslims in the Media (*The Age *and* Herald Sun *Newspapers)*. Melbourne: Monash University.

al-'Asqalāni, *Bulūgh al-Marām min Adillat al-Aḥkām*, (2007), 2nd Edition, Sharikah Dār al-Mashārī'a, Beirut.

al-'Asqalāni, ibn H. n.d., *Fatḥ Al-Bārī̱*. Dār al-Bayān lil-Turāth.

al-'Aziz (ibn 'Ābidīn), M. 2009, *Sharḥ 'Uqūd Rasm al-Mufti*. Karachi: Maktabah al-Bushra.

Al-Anṣāri, Z. 2001, *Asnā̱ Al-Maṭā̱lib Sharḥ Rawḏ Al-Ṭālib*. Beirut: Dār al-Kutub al-'Ilmiyyah.

al-Anṣāri, Z. n.d., *Fatḥ al-'Allā̱m bi-Sharḥ Al'ilām bi-aḥā̱dith al-Aḥkām*. Beirut: Dār al-Kutub al-'Ilmiyyah.

al-Aşfahāni, A.N. 2010, *Ḥilyat al-Awliyā wa Ṭabaqāt al-Asfiyā'*, vol. 1. Beirut: Dār al-Kutub al-ʿIlmiyyah.

al-Baghawi, al-H. 1997, *At-Tahdheeb fi Fiqh al-Imām al-Shāfi'*, vol. 1. Beirut, Dār al-Kutub al-'Ilmiyyah.

al-Baghdadi, al-K. n.d., *Al-Faqih wal Mutafaqqih*. 1997, Dār al-Watn l-il Nashr; Riyad.

Al-Bār, M. 1994, *Al-Khitān*. Jiddah and Mekkah, Dār al-Manār.

al-Dusuqi, M. 2011, *Ḫāshiyah Al-Dusuqi 'alā Sharḫ al-Kabir*, 3rd edn. Beirut: Dār al-Kutub al-ʿIlmiyyah

al-Ghazāli, Abu H. 1937, *Al-Muṣṭasfa min 'ilm Al-Uṣūl*. Cairo: Al-Maktabah al-Tijaniyya.

al-Ghazāli, Abu H. 2007, *The Proper Conduct of Marriage in Islam, adab an-nikāḥ, Book 12 of Ihya' Ulum Ad-din*, trans. M. Holland. North Miami Beach, FL: Al-Baz Publishing.

al-Harari, A. 2012, *Bughiat at-Ṭālib*. Beirut: Dār al-Māsharī'ah.

al-Haytami, ibn H. n.d., *Al-Fatāwā Al-Kubrā Al-Fiqhiyat 'alā Madhhab Al-Imām Al-Shāfi'i*. Beirut: Dār al-Kutub al-'Ilmiyyah.

al-Hibri, A. 2005, 'The nature of the Islamic marriage: Sacramental, covenantal, or contractual?', in J. Witte Jr. and E. Ellison (eds), *Covenant Marriage in Comparative Perspective*. Grand Rapids, MI: William B. Eerdmans Publishing Company.

Al-Husari, A. 1977, *'Ilm al-Qāḏi*. Egypt: Maktabah Al-Kulliyyah Azhariyyah.

Ali, S. 2000, *Gender and Human Rights in Islam and International Law*. The Hague: Kluwer Law International.

Alini, E. 2012, 'Does Islamic finance have a place in Canada?', *Maclean's*, at: www.macleans.ca/economy/economicanalysis/does-islamic-finance-have-a-place-in-canada/ (accessed 7 April 2015).

Al-Kawthari, M. 1993, *Maqalāt al-Kawthari*. Beirut: Dār al-Aḥnāf.

Alkhatib, I.A. 2013, 'Shariah law and American family courts: Judicial inconsistency on the talaq and mahr issues in Wayne Country, Michigan', *The Journal of Law and Society*, 14: 83–105.

Allen, C. 2010, *Islamophobia*. Farnham, Surrey: Ashgate Publishing.

Al-Maidani, A. 2001, *Al-Lubāb fi Sharḥ Al-Kitāb*. Beirut: Dār Al-Kitab Al-Arabi.

Al-Marghinani, B. n.d., *Al-Hidāyah Sharḥ Bidāyat Al-Mubtadi*. Beirut: Dār Al-Arqam.

Al-Misri, A. 1999, *Reliance of the Traveller: A Classic Manual of Islamic Sacred Law*, trans. N.H.M. Keller. Beltsville, MD: Amana Publications.

Al-Munajjid, M.S. n.d., '34497: Ruling on standing up for who comes in, and kissing him', *Islam Question and Answer*, at: http://islamqa.info/en/34497 (accessed 17 February 2015).

Al-Qarāfi, S. 2000, *Nafā'is Al-Uṣūl fi Sharḥ al-Maḥṣūl*. Beirut: Dār al-Kutub al-ʿIlmiyyah.

Al-Rāzi, A-F. 1999, n.d., *Al-Tafsir Al-Kabir*. Beirut, Dār Ihyā' At-Turāth al-'Arabi'.

Al-Shāfiʿi, M. 2005, *Kitāb Al-Umm*. Beirut: Dār Ibn Ḥazm.

Al-Shirāzi, A.I. 2006, *Al-Luma' Fi Uṣūl al-Fiqh*. Beirut: Sharikah Dār al-Mashārī'ah.

Al-Siyūṭī, J. n.d., *Sharḫ At-Tanbih*, vol. 1, Beirut: Dār al-Fikr.

Al-Yaqoubi, Shaykh M. 2015, *Refuting ISIS: A Rebuttal of its Religious and Ideological Foundations*. UK: Sacred Knowledge.

al'Umrāni, Y. 2002, *Al-Bayān fi Fiqh al-Imām al-Shāfi'i*, vol. 1. Beirut, Dār al-Kutub al-'Ilmiyyah.

American Civil Liberties Union 2011, *Nothing to Fear: Debunking the Mythical 'Sharia Threat' to our Judicial System*, ACLU Program on Freedom of Religion and Belief, USA, at: www.aclu.org/sites/default/files/field_document/Nothing_To_Fear_Report_FINAL_MAY_2011.pdf (accessed July 2015).

Amirthalingam, K. 2009, 'Culture, crime and culpability: Perspectives on the defence of provocation', in M-C. Foblets and A.D. Renteln (eds), *Multicultural Jurisprudence: Comparative Perspectives on the Cultural Defense*. Portland, OR: Hart Publishing.

An-Na'im, A. 1990, *Towards an Islamic Reformation: Civil Liberties, Human Rights and International Law*. Syracuse, NY: Syracuse University Press.

An-Nabahani, T. 1998, *The Islamic State*, Khilafah Publications, at: www.hizb-ut-tahrir.org/PDF/EN/en_books_pdf/05_The_Islamic_State.pdf (accessed 21 August 2015).

An-Nasafi, A. 2008, *Madarik At-Tanzil wa Haqa'iq At-Ta'weel*, vol. 1. Beirut: Dār al-Kutub al-'Ilmiyyah.

An-Nawawi, M. 2002, *Al-Arba'ūna An-Nawawiyyah fi-l Aḥādith An-Nabawiyyah*. Beirut: Dār al-Masharī'a.

An-Nawawi, M. 2005, *Minhāj al-Ṭalibeen*, 1st edn. Jeddah: Dār al-Minhaj.

An-Nawawi, M. 2010, *Al-Majmū' Sharḥ al-Muhadhdhab*. Beirut: Dār al-Fikr.

Ansari, F. 2005, 'British anti-terrorism: A modern day witch-hunt', Islamic Human Rights Commission, at: www.ihrc.org (accessed July 2015).

Anthony, A. 2014, 'Anjem Choudary: The British extremist who backs the caliphate', *Guardian*, 7 September, at: www.theguardian.com/world/2014/sep/07/anjem-choudary-islamic-state-isis (accessed July 2015).

Arnold, E. and Sorriano, E. 2013, 'The Recent Revolution of Expert Evidence in Selected Common Law Jurisdictions Around the World', CVPL, at: https://cicbv.ca/wp-content/uploads/2010/10/2012-CICBV-Research-Paper-CVPL-FINAL.pdf (accessed 8 October 2015).

Aslam, J. 2006, 'Judicial oversight of Islamic family law arbitration in Ontario', *International Law and Politics*, 38: 841–76.

At-Ṯabari, ibn J. n.d., *Jāmi'u Al-Bayān Fi Ta'wil Al-Qur'ān*, vol. 9, Darussalam, Egypt.

At-Tirmidhi, M. I. 1998 n.d., *Al-Jami' Al-Kabir Sunan At-Tirmidhi'*, Dār al-Gharb al-Islāmi', Beirut.

Attorney-General's Department 2013, *Review of Australia's Female Genital Mutilation Legal Framework, Final Report*, Australian Government, Australia.

Australian Bureau of Statistics 2012, *Reflecting a nation: Stories from the 2011 census, 2012–2013*, 2071.0, ABS, at: www.abs.gov.au/ausstats/abs@.nsf/Lookup/2071.0main+features902012-2013 (accessed 30 August 2015).

Awad, A. 2012, 'The true story of Sharia in American courts', *The Nation*, 14 June, at: www.thenation.com/article/true-story-sharia-american-courts/ (accessed July 2015).

Awad, A. 2014 'Islamic family law in American courts: A rich diverse and evolving jurisprudence', in E Giunchi (ed.), *Muslim Family Law in Western Courts*. London: Routledge.

Awan, A. 2007, 'Transitional religiosity experiences: Contextual disjuncture and Islamic political radicalism', in Tahir Abbas (ed.), *Islamic Political Radicalism: A European Perspective*. Edinburgh: Edinburgh University Press.

Awan, I. and Zempi, I. 2015, *We fear for our lives: Offline and online experiences of anti-Muslim hostility*, Birmingham City University, Nottingham Trent University and Tell MAMA, UK, at: http://tellmamauk.org/wp-content/uploads/resources/We%20Fear%20For%20Our%20Lives.pdf (accessed July 2015).

Badawi, Z. 1995, 'Muslim justice in a secular state', in M. King (ed.), *God's Law Versus State Law: The Construction of Islamic Identity in Western Europe*. London: Grey Seal.

Baird, D. and Rasmussen, R. 2002, 'The end of bankruptcy', *Stanford Law Review*, 55: 751–90.

Bakht, N. 2004, 'Family arbitration using Sharia law: Examining Ontario's arbitration act and its impact on women', *Muslim World Journal of Human Rights*, 1 (1): 1–24.

Bakht, N. 2005, 'Were Muslim barbarians really knocking on the gates of Ontario?: The Religious Arbitration Controversy – Another Perspective', *Ottawa Law Review*, (Summer): 67–82.

Ballantyne, W.M. 2000, *Essays and Addresses on Arab Laws*. Richmond, Surrey: Curzon Press.

Ballard, R. 2011, 'Honour killing? Or just plain homicide?,' in L. Holden (ed.), *Cultural Expertise and Litigation*. London: Routledge.

Bano, S. 2012, *Muslim Women and Shari'ah Councils: Transcending the Boundaries of Community and Law*. Basingstoke: Palgrave Macmillan.

Baumeister, A. 2003, 'Ways of belonging: Ethnonational minorities and models of differentiated citizenship', *Ethnicities*, 3 (3): 393–416.

BBC News 2008, 'Cameron steps into Sharia law row', *BBC News*, 26 February, at: http://news.bbc.co.uk/2/hi/uk_news/politics/7264740.stm (accessed September 2008).

Beatty, M. 2014, 'Property settlement: The 4 steps courts use to decide property division', DIY Family Law Australia, at: www.diyfamilylawaustralia.com/Topic/property_settlement_how_courts_decide_property_division_4steps.html (accessed July 2015).

Beck, F.F.M. 2004, 'Liberalism, minorities and the politics of societal differentiation', Proceedings of the Second Pavia Graduate Conference in Political Philosophy, 15–16 April.

Beyer, P. 2005, 'Religious identity and educational attainment among recent immigrants to Canada: Gender, age and 2nd generation', *Journal of International Migration and Integration*, 6 (2): 177–99.

bin Bayyah, A. 2007, *Ṣinā'at al-Fatwa wa-Fiqh Al-'Aqalliyyāt* [The craft of fatwa and the law of Muslim minorities]. Beirut: Dār al-Minhaj.

bin Bayyah, A. n.d.a, *Advice from Shaykh Abdallah Bin Bayyah to the Muslim community of America: Four obstacles that Muslims face in America*, The official website of His Eminence Shaykh Abdallah bin Bayyah, at: http://binbayyah.net/english/2014/05/29/advice-from-shaykh-abdallah-bin-bayyah-to-the-muslim-community-of-america-four-obstacles-that-muslims-face-in-america/ (accessed 10 August 2015).

bin Bayyah, A. n.d.b, *On the fiqh of Muslim minorities*, The official website of His Eminence Shaykh Abdallah bin Bayyah, at: http://binbayyah.net/english/2012/02/20/on-the-fiqh-of-muslim-minorities/ (accessed 11 August 2015).

Black, A. and Hosen, N. 2009, 'Fatwas: Their role in contemporary secular Australia', *Griffith Law Review*, 18 (2): 405–27.

Black, A. and Sadiq, K. 2011, 'Good and bad sharia: Australia's mixed response to Islamic law', *UNSW Law Journal*, 34 (1): 383–412.

Blakkarly, J. 2015, 'Unease with Australia's Islamophobia', *Aljazeera*, 12 April, at: www.aljazeera.com/indepth/features/2015/04/unease-australia-islamophobia-150409075748404.html (accessed July 2015).

Bodkin, P. and Dale, A. 2013, 'Court stand-off as magistrate berates then placates "disrespectful" rioter Mohammed Issai Issaka', *Daily Telegraph*, 21 May.

Bowen, J.R. 2010, 'How English courts recognise shariah?', *University of St Thomas Law Journal*, 7 (3): 411–35.

Boyd, M. 2004, *Dispute Resolution in Family Law: Protecting Choice, Promoting Inclusion*, Ontario Ministry of the Attorney-General, Canada.

Boyd, M. 2006, 'Arbitration in family law: Difficult choices', *Inroads*, 18: 58–63, at: http://inroadsjournal.ca/arbitration-in-family-law-difficult-choices/ (accessed April 2010).

Breslow, J. 2012, 'More Deaths Go Unchecked as Autopsy Rate Falls to "Miserably Low" Levels', *Frontline*, 8 August, at: www.pbs.org/wgbh/pages/frontline/criminal-justice/post-mortem/more-deaths-go-unchecked-as-autopsy-rate-falls-to-miserably-low-levels/ (accessed 6 September 2015).

Brown, D. 2007, 'A destruction of Muslim identity: Ontario's decision to stop Sharia based arbitration', *North Carolina Journal of International and Commercial Regulation*, 32: 495–546.

Brown, D. 2013, 'Criminalisation and normative theory', *Current Issues in Criminal Justice*, 25 (2): 605–25.

Brown, D., Farrier, D., McNamara, L., Steel, A., Grewcock, M., Quilter, J. and Schwartz, M. 2015, *Criminal Laws*, 6th edn. Leichhardt, NSW: Federation Press.

Brown, L. 1993, *New Shorter Oxford English Dictionary*. Oxford: Oxford University Press.

Browne, R. 2015, 'Against their will: Inside Canada's forced marriages', *Maclean's*, at: www.macleans.ca/news/canada/against-their-will/. (accessed July 2015).

Bunting, M. 2008, 'A noble, reckless rebellion', *Guardian*, 9 February, at: www.theguardian.com/commentisfree/2008/feb/09/religion.politics (accessed July 2015).

Byman, D. 2015, *Comparing Al-Qaeda and ISIS: Different Goals, Different Targets*, Brookings, at: www.brookings.edu/research/testimony/2015/04/29-terrorism-in-africa-byman (accessed 4 December 2015).

CagePrisoners 2012, Home Office schedule 7 review, Cage, 6 December, at: www.cageuk.org/sites/files/reports/CP_Schedule_7_review.pdf (accessed July 2015).

Carpenter, B. and Tait, G. 2010, 'The Autopsy Imperative: Medicine, Law and the Coronial Investigation', *Journal of Medical Humanities*, 31: 205–21.

Carpenter, B., Tait, G. and Quadrelli, C. 2014, 'The body in grief: Death investigations, objections to autopsy and the religious and cultural 'other' ", *Religions*, 5: 165–78.

Caughey, J. 2009, 'The anthropologist as expert witness: A murder in Maine', in M-C. Foblets and A.D. Renteln (eds), *Multicultural Jurisprudence: Comparative Perspectives on the Cultural Defense*. Portland, OR: Hart Publishing.

CBC News 2013, 'Low autopsy rate in B.C. alarms experts: Too many deaths inadequately investigated, former coroners say', CBC News, 6 February, at: www.cbc.ca/news/canada/british-columbia/low-autopsy-rate-in-b-c-alarms-experts-1.1335613 (accessed 6 September 2015).

Çelik, M. 2014, 'Is Islamophobia rising in Canada?', *Daily Sabah Opinion*, 16 June, at: www.dailysabah.com/opinion/2014/06/16/is-islamophobia-rising-in-canada (accessed July 2015).

Centre for Muslim Minorities and Islam Policy Studies 2009, *Mapping Employment and Education Among Muslim Australians*. Monash University, Victoria Australia, at: www.dss.gov.au/sites/default/files/documents/01_2014/muslim-mapping-report.pdf (accessed July 2015).

Cesari, J. 2013, *Why the West Fears Islam: An Exploration of Muslims in Liberal Democracies*. New York: Palgrave Macmillan.

Chalabi, M. 2013, 'Attacks on Muslims: Numbers in detail', *Guardian*, 28 May, at: www.theguardian.com/news/datablog/2013/may/28/attacks-on-muslims-numbers-detail (accessed July 2015).

Cherney, A. and Murphy, K. 2014, 'Fairness and trust make all the difference in countering terrorism, The Conversation', 3 October, at: http://theconversation.com/fairness-and-trust-make-all-the-difference-in-countering-terrorism-32319 (accessed July 2015).

Cherney, A., Sergeant, E. and Murphy, K. 2015, 'The importance of procedural justice and police performance in shaping intentions to cooperate with the police: Does social identity matter?', *European Journal of Criminology*, 12 (6) 719–38.

Chiba, M. 1989, *Legal Pluralism: Towards a General Theory Through Japanese Legal Culture*. Tokyo: Tokai University Press.

The Chicago Council on Global Affairs 2007, 'Strengthening America: The civic and political integration of Muslim Americans, report of the task force on Muslim American civic and political engagement', The Chicago Council on Global Affairs, at: www.centerforglobalunderstanding.org/pdf/Strengthening_America_%20Exec_Summary.pdf (accessed July 2015).

Choudhary, T. and Fenwick, H. 2012, 'The impact of counter-terrorism measures on Muslim communities', in H. Fenwick (ed.), *Developments in Counter-Terrorism Measures and Uses of Technology*. Oxford: Routledge, pp. 45–76.

Clarkson, C.M.V. and Hill, J. 2011, *The Conflict of Laws*, 4th edn. Oxford: Oxford University Press.

Cole, D. 2006, 'Are we safer?', *The New York Review of Books*, at: www.nybooks.com/articles/2006/03/09/are-we-safer/ (accessed July 2015).

Collins, J., Noble, G., Poynting, S. and Tabar, P. 2000, *Kebabs, Kids, Cops and Crime: Youth, Ethnicity and Crime*. Sydney: Pluto Press.

Colon, J.C. 2011, 'Choice of law and Islamic finance', *Texas International Law Journal*, 46 (2): 412–35.

Cook, M. 2010, *Commanding Right and Forbidding Wrong in Islamic Thought*. Cambridge: Cambridge University Press.

Costello, P. 2006, 'Worth promoting, worth defending: Australian citizenship, what it means and how to nurture it', Address to the Sydney Institute, 23 February, at: www.petercostello.com.au/speeches/2006/2111-worth-promoting-worth-defending-australian-citizenship-what-it-means-and-how-to-nurture-it-address-to-the-sydney-institute sydney (accessed 6 April 2016).

Cranmer, F. 2015, 'Theresa May, the Home Office and sharia', *Law & Religion UK*, 23 March, at: www.lawandreligionuk.com/2015/03/23/theresa-may-the-home-office-and-sharia/ (accessed July 2015).

Cristillo, L. 2008, *Religiosity, Education and Civic Belonging: Muslim Youth in New York City Public Schools Study*. New York: Teachers College Columbia University.

CTV News 2004, 'Islamic group against Ontario use of Sharia law', *CTV News*, 22 August.

David, R. and Brierley, J.E.C. 1978, *Major Legal Systems in the World Today: An Introduction to the Study of Comparative Law*. New York: Simon & Schuster.

Davies, L. 2013, 'Sydney sharia whipping case: Man jailed for dishing out 40 lashes', *Sydney Morning Herald*, 14 June.

Davies, M. 2005, 'Ethos of pluralism', *Sydney Law Review*, 27 (1): 87–112.

Davies, M., Bell, A. and Brereton, P. 2013, *Nygh's Conflicts of Laws in Australia*, 9th edn. Australia: LexisNexis.

Dawn 2006, *Britain: London's Muslims Face Bias, Says Mayor*. UCLA Asia Institute, 24 October, at: www.international.ucla.edu/asia/article/56140 (accessed July 2015).

De Jong, F. 1983, 'The Sufi orders in nineteenth and twentieth-century Palestine', *Studia Islamica*, 58: 149–81.

Dearden, L. 2015, 'Anzac Day terror plot: British teenager sentenced to life in prison for planning to behead police in Australia', *Independent*, 2 October, at: www.independent.co.uk/news/uk/crime/anzac-day-terror-plot-british-teenager-sentenced-to-life-in-prison-for-planning-to-behead-police-in-a6676616.html (accessed 18 October 2015).

De Brennan, S. 2006, 'Sharia law and Australia', *On Line* Opinion, 22 March, at: www.onlineopinion.com.au/view.asp?article=4282 (accessed 6 April 2016).

Deckha, M. 2009, 'The paradox of cultural defence: Gender and cultural othering in Canada', in M-C. Foblets and A.D. Renteln (eds), *Multicultural Jurisprudence: Comparative Perspectives on the Cultural Defense*. Portland, OR: Hart Publishing.

Department of Immigration and Citizenship 2009, *The Australia Journey – Muslim Communities*. Australia: Australian Government.

Divorce-Canada.ca 2015a, 'Child custody in Canada', Divorce Canada, at: http://divorce-canada.ca/child-custody-in-canada (accessed July 2015).

Divorce-Canada.ca 2015b, 'Divorce in Canada: FAQ', Divorce Canada, at: http://divorce-canada.ca/divorce-in-canada-faq (accessed July 2015).

Divorce-Canada.ca 2015c, 'Property division in a divorce in Canada', Divorce Canada, at: http://divorce-canada.ca/property-divorce-laws (accessed July 2015).

Doi, A.R. 2006, *Women in Shari'ah*. Kuala Lumpur: Noordeen.

Doré, L. 2015, 'More Britons believe that multiculturalism makes the country worse – not better, says poll', *Independent*, 4 July, at: www.independent.co.uk/news/uk/home-news/more-britons-believe-that-multiculturalism-makes-the-country-worse-not-better-says-poll-10366003.html (accessed 6 April 2016).

Doskow, E. n.d., 'The best interests of the child: Factors a judge may consider in deciding custody', NOLO, US, at: www.divorcenet.com/resources/divorce/divorce-and-children/the-best-interests-child-factors-a-#b (accessed July 2015).

Dranoff, L. 2005, 'Setting a dangerous precedent: Comment on the Boyd report to the Ontario Government', *Matrimonial Affairs*, at: http://jura123.com/pcwo/documents/Justice/zdranoff_reM_BoydonSharia_05.pdf (accessed January 2011).

Dubai International Financial Centre 2015, 'Laws & regulations', Dubai International Financial Centre, Dubai, at: www.difc.ae/laws-regulations (accessed July 2015).

Duff, A. 2007, *Answering for Crime: Responsibility and Liability in the Criminal Law*. Oxford: Hart Publishing.

Duffy, R. 2015, 'Is this letter to Muslim leaders Islamophobic or "reasonable, sensible and moderate"?', *The Journal*, 19 January, at: www.thejournal.ie/eric-pickles-letter-1890225-Jan2015/ (accessed July 2015)

Dunn, K. 2001, 'Representations of Islām in the politics of mosque development in Sydney', *Tijdschrift voor economische en sociale geografie*, 92 (3): 291–308.

Dunn, K., Atie, R., Mapedzahamam, V., Ozalp, M. and Aydogan, A. 2015, *The Resilience and Ordinariness of Australian Muslims: Attitudes and Experiences of Muslims Report*. Western Sydney University and Islamic Sciences and Research Academy Australia, Australia.

Dworkin, R. 1988, *Law's Empire*. Cambridge, MA: Harvard University Press.

Dworkin, R. 1995, 'Foundations of liberal equality', in S. Darwall (ed.), *Equal Freedom*. Ann Arbor, MI: University of Michigan Press.

Edge, I. 2013, 'Islamic finance, alternative dispute resolution and family law: Developments towards legal pluralism?', in R. Griffith-Jones (ed.), *Islām and English Law: Rights, Responsibilities and the Place of Shari'a*. Cambridge and New York: Cambridge University Press.

Edmond, G. 2009, 'Merton and the Hot Tub: Scientific Conventions and Expert Evidence in Australian Civil Procedure', *Law and Contemporary Problems*, 72: 158–89.

El Dareer, A. 1983, *Woman, Why do you Weep? Circumcision and its Consequences*. London: Zed Books.

Elewa, A. and Silvers, L. 2010, '"I *am* one of the people": A survey and analysis of legal arguments on woman-led prayer in Islam', *Journal of Law and Religion*, 26 (1): 141–71.

Elgot, J. 2014, 'Anti-Muslim hate crime soars in London, according to new police figures', *The Huffington Post UK*, 1 October, at: www.huffingtonpost.co.uk/2014/10/01/antimuslim-hate-crime-london_n_5914700.html (accessed July 2015).

Ely, J.H. 1980, *Democracy and Distrust: A Theory of Judicial Review*. Cambridge, MA: Harvard University Press.

Emmett, S., Ibrahim, S., Charles, A. and Ranson, D. 2004, 'Coronial autopsies: A rising tide of objections', *Medical Journal of Australia*, 181 (3): 173.

Environics Research Group n.d., Focus Canada Report 2006–2004, Environics Research Group, Canada, at: www.environicsinstitute.org/uploads/institute-projects/focus%20canada%202006-4%20report.pdf (accessed July 2015).

Essof, I. 2011, 'Divorce in Australia: From an Islamic law perspective', *Alternative Law Journal*, 36 (3): 182–86, at: http://search.informit.com.au/documentSummary;dn=250243360012502;res=IELAPA (accessed July 2015).

Euro-Islam.info n.d., *Islam in the United States*, Euro-Islam.info, Europe, at: www.euro-islam.info/country-profiles/united-states/ (accessed July 2015)

'Fakhr al-Din al-Razi' 1960–2002, *The Encyclopaedia of Islam*, 2nd edn, H.A.R. Gibbs, B. Lewis, Ch. Pellat, C. Bosworth *et al.* (eds), 11 vols. Leiden: E.J. Brill.

Family Law Council 2001, *Cultural-Community Divorce and the Family Law Act 1975: A Proposal to Clarify the Law*. report to the Attorney-General, Family Law Council, Australia.

Farrar, S. 2003, 'Islamic jurisprudence and the role of the accused: A re-examination', *Legal Studies*, 23 (4): 587–604.

Farrar, S. 2011, 'Accommodating Islamic banking and finance in Australia', *UNSW Law Journal*, 34: 413–42.

Farrar, S. 2014, 'The Organisation of Islamic Cooperation: Forever on the Periphery of Public International Law?', *Chinese Journal of International Law*, 13 (4): 787–817.

Faucon, C. 2014, 'Marriage outlaws: Regulating polygamy in America', *Duke Journal of Gender Law and Policy*, 22 (1): 1–54, at: http://scholarship.law.duke.edu/cgi/viewcontent.cgi?article=1288&context=djglp (accessed July 2015).

Favazza, A.F. 1996, *Bodies under Siege: Self-mutilation and Body Modification in Culture and Psychiatry*. Baltimore, MD: John Hopkins University Press.

Federal Bureau of Investigation n.d., *USA Uniform Crime Reports, 2013 Hate Crime Statistics, Victims*. FBI, at: www.fbi.gov/about-us/cjis/ucr/hate-crime/2013/topic-pages/victims/victims_final (accessed July 2015).

Federal Circuit Court of Australia 2014, 'How do I apply for a divorce?', Federal Circuit Court of Australia, 11 November, at: www.federalcircuitcourt.gov.au/wps/wcm/connect/fccweb/how-do-i/apply-for-a-divorce/apply-for-divorce (accessed July 2015).

Feldman, N. 2008, 'Why Sharia?', *The New York Times*, 6 March.

Fielding, A. 2008, 'When rights collide: Liberalism, pluralism and freedom of religion in Canada', *Appeal*, 13: 28–50.

Fife-Yeomans, J. and Kent, P. 2011, 'Muslim woman Carnita Matthews escapes jail by remaining behind her burqa', *Daily Telegraph*, 21 June, at: www.dailytelegraph.com.au/judge-could-not-be-sure-who-was-behind-the-veil/story-e6freuy9-1226078801032 (accessed 7 December 2015).

Forced Marriage Unit 2015, 'Statistics January to December 2014', Foreign and Commonwealth Office & Home Office, UK, at: www.gov.uk/government/uploads/system/uploads/attachment_data/file/412667/FMU_Stats_2014.pdf (accessed July 2015).

Foreign and Commonwealth Home Office & Home Office 2013, 'Law and the justice system – guidance: Forced marriage: Information and practice guidelines for professionals protecting, advising and supporting victims', UK Government, UK, at: www.gov.uk/guidance/forced-marriage (accessed July 2015).

Fournier, P. 2002, 'The ghettoization of difference in Canada: "Rape by culture" and the danger of a "cultural defence" in criminal law trials', *Manitoba Law Journal*, 29: 81–119.

Fournier, P. 2004, 'The reception of Muslim family law in western liberal states', Canadian Council of Muslim Women Sharia/Muslim Law Project, at: www.ccmw.com/documents/Pascalepaper.pdf (accessed July 2015).

Fournier, P. 2010, *Muslim Marriage in Western Courts: Lost in Transplantation*. Farnham, Surrey: Ashgate.

Freeland, R. 2006, 'Islamic personal law in American courts', in A. Sonbol (ed.), *Beyond the Exotic: Women's Histories in Islamic Societies*. Cairo: American University of Cairo Press, pp. 227–46.

Fukurai, H. and Davies, D. 1997, 'Affirmative action in jury selection: Racially representative juries, racial quotas, and affirmative juries of the Hennepin Model and the Jury De Medietate Linguae', *Virginia Journal of Social Policy and the Law*, 4: 645–81.

Gallagher, P. 2015, 'Coroners must send bodies for scans rather than autopsies if religion demands they stay intact, High Court rules', *Independent*, 28 July.

Gallup 2011, *Muslim Americans: Faith, Freedom, and the Future Examining U.S. Muslims' Political, Social, and Spiritual Engagement 10 Years after September 11*. Gallup Center for Muslim Studies and the Abu Dhabi Gallup Center.

Gallup n.d., *Islamophobia: Understanding Anti-Muslim Sentiment in the West*. Gallup, US, at: www.gallup.com/poll/157082/islamophobia-understanding-anti-muslim-sentiment-west.aspx (accessed July 2015).

Gerges, F. 2005, *The Far Enemy: Why Jihad went Global*. Cambridge: Cambridge University Press.

Ghobadzaeh, N. 2009, 'Multiculturalism and Muslim Women: Shariah Debate in Australia and Canada', Proceedings at the Annual Conference Canadian Political Association, 29 May.

Giunchi, E. 2014, 'Muslim family law and legal practice in the West', in Elisa Giunchi (ed.), *Muslim Family Law in Western Courts*. London: Routledge.

Glenn, H.P. 2010, *Legal Traditions of the World*. Oxford: Oxford University Press.

Gould, B. 2006, 'Peter Costello, Muslims and Sharia Law', *Ozleft*, 6 March, at: www.marxists.org/archive/gould/2006/20060306.htm (accessed September 2007).

Government of Canada 2015, *Annual Report on the Operation of the Canadian Multiculturalism Act – 2013–2014*, Government of Canada, at: www.cic.gc.ca/english/resources/publications/multi-report2014/3.asp (accessed July 2015).

Griffith-Jones, R. (ed.) 2013, *Islam and English Law: Rights, Responsibilities and the Place of Shari'a*. Cambridge and New York: Cambridge University Press.

Ha, T.T. 2014, 'RCMP charge missing Toronto financier with $4.3 mortgage fraud', *The Globe and Mail*, 19 February, at: www.theglobeandmail.com/news/national/rcmp-charge-missing-toronto-financier-with-43-million-mortgage-fraud/article16972349/ (accessed 7 April 2015).

Hagopian, E. 2004, *Civil Rights in Peril: The Targeting of Arabs and Muslims*. London: Pluto Press.

Halim, F. 2006, 'Pluralism of American Muslims and the Challenge of Assimilation,' *Journal of Muslim Minority Affairs*, 26 (2) 235–44.

Hall, L. 2014, 'First female genital mutilation case to go to trial in NSW Supreme Court', *Sydney Morning Herald*, 9 December, at: www.smh.com.au/nsw/first-female-genital-mutilation-case-to-go-to-trial-in-nsw-supreme-court-20141209-1237h7.html (accessed July 2015).

Hallaq, W. 1984, 'Was the gate of ijtihad closed?' *International Journal of Middle East Studies*, 16 (1): 3–41.

Hallaq, W. 2009, *Shari'a: Theory, Practice, Transformations*. Cambridge: Cambridge University Press.

Hals, T. 2013, 'Arcapita's novel sharia bankruptcy plan approved', *Reuters*, 11 June, at: www.reuters.com/article/2013/06/11/arcapita-bankruptcy-approval-idUSL2N0EN1EQ20130611 (accessed July 2015).

Hamdani, D. 2014, *Canadian Muslim Women: A Decade of Change – 2001 to 2011*, Canadian Council of Muslim Women, 21 September, at: http://ccmw.com/canadian-muslim-women-a-decade-of-change-2001-to-2011/ (accessed July 2015).

Hamdani, D. 2015, 'Canadian Muslims: A statistical review', The Canadian Dawn Foundation, Canada, at: http://youthblast.ca/wp-content/uploads/2015/06/Canadian-Muslims-A-Statistical-Review-Final.pdf (accessed July 2015).

Hannah, F. 2015, 'Sharia-compliant savings and bank accounts rocket in popularity across Britain', *Independent*, 3 May, at: www.independent.co.uk/news/business/shariacompliant-savings-and-bank-accounts-rocket-in-popularity-across-britain-10220992.html (accessed 4 May 2015).

Hanshaw, M.E. 2010, *Muslim and American? Straddling Islamic Law and U.S. Justice*, El Paso, TX: LFB Scholarly Pub.

Hanzlick, R. 2007, *Death Investigation: Systems and Procedures*. Boca Raton, FL: CRC Press.

Hanzlick, R. and Combs, D. 1998, 'Medical examiner and coroner systems: History and trends', *JAMA*, 279 (11): 870–74.

Harris, D. 2002, *Profiles in Injustice: Why Racial Profiling Cannot Work*. New York: The New Press.

Hartford, H. 2007, *Initiating and Upholding an Islamic Marriage*, 3rd edn. Damascus: Dār al-Fikr.

Hartford, H. and Muneeb, A. 2007, *Your Islamic Marriage Contract*. Amman: Al-Fath Research and Publishing.

Hassan, R. 2009, 'Social and economic conditions of Australian Muslims: Implications for social inclusion', *NCEIS Research Papers*, 2 (4), National Centre of Excellence for Islamic Studies, Australia.

Hassan, R. 2015, *Australian Muslims: A Demographic, Social and Economic profile of Muslims in Australia 2015*. Adelaide, SA: University of South Australia, at: www.unisa.edu.au/Global/EASS/MnM/Publications/Australian_Muslims_Report_2015.pdf (accessed July 2015).

Hassan, S.F. 2013, *Fiqh al-Aqalliyat: History, Development, and Progress*. New York: Palgrave Macmillan.

Hay, D. and Snyder, F. 1989, *Policy and Prosecution in Great Britain: 1750–1850*. Oxford: Oxford University Press.

Helm, T., Taylor, M. and Davis, R. 2011, 'David Cameron sparks fury from critics who say attack on multiculturalism has boosted English Defence League', *Guardian*,

6 February, at: www.theguardian.com/politics/2011/feb/05/david-cameron-speech-criticised-edl (accessed July 2015).

Heron, J. and Reason, P. 1997, 'A participatory inquiry paradigm', *Qualitative Inquiry*, 3 (3): 274–94.

HG.org Legal Resources 2015a, 'Bankruptcy Law – Chapter 7, 11, 13', HG.org, at: www.hg.org/bankrpt.html (accessed 22 April 2015).

HG.org Legal Resources 2015b, 'U.S. divorce law center', HG.org, at: www.hg.org/divorce-law-center.html (accessed July 2015).

Hickey, M. 2008, 'Islamic sharia courts in Britain are now legally binding', *Mail Online*, 15 September, at: www.dailymail.co.uk/news/article-1055764/Islamic-sharia-courts-Britain-legally-binding.html (accessed December 2010).

Hirsch, A. 2010, 'Fears of over non-Muslim's use of Islamic law to resolve disputes', *Guardian*, 15 March, at: www.theguardian.com/uk/2010/mar/14/non-muslims-sharia-law-uk (accessed July 2015).

Holmes, O.W. 2000, 'The Common Law', Lecture 1, para. 1, at: www.hourofthetime.com/1-LF/November2012/Hour_Of_The_Time_11132012-The%20Common%20Law_Holmes.pdf (accessed 30 September 2015).

Hooker, M.B. 1975, *Legal Pluralism: An Introduction to Colonial and Neo-Colonial Laws*. Oxford: Clarendon Press.

Hooker, V. 2004, 'Developing Islamic arguments for change through "liberal Islam"', in V. Hooker and A. Saikal (eds), *Islamic Perspectives in the New Millennium*. ISEAS, Singapore, pp. 231–51.

Horder, J. 1992, *Provocation and Responsibility*. Oxford: Oxford University Press.

Hunter, J., Henning, T., Edmond, G., McMahon, R., Metzger, J. and San Roque, M. 2015, *The Trial: Principles, Process and Evidence*. Leichhardt, NSW: Federation Press.

Huntington, S. 1996, *The Clash of Civilizations and the Remaking of World Order*. New York: Simon & Schuster.

Husak, D. 2008, *Overcriminalization: The Limits of the Criminal Law*. Oxford: Oxford University Press.

Hussain, J. 2011, *Islam: Its law and Society*. Leichhardt, NSW: The Federation Press.

Hussain, M. 2010, *Demystifying Islamic Finance: Correcting Misconceptions, Advancing Value Propositions*. Malaysia: Zaid lbrahim & Co.

ibn ʿĀbidīn, M. 1994, *Radd Al-Muḥtār ʿalā Al-Durr Al-Mukhtār Sharḥ Tanweer Al-Abṣār*. Beirut: Dār al-Kutub al-ʿIlmiyyah.

ibn Athir M. n.d., 1979, *An-Nihayat fi ghareeb al-ḥadīth wal Athar*. Beirut, 'Maktabah al-'Ilmiyyah.

Ibn Daqiq al-ʿId 2012 *Sharḥ al-Arba'una An-Nawawiyyah fi-l Aḥādīth An-Nabawiyyah*. Beirut: Dār al-Mashari'a.

Ibn Rushd 1996, *The Distinguished Jurist's Primer*, vol. 2, trans. I.A.K. Nyazee. London: Garnet Publishing.

Illaysh, M. n.d., *Manḥ al-Jalil Sharḥ Mukhtaṣar Khalil*. Beirut, Dār al-Fikr.

In Brief n.d., 'Access to children', *In Brief: Helping with Life's Legal Issues*, UK, at: www.inbrief.co.uk/divorce-law/access-to-children.htm (accessed July 2015).

International Centre for Human Rights and Democratic Development 2005, 'Behind closed doors: How faith based arbitration shuts out women's rights in Canada and abroad', *Rights and Democracy*, at: www.dd-rd.ca/english/commdoc/publications/women/arbifaith.htm (accessed March 2010).

Ipgrave, J. 2010, 'Including the religious viewpoints and experiences of Muslim students in an environment that is both plural and secular', *Journal of International Migration and Integration*, 11 (1): 5–22.

Islamic Sharia Council n.d., 'ISC stand on the marriage contract', Islamic Sharia Council, UK, at: www.islamic-*sharia*.org/index2.php?option=com_docman&gid=4&task=doc_view&Itemid=99999999 (accessed January 2011).

Islamophobia Register Australia 2015, Islamophobia Register Australia, Australia, at: www.islamophobia.com.au/index.php (accessed July 2015).

Jaan, H. 2014, *Equal and Free, 50 Muslim Women's Experiences of Marriage in Britain Today*, at: www.secularism.org.uk/uploads/aurat-report-dec2014.pdf (accessed December 2015).

Jabour, B. 2015a, 'Australian FGM case: Girl describes pain after alleged procedure', *Guardian*, 17 September, at: www.theguardian.com/society/2015/sep/17/australian-fgm-case-girl-describes-hurting-in-my-bottom (accessed 17 September 2015).

Jabour, B. 2015b, 'Australia's first female genital mutilation trial: How a bright young girl convinced a jury', *Guardian*, 13 November, at: www.theguardian.com/society/2015/nov/13/female-genital-mutilation-trial-young-girl-convinced-jury-australia (accessed 6 December 2015).

Jackson, S.A. 2003, 'Shari'ah, democracy, and the modern nation-state: Some reflections on Islam, popular rule, and pluralism,' *Fordham International Law Journal*, 27 (1): 88–107.

Jackson, S.A. 2010, 'What is Shari'a and why does it matter?', *Huffington Post*, 9 November, at: www.huffingtonpost.com/sherman-a-jackson/what-is-shariah-and-why-d_b_710976.html (accessed 1 June 2015).

Jacobsen, D., Olmsted, E., Deckard, N. and Woodward, M. 2012, *Survey of Muslims in Western Europe, West Africa and Malaysia. Sample Characteristics*. The Center for the Study of Religion and Conflict, Arizona State University, at: https://csrc.asu.edu/sites/default/files/download/2012/06/Minerva%20Sample%20Characteristics-6-11-12%20meo.pdf (accessed 26 February 2015).

Johnson, C. 2014, 'A bank, a bankruptcy, and the world of Shariah law', *The American Lawyer*, 29 September, at: www.americanlawyer.com/id=1202671042434/A-Bank-a-Bankruptcy-and-the-World-of-Shariah-Law#ixzz3VXVR1qkc (accessed July 2015).

Johnston, R. 2016, 'Terrorist attacks and related incidents in the United States', compiled by W. Robert Johnston, last updated 16 February 2016, at: www.johnstonsarchive.net/terrorism/wrjp255a.html (accessed 6 April 2016).

Jones, M. (ed.) 1993, *An Australian pilgrimage: Muslims in Australia from the Seventeenth Century to the Present*. Melbourne: The Law Printer.

Jones, S. and agency 2013, 'Muslim vigilantes jailed for "sharia law" attacks in London', *Guardian*, 7 December, at: www.theguardian.com/uk-news/2013/dec/06/muslim-vigilantes-jailed-sharia-law-attacks-london (accessed July 2015).

Joppke, C. 2004, 'The retreat of multiculturalism in the liberal state', *The British Journal of Sociology*, 55 (2): 237–57.

Justice NSW n.d., *Inquest into the Deaths Arising from the Lindt Café Siege*. Justice NSW, Australia, at: www.lindtinquest.justice.nsw.gov.au/ (accessed July 2015).

Kamali, M.H. 2015, *The Middle Path of Moderation in Islam: The Qur'ānic Principle of Wasaṭiyyah*. Oxford and New York: Oxford University Press.

Kazmi, N. 2008, 'Why self-flagellation matters to Shias', *Guardian*, 28 August, at: www.theguardian.com/commentisfree/2008/aug/28/religion.islam (accessed 6 April 2016).

Keppel, G. 2009, *Jihad: The Trial of Political Islam*. London and New York: I.B. Tauris.

Khan, S. 1993, 'Canadian Muslim women and Shari'a law: A feminist response to "Oh! Canada!"', *Canadian Journal of Women and the Law*, 6 (1): 52–65.

Kim, E-J. 2014, 'Islamic law in American courts: Good, bad, and unsustainable', *Notre Dame Journal of Law, Ethics and Public Policy*, 28 (1): 287–307.

Kirkup, J. 2011, 'Baroness Warsi: David Cameron won't back "Islamophobia" claims', *Telegraph*, 20 January, www.telegraph.co.uk/news/religion/8272273/Baroness-Warsi-David-Cameron-wont-back-Islamophobia-claims.html (accessed July 2015).

Koenig, M. 2005, 'Incorporating Muslim migrants in Western nation states: A comparison of the United Kingdom, France and Germany', *Journal of International Migration and Integration*, 6 (2): 219–34.

Koern, S. 2015, *UK: Anjem Choudary Charged with Supporting Islamic State*. Gatestone Institute, 9 August, at: www.gatestoneinstitute.org/6315/anjem-choudary-islamic-state (accessed 23 August 2015).

Korteweg, A. 2008, 'The Sharia debate in Ontario: Gender, Islam and representations of Muslim women's agency', *Gender and Society*, 22: 434–54.

Korteweg, A. 2011, 'Understanding honour killing and honour-related violence in the immigration context: Implications for the legal profession and beyond', *Canadian Criminal Law Review*, 16: 135–60.

Krayem, G. 2014, *Islamic Family Law in Australia*. Carlton, VIC: Melbourne University Publishing.

Kumpf, S.N. 2014, 'Lasting infancy or coming of age? Insolvency considerations when Islamic finance vehicles fail', *INSOL World*, vol. 4th Quarter: 20–23.

Kureshi, H. 2013,'Case study – Arcapita', Islamic Finance, weblog post, at: http://islamicfinancialsystems1.blogspot.com.au/2013/08/case-study-arcapita-by-hussain-kureshi.html (accessed 27 March 2015).

Kurzman, C. 1998, *Liberal Islam: A Source Book*. Oxford and New York: Oxford University Press.

Kutty, A. and Kutty, F. 2004, 'Shariah courts in Canada, myth and reality', *IslamiCity*, 9 March, at: www.islamicity.org/2252/shariah-courts-in-canada-myth-and-reality/ (accessed July 2010).

Kuwait Financial Centre 'Markaz' 2013, *Dealing with Bankruptcy in the GCC: A Key Missing Block in the Reform Agenda*, Markaz, at: www.markaz.com/DesktopModules/CRD/Attachments/BankruptcyintheGCC-MarkazResearch.pdf (accessed 27 March 2015).

Kymlicka, W. 1989, *Liberalism, Community and Culture*. Oxford: Oxford University Press.

Kymlicka, W. 1996, *Multicultural Citizenship*. Oxford: Oxford University Press.

Kymlicka, W. 1998, *Finding Our Way, Rethinking Ethnocultural Relations in Canada*. Toronto: Oxford University Press.

Kymlicka, W. 2007a, 'Ethnocultural diversity in a liberal state: Making sense of the Canadian model(s)', in K. Banting, T. Courchene and L. Seidle (eds), *Belonging? Diversity, Recognition and Shared Citizenship in Canada*. Montreal: Institute for Research on Public Policy.

Kymlicka, W. 2007b, *Multicultural Odysseys: Navigating the New International Politics of Diversity*. Oxford: Oxford University Press.

Lacey, N. 2012, 'Principles, policies and politics of the criminal law', in L. Zedner and J. Roberts (eds), *Principles and Values in Criminal Law and Criminal Justice: Essays in Honour of Andrew Ashworth*. Oxford: Oxford University Press.

Lalani, S. 2013, 'Establishing the content of foreign law: A comparative study', *Maastricht Journal*, 20 (1): 75–112.

Lalla-Maharajh, J. 2010, 'Female genital mutilation in Georgia, USA', *Huffington Post*, 15 May, at: www.huffingtonpost.com/julia-lallamaharajh/female-genital-mutilation_b_498529.html (accessed July 2015).

Lambert, R. and Githens-Mazer, J. 2010, *Islamophobia and Anti-Muslim Hate Crimes: UK Case Studies – An Introduction to a 10 year Europe Wide Research Project*, University of Exeter European Muslim Research Centre, UK.

Lamont, L. 2007, 'Terrorism accused refuse to stand', *Sydney Morning Herald*, 1 June, at:www.smh.com.au/news/national/terrorism-accused-refuse-to-stand/2007/05/31/1180205431045.html (accessed 17 February 2015).

Lane, E. 2010, *An Arabic–English lexicon: Derived from the Best and the Most Copious Eastern Sources*. Charleston, SC: Nabu Press.

Laville, S. 2015a, 'Decision to prosecute doctor for FGM "left me with no faith in British justice"', *Guardian*, 5 February, at: www.theguardian.com/society/2015/feb/04/prosecuting-dr-dhanuson-dharmasena-female-genital-mutilation-mistake-consultant (accessed July 2015).

Laville, S. 2015b, 'First FGM prosecution: How the case came to court', *Guardian*, 5 February, at: www.theguardian.com/society/2015/feb/04/first-female-genital-mutilation-prosecution-dhanuson-dharmasena-fgm (accessed July 2015).

Lavin, T. 2013, 'Do Jews practice female genital mutilation? One Guardian writer thinks so', *Jewish Telegraphic Agency*, 9 September, at: www.jta.org/2013/09/09/news-opinion/the-telegraph/guardian-article-claims-that-jews-practice-female-genital-mutilation (accessed July 2015).

Lawrence, J., Morton, P.R. and Khan, S.H. 2013, 'Resolving Islamic finance disputes', *Legal Insight*, 23 September, K&L Gates, at: www.klgates.com/resolving-islamic-finance-disputes-09-19-2013/ (accessed 6 April 2016).

Layish, A. 2005,'The fatwa as an instrument of accommodation', in M.K. Masud, B. Messick and D.S. Powers (eds), *Islamic Legal Interpretation: Muftis and Their Fatwas*. Cambridge: Harvard University Press, pp. 270–77.

Le Gall, D. 2010, 'Recent thinking on Sufis and saints in the lives of Muslim societies, past and present', *International Journal of Middle East Studies*, 42: 673–87.

Lebanese Muslim Association 2015, 'LMA rejects aggressive rhetoric against Muslims', media release, 24 February, at: www.lma.org.au/wp-content/uploads/2015/08/LMA-MEDIA-RELEASE_PM-address_Feb24_2015.pdf (accessed 6 April 2016).

Legal Information Institute, n.d., 'Federal rules of evidence', Legal Information Institute, at: www.law.cornell.edu/rules/fre 5 (accessed 5 December 2015).

Legrand, P. 1997, 'The impossibility of "legal transplants"', 4 *Maastricht Journal European and Comparative Law*, 111.

Lepore, C. 2012, 'Asserting state sovereignty over national communities of Islam in the United States and Britain: Sharia courts as a tool of Muslim accomodation [sic] and integration', *Washington University Global Studies Law Review*, 11 (3): 669–92.

Lewis, H. 1995, 'Between Irua and "Female Genital Mutilation": Feminist Human Rights Discourse and the Cultural Divide', *Harvard Human Rights Journal*, 8 (1): 1–55.

Lindsey, T. and Steiner, K. 2012, *Islam, Law and the State in Southeast Asia: Volume II: Singapore*. New York: I.B. Tauris.

Macfarlane, J. 2012, *Islamic Divorce in North America: A* Shari'a *Path in a Secular Society*. New York: Oxford University Press.

Macfarlane, J. n.d., 'Faith-based dispute resolution – Transcription', *Windsor Law*, at:

http://www1.uwindsor.ca/law/IslamicdivorceinNorthAmerica/faith-based-dispute-resolution-transcription (accessed July 2015).

Macklin, A. 2006, 'Post-neoliberal multiculturalism: The case of faith-based arbitration', Proceedings of the annual meeting of the Canadian Political Science Association, York University, Toronto, 1–3 June.

Mahmoudjafari, N. 2014, 'Religion and family law: The possibility of pluralistic cooperation', *UMKC Law Review*, 82 (4): 1077–84, at: http://connection.ebscohost.com/c/articles/110195102/religion-family-law-possibility-pluralistic-cooperation (accessed July 2015).

Malik, N. 2011, 'What is Lady Cox's bill really about?', *Guardian*, 21 June, at: www.theguardian.com/commentisfree/belief/2011/jun/20/lady-cox-bill-womens-rights (accessed July 2015).

Mallat, C. 1988, 'The debate on riba and interest in twentieth century jurisprudence', in C. Mallat (ed.), *Islamic law, and Finance*. London: Graham & Trotman.

Mallick, H. 2004, 'Boutique law: It's the latest thing', *The Globe and Mail*, 15 May.

Maloney, R. 2015, 'Jason Kenney references Shariah law to defend niqab position', *Huffington Post Canada*, 23 June, at: www.huffingtonpost.ca/2015/06/23/jason-kenney-shariah-law-niqab-ban_n_7646004.html (accessed July 2015).

Manning, P. 2004, *Dog Whistle Politics and Journalism: Reporting Arabic and Muslim People in Sydney Newspapers*. Sydney: Southwood Press.

Maret, R.E. 2013, 'Mind the gap: The Equality Bill and Sharia arbitration in the United Kingdom', *Boston College International and Comparative Law Review*, 36 (1): 255–83.

Markus, A. 2014, 'Mapping social cohesion: The Scanlon Foundation surveys 2014', Monash University, Australia, at: http://monash.edu/mapping-population/ (accessed July 2015).

Marranci, G. 2009, *Faith, Ideology and Fear: Muslim Identities Within and Beyond Prisons*. London and New York: Continuum.

McConville, M., Sanders, A. and Leng, R. 1991, *The Case for the Prosecution*. London: Routledge.

McCulloch, J. and Pickering, S. 2009, 'Pre-crime and counter-terrorism: Imagining future crime in the "War on Terror" ', *The British Journal of Criminology*, 49 (5): 628–45.

McGuire, M. 2014, *The Right to Refuse: Examining Forced Marriage in Australia*, Good Shepherd Youth & Family Service, Domestic Violence Victoria, at: www.goodshepvic.org.au/Assets/Files/Right_to_Refuse_final_report.pdf (accessed July 2015).

McMillen, M.J.T. 2001, 'Islamic Shari'ah-compliant project finance: Collateral security and financing structure case studies', *Fordham Journal of International Law*, 24: 1184–232.

McQuire, A. 2014, *Islamophobia: Australia's Newest National Sport*. *New Matilda*, 23 September, at: https://newmatilda.com/2014/09/23/islamophobia-australias-newest-national-sport (accessed July 2015).

Meer, N. and Modood, T. 2012, 'For "Jewish" Read "Muslim"? Islamophobia as a form of racialisation of ethno-religious groups in Britain today', *Islamophobia Studies Journal*, 1 (1): 34–53.

Meetoo, V. and Mirza, H.S. 2011, 'There is nothing "honourable" about honour killings: Gender, violence and the limits of multiculturalism', in M.M. Idriss and T. Abbas (eds), *Honour, Violence, Women and Islam*. London: Routledge, pp. 42–66.

Mernissi, F. 1991, *The Veil and the Male Elite: A Feminist Interpretation of Women's Rights in Islam*, trans. J. Lakeland. Reading, MA: Addison-Wesley Publishing.

Mernissi, F. 2009, *Islam and Democracy*. Cambridge, MA: Basic Books.

Michalski, R.M. 2011, 'Pleading and proving foreign law in the age of plausibility pleading', *Buffalo Law Review*, 59: 1207–66.

Millar, R. 2014, *Designate Canada a Sharia-free Zone*, petition, at: www.change.org/p/the-rt-hon-stephen-harper-prime-minister-of-canada-designate-canada-a-sharia-free-zone (accessed July 2015).

Mills, R. 1995, 'Interview [with Syed Mumtaz Ali]: A review of the Muslim personal/family law campaign', at: http://muslim-canada.org/pfl.htm (accessed February 2010).

Ministry of the Attorney General 2005, 'Statement by Attorney General on the Arbitration Act, 1991', 8 September, at: http://news.ontario.ca/archive/en/2005/09/08/Statement-by-Attorney-General-on-the-Arbitration-Act-1991.html (accessed 6 April 2016).

Ministry of Religious Endowments and Islamic Affairs 1983, *al-Mawsu'a al-Kuwaytiya*, 2nd edn. Kuwait: Dhat al-Salasil.

Modood, T. 1993, 'Kymlicka on British Muslims', *Analyse & Kritik*, 15: 87–91.

Modood, T. 2007, *Multiculturalism: A Civic Idea*. Cambridge: Polity Press.

Modood, T. 2008, 'Multicultural citizenship and the anti-Sharia storm', openDemocracy, 14 February, at: www.opendemocracy.net/article/faith_ideas/europe_islam/anti_sharia_storm (accessed July 2015).

Modood, T. 2009, 'Muslims, religious equality and secularism', in G.B. Levey and T. Modood (eds), *Secularism, Religion and Multicultural Citizenship*. New York: Cambridge University Press, pp. 164–85.

Moghul, U.F. and Ahmed, A.A. 2003, 'Contractual forms in Islamic Finance Law and *Islamic Inv. Co. of the Gulf (Bahamas) Ltd.* v. *Symphony Gems N.V. & Ors.*: A first impression of Islamic finance', *Fordham International Law Journal*, 27: 150–94, at: http://ir.lawnet.fordham.edu/ilj/vol. 27/iss1/ (accessed 10 December 2015).

Mohammad, M. and Kharoshah, K. 2014, 'Autopsy in Islam and current practice in Arab Muslim countries', *Journal of Forensic and Legal Medicine*, 23: 80–83.

More, K. 2010, *The Unfamiliar Abode: Islamic Law in the United States and Britain*. Oxford: Oxford University Press.

Morris, L. 2007, 'Not all of the old school', *Sydney Morning Herald*, 2 May, at: www.smh.com.au/news/national/not-all-of-the-old-school/2007/05/01/1177788142524.html (accessed July 2015).

Muslim Arbitration Tribunal 2015, Muslim Arbitration Tribunal, UK, at: www.matribunal.com/. (accessed October 2010).

Muslim Council of Britain Research & Documentation Committee 2015, *British Muslims in Numbers*, The Muslim Council of Britain, at: www.mcb.org.uk/wp-content/uploads/2015/02/MCBCensusReport_2015.pdf (accessed July 2015).

Muslim Marriage Contract 2008, The Muslim Institute, London, at: www.muslimparliament.org.uk/Documentation/Muslim%20Marriage%20Contract.pdf (accessed January 2011).

The Muslim Marriage Mediation & Arbitration Service n.d., *An essential Islamic service in Canada: Muslim marriage mediation and arbitration service*, at: http://muslim-canada.org/brochure.htm (accessed October 2010).

Muslim Women's Network UK 2015, *Forced Marriage & Honour Based Violence is Against the Law*. Communities and Local Government, UK, www.mwnuk.co.uk//go_files/factsheets/758400-Focrced%20Marriage%20Booklet%20v.4.1.pdf (accessed July 2015).

Mythen, G., Walklate, S. and Khan, F. 2009, '"I'm a Muslim, but I'm not a terrorist": Victimization, risky identities and the performance of safety', *The British Journal of Criminology*, 49 (6): 736–54, doi: 10.1093/bjc/azp032.

Nagra, B. 2011, 'Unequal citizenship: Being Muslim and Canadian in the post 9/11 era', PhD thesis, University of Toronto, Canada.

Nardelli, A. and Arnett, G. 2014, 'Today's key fact: You are probably wrong about almost everything', *Guardian*, 29 October, at: www.theguardian.com/news/datablog/2014/oct/29/todays-key-fact-you-are-probably-wrong-about-almost-everything (accessed 16 November 2015).

Nasir, J. 1986, *The Islamic Law of Personal Status*. London: Graham & Trotman.

Nawaz, M. 2015, 'Why the survey of British Muslim attitudes is so profoundly disconcerting', *Independent*, 26 February, at: www.independent.co.uk/voices/comment/why-the-survey-of-british-muslim-attitudes-is-so-profoundly-disconcerting-10070358.html (accessed July 2015).

NHS Choices 2014, 'Labiaplasty', NHS, 20 August, www.nhs.uk/conditions/labiaplasty/Pages/Introduction.aspx (accessed 26 February 2015).

Nichols, J. 2012, 'Introduction', in J. Nichols (ed.), *Marriage & Divorce in a Multicultural Context: Multi-Tiered Marriage and the Boundaries of Civil Law and Religion.* Cambridge: Cambridge University Press.

Nickson, C. 2015, 'Shared custody of your children', Equal Rights for Separated Dads, UK, at: www.separateddads.co.uk/sharedcustodyofyourchildren.html (accessed July 2015).

Norrie, A. 2014, *Crime, Reason and History: A Critical Introduction to Criminal Law*. Cambridge: Cambridge University Press.

O'Connor, M. 2008, 'Reconstructing the hymen: Mutilation or restoration?', *Journal of Law and Medicine*, 16 (1): 161–75.

Office for National Statistics 2012, *Religion in England and Wales 2011*, 11 December, Government of Great Britain, UK.

Office for National Statistics 2013, *The Full Story: What does the Census Tell us About Religion in 2011*, 16 May, Government of Great Britain.

Ogan, C. 2014, 'The rise of anti-Muslim prejudice: Media and Islamophobia in Europe and the United States', *The International Communication Gazette*, 76 (1): 27–46.

One Law for All n.d., *No Sharia Law Campaign*, One Law for All, UK, at: www.onelawforall.org.uk (accessed October 2010).

Örücü, E. 1996, 'Mixed and mixing systems: A conceptual search', in E. Örücü, E. Attwooll and S. Coyle (eds), *Studies in Legal Systems: Mixed and Mixing*. London: Kluwer Law International, pp. 335–52.

Örücü, E. 2002, 'Law as transposition', *International & Comparative Law Quarterly*, 51 (2): 205–23.

Othman, A. 2007, '"And amicable settlement is best": Sulh and dispute resolution in Islamic law', *Arab Law Quarterly*, 21 (1): 64–90.

Paciocco, D. and Stuesser, L. 2015, *The Law of Evidence*, 7th edn. Toronto: Irwin Law.

Parekh, B. 2006, 'Europe, liberalism and the "Muslim question"', in T. Modood, A. Triandafyllidou and R. Zapato-Barrer (eds), *Multiculturalism, Muslims and Citizenship: A European Approach*. London: Routledge.

Parkinson, P. 1996, 'Multiculturalism and the Regulation of Marital Status in Australia' in N. Lowe and G. Douglas, *Families Across Frontiers*. The Hague: Kluwer.

Patel, F. 2013, 'NYPD must ditch discriminatory Muslim surveillance for its own good', *Al Jazeera America*, 30 October, at: http://america.aljazeera.com/articles/2013/10/30/nypd-muslim-surveillancediscrimination.html (accessed July 2015).

Pearl, D. 1972, 'Muslim marriages in English law', *Cambridge Law Journal*, 30 (1): 120–43.

Pearl, D. 1985–86, 'Islamic family law and Anglo-American public policy', *Cleveland State Law Review*, 34: 113–27.

Pearl, D. 1987, *A Textbook on Muslim Personal Law*, 2nd edn. London: Croom Helm.

Pearl, D. 2000, 'Ethnic diversity in English law', in S. Cretney (ed.), *Family Law: Essays for the New Millennium*. Bristol: Jordans Publishing Ltd.

Pearl, D. and Menski, W. 1998, *Muslim Family Law*, 3rd edn. London: Sweet & Maxwell.

Pedersen, A. and Hartley, L. 2012, 'Prejudice against Muslim Australians: The role of values, gender and consensus', *Journal of Community and Applied Social Psychology*, 22 (3): 239–55.

Pew Research Center 2007, *Muslim Americans: Middle class and mostly mainstream*, May 22, Pew Research Center, US, at: www.pewresearch.org/2007/05/22/muslim-americans-middle-class-and-mostly-mainstream/ (accessed July 2015).

Pew Research Center 2010, 'Radical Islamist movements: Jihadi networks and Hizb ut-Tahrir', 15 September, at: www.pewforum.org/2010/09/15/muslim-networks-and-movements-in-western-europe-radical-islamist-movements-jihadi-networks-and-hizb-ut-tahrir/ (accessed 4 December 2015).

Pew Research Center 2011, 'Muslim Americans: No signs of growth in alienation of support for extremism', 30 August, Pew Research Center, US, at: www.people-press.org/2011/08/30/section-1-a-demographic-portrait-of-muslim-americans/ (accessed July 2015).

Pew Research Center Forum on Religion and Public Life 2011, 'The future of the global Muslim population: Projectsions for 2010–2030', Pew Research Center, Washington, DC, at: www.pewforum.org/files/2011/01/FutureGlobalMuslimPopulation-WebPDF-Feb10.pdf (accessed July 2015).

Pieri, Z., Woodward, M., Hassan, I.H., Yahya, M., Hassan, I. and Rohmaniyah, I. 2014, 'Commanding good and prohibiting evil in contemporary Islam: Cases from Britain, Nigeria, and Southeast Asia', *Contemporary Islam*, 8 (1): 37–55.

Pilon, M. 2001, 'Canada's legal age of consent to sexual activity', revised, Parliament of Canada, Canada, at: www.parl.gc.ca/Content/LOP/ResearchPublications/prb993-e.htm (accessed 6 April 2015).

Posner, R. 1996, 'Pragmatic adjudication', *Cardozo Law Review*, 18: 1–20.

Poulter, S. 1998, *Ethnicity, Law and Human Rights: The English Experience*. Oxford: Clarendon Press.

Poynting, S. and Mason, V. 2006, '"Tolerance, freedom, justice and peace"?: Britain, Australia and anti-Muslim racism since 11 September 2001', *Journal of Intercultural Studies*, 27 (4): 365–91, DOI 10.1080/07256860600934973.

Poynting, S. and Perry, B. 2007, 'Climates of hate: Media and state inspired victimisation of Muslims in Canada and Australia since 9/11', *Current Issues in Criminal Justice*, 19 (2): 151–71.

Poynting, S., Noble, G., Tabar, P. and Collins, J. 2004, *Bin Laden in the Suburbs: Criminalising the Arab 'Other'*. Sydney: Federation Press.

Press Association 2015, 'Councils must be more proactive to prevent FGM, says top judge', *Guardian*, 15 January, at: www.theguardian.com/society/2015/jan/14/councils-proactive-prevent-fgm-judge (accessed July 2015).

Queensland Law Reform Commission 1993, *Female Genital Mutilation, MP7*, QLRC, Brisbane, at: www.qlrc.qld.gov.au/_data/assets/pdf_file/0019/372511/r47.pdf (accessed 6 December 2015).

Qutb, S. 1980 *Fi Dhilāl al-Qur'ān*, vol. 2, Beirut: Dār al-Shurūk.

Qutb, S. 2006, *Milestones – Ma'alim fil Tareeq*, A.B. Al-Mehri (ed.). Birmingham: Maktabah Publishers.

Racismnoway n.d., *About racism: Australia' cultural diversity*, NSW Government Department of Education, at: www.racismnoway.com.au/about-racism/population/ (accessed July 2015).

Rafiq, A. 2014, 'Child Custody in Classical Islamic Law and Laws of Contemporary Muslim World; An Analysis', *International Journal of Humanities and Social Science*, 4 (5): 267–77.

Rahim, L.Z. 2006, 'Discursive contest between liberal and literal Islam in South East Asia', *Policy and Society*, 25 (4): 77–98.

Ramadan, T. 2004, *Western Muslims and the Future of Islam*. Oxford: Oxford University Press.

Rawls, J. 1999, *A Theory of Justice*, revised edn. Oxford: Oxford University Press.

Raz, J. 1988, *The Morality of Freedom*. Oxford: Oxford University Press.

Reifert, E. 2011, 'Getting into the Hot Tub: How the U.S. Could Benefit from Australia's Concept of "Hot Tubbing" ', *University of Detroit Mercy Law Review*, 89 (103).

Reiss, F. 2015, 'America's child-marriage problem', *The New York Times*, 13 October, at: www.nytimes.com/2015/10/14/opinion/americas-child-marriage-problem.html?ref=opinion&_r=0 (accessed July 2015).

Religious Law in Canada 2005, radio program, ABC Radio, The Religion Report, 21 September.

Reuters 2012, 'Mom gets probation for locking up daughter for talking to a boy', NBC News, 6 November, at: http://usnews.nbcnews.com/_news/2012/11/07/14984748-mom-gets-probation-for-locking-up-daughter-for-talking-to-a-boy?lite (accessed 21 February 2015).

Rispler-Chaim, V. 1993, *Islamic Medical Ethics in the Twentieth Century*. Leiden: Brill.

Roark, M. 2008, 'Reading Mohammed in Charleston: Assessing the U.S. courts' approach to the convergence of law, language, and norms', *Widener Law Review*, 14 (205).

Roberts, P. and Zuckerman, A. 2010, *Criminal evidence*, 2nd edn. Oxford: Oxford University Press.

Roberts, R. 2014, 'American Muslims' ongoing civil rights fight Muslims and Arabs in the US say they face discrimination in many areas of life, 13 years after the 9/11 attacks', *Aljazeera*, 13 July, at: www.aljazeera.com/indepth/features/2014/07/american-muslims-ongoing-civil-rights-fight-2014713883896279.html (accessed July 2015).

Robertson, J. 2015, 'FGM: Brisbane couple charged with taking two girls to Africa for procedure', *Guardian*, 2 December, at: www.theguardian.com/society/2015/dec/02/fgm-brisbane-couple-charged-with-taking-two-girls-to-africa-for-procedure (accessed 6 December 2015).

Rubin, P. 2011, 'Iraq native Faleh Almaleki gets 34 years in prison for murdering his Americanized daughter', *Phoenix New Times*, 21 April, at: www.phoenixnewtimes.com/2011-04-21/news/iraqi-faleh-almaleki-gets-34-years-in-prison-for-murdering-his-americanized-daughter/2/ (accessed 21 February 2015).

Ruhl, G. 2007, *Party Autonomy in the Private International Law of Contracts: Transatlantic Convergence and Economic Efficiency*. Research Report no. 4/2007, Osgood Digital Commons, at: http://digitalcommons.osgoode.yorku.ca/cgi/viewcontent.cgi?article=1227&context=clpe (accessed 10 December 2015).

Sahgal, N. 2013, *Study: Muslim Job Candidates may Face Discrimination in Republican States*. Pew Research Center, at: www.pewresearch.org/fact-tank/2013/11/26/study-muslim-job-candidates-may-face-discrimination-in-republican-states/ (accessed July 2015).

Sahih Muslim n.d., *Book of Faith*, Sunnah.com, at: http://sunnah.com/muslim/1 (accessed 28 February 2015).

Said, E. 1978, *Orientalism*. London: Vintage Books.

Said, E. 1997, *Covering Islam: How the Media and the Experts Determine How We See the Rest of the World*, revised edn. London: Vintage Books.

Saleh, N. 1986, *Unlawful Gain and Legitimate Profit in Islamic Law: Riba, Gharar and Islamic Banking*. London and New York: Cambridge University Press.

Saleh, N. 2001, 'Freedom of contract: What does it mean in the context of Arab laws?', *Arab Law Quarterly*, 16: 346–47.

The Saudi Network n.d., 'Saudi labor and workmen law', The Saudi Network, Saudi Arabia, at: www.the-saudi.net/business-center/labor_law.htm (accessed July 2015).

Schleifer, T. 2015, 'Carson: I can support a Muslim who denounces Sharia law', CNN politics, 22 September, at: http://edition.cnn.com/2015/09/21/politics/ben-carson-muslim-sharia-law-presidency/ (accessed July 2015).

Shachar, A. 1998, 'Reshaping the multicultural model: Group accommodation and individual rights', *Windsor Review of Legal and Social Issues*, 8: 83–111.

Shachar, A. 2008, 'Privatizing diversity: A cautionary tale from religious arbitration in family law', *Theoretical Inquiries in Law*, 9: 573–607.

Shah, S. 2014, 'Islamic education and the UK Muslims: Options and expectations in a context of multi-locationality', *Studies in Philosophy and Education*, 33: 233–49.

Shepherd, S. 2009, 'Western philosophies of law: The Common Law', in 'Law', *Encyclopedia of Life Support Systems*, developed under the auspices of the UNESCO. Paris: Eols Publishers, at: www.eols.net (accessed 6 April 2016).

Siddiqui, S. 2013, 'Florida state senator: Sharia law like disease we should vaccinate against', *Huffington Post Australia*, 2 April, at: www.huffingtonpost.com.au/2013/04/01/alan-hays-sharia_n_2992532.html?ir=Australia (accessed July 2015).

Siddiqui, T.R. 2007, 'Interpretation of Islamic Marriage Contracts by American Courts,' *Family Law Quarterly*, 41: 639–58.

Siegel, M. 2015, 'Australian Muslim leader blasts government's deradicalization drive', *Reuters*, 22 July, at: www.reuters.com/article/2015/07/22/us-mideast-crisis-australia-idUSKCN0PW0C920150722 (accessed July 2015).

Sizemore, C.A. 2011, 'Enforcing Islamic *mahr* agreements: The American judge's interpretational dilemma', *George Mason Law Review*, 18 (4): 1085–116.

Skeel, D.A. 1998, 'Bankruptcy lawyers and the shape of American bankruptcy law', *Fordham Law Review*, 67 (2): 497–522, at: ir.lawnet.fordham.edu/cgi/viewcontent.cgi?article=3511&context=flr (accessed 22 April 2015).

Smith, J. 2004, 'The shipman inquiry: Death certification', *Science, Medicine and Law*, 44 (4): 280–87.

Soliman, Y. 2008, 'Embarrassing to Muslims', *Herald Sun*, 10 February, at: www.news.com.au/heraldsun/story/0,21985,23186972-5000117,00.html (accessed March 2010).

Steinhardt, G. 2013, 'Rawls on Religion and Public Reason', *Colloquium*, 5 September, at: https://lucian.uchicago.edu/blogs/colloquium/2013/09/05/rawls-on-religion-and-public-reason/ (accessed 30 September 2015).

Strawson, J. 2003, 'Revisiting Islamic Law: Marginal notes from colonial history', *Griffith Law Review*, 12 (2): 362–83.

Stuart, H. 2015, 'Understanding CAGE: A public information dossier. An examination of ideology, campaigns and support network', Centre for the Response to Radicalisation and

Terrorism, Policy Paper no. 5, The Henry Jackson Society, at: http://henryjacksonsociety.org/wp-content/uploads/2015/04/Understanding-CAGE.pdf (accessed 5 December 2015).

Styles, A. 2010, 'Judge bans burqa from Perth court', *WAtoday*, 19 August, at: www.watoday.com.au/wa-news/judge-bans-burqa-from-perth-court-20100819-12k2c.html (accessed 16 February 2015).

Sunday Life 2013, 'Labiaplasty surgery on the rise in Australia but a backlash looms', *Daily Life*, 17 November, at: www.dailylife.com.au/health-and-fitness/dl-wellbeing/labiaplasty-surgery-on-the-rise-in-australia-but-a-backlash-looms-20131115-2xldg.html (accessed 6 December 2015).

Take on Hate n.d., National Network for Arab American Communities, US, at: www.takeonhate.org/ (accessed July 2015).

Tamanaha, B. 2000, 'A non-essentialist version of legal pluralism', *Journal of Law and Society*, 27: 296.

Tan, C. 2011, 'Where tradition and "modern" knowledge meet: exploring two Islamic schools in Singapore and Britain', *Intercultural Education*, 22 (1): 55–68, doi: 10.1080/14675986.2011.549645.

Tapper, C. 2010, *Cross and Tapper on Evidence*, 12th edn. Oxford: Oxford University Press.

Taylor, C. 2009, 'What is secularism?', in G.B. Levey and T. Modood (eds), *Secularism, Religion and Multicultural Citizenship*. Cambridge: Cambridge University Press.

Tellmama 2014, 'Infographic showing the peaks and troughs on anti-Muslim hate crimes', Tellmama, 10 November, at: http://tellmamauk.org/infographic-showing-the-peaks-and-troughs-on-anti-muslim-hate-crimes/ (accessed July 2015).

Thompson, E. and Yunus, F.S. 2007, 'Choice of laws or choice of culture: How Western nations treat Islamic marital contracts in domestic courts', *Wisconsin International Law Journal*, 25 (2): 361–95.

Thomson, A. 2007, *Islamic law for family lawyers*, Family Law Week, 22 January, at: www.familylawweek.co.uk/site.aspx?i=ed2215 (accessed October 2010).

TNN 2014, 'Shias debate court remark on Muharram "atrocities"', *Times of India*, 26 November, at: http://timesofindia.indiatimes.com/city/mumbai/Shias-debate-court-remark-on-Muharram-atrocities/articleshow/45276791.cms (accessed July 2015).

Trigg, R. 2012a, *Equality, Freedom and Religion*. Oxford: Oxford University Press.

Trigg, R. 2012b, 'Religious Freedom in a Secular Society', *International Journal for Religious Freedom*, 5 (1): 45–58.

Trimingham, J.S. 1972, *The Sufi orders in Islam*. Oxford: Oxford University Press.

Tyler, T., Schulhofer, S. and Huq, A. 2010, 'Legitimacy and deterrence effects in counterterrorism policies: A study of Muslim Americans', *Law & Society Review*, 44 (2): 365–402.

UK Government 2015, 'Get a divorce', UK Government, at: www.gov.uk/divorce/overview (accessed July 2015).

UK Government and Parliament 2014, 'Ban all sharia law in the U.K.', petition, at: https://petition.parliament.uk/archived/petitions/48352 (accessed July 2015).

UK Home Office 2012, *Hate Crimes, England and Wales 2011 to 2012*, UK Government, at: www.gov.uk/government/publications/hate-crimes-england-and-wales-2011-to-2012-2/hate-crimes-england-and-wales-2011-to-2012 (accessed July 2015).

UK Parliament n.d., 'Relationships: The law of marriage', UK Parliament, UK, at: www.parliament.uk/about/living-heritage/transformingsociety/private-lives/relationships/overview/lawofmarriage-/ (accessed July 2015).

Underabi, H. 2014, *Mosques of Sydney and NSW*, Charles Sturt University, ISRA

Australia and University of Western Sydney, Australia, at: http://uws.edu.au/__data/assets/pdf_file/0003/754140/IS0001_ISRA_NSW_Msq_Rprt.pdf (accessed July 2015).

Veiszadeh, M. 2014, 'Muslim women scared to go outdoors in climate of hate', weblog, at: http://mariamveiszadeh.com/2014/11/11/muslim-women-scared-to-go-outdoors-in-climate-of-hate/ (accessed July 2015).

Veiszadeh, M. 2015, 'Death threats in the virtual world meant I had to worry about my safety in the real one', *Mamamia*, at: www.mamamia.com.au/lifestyle/the-online-abuse-mariam-endured-became-so-horrific-police-had-to-guard-her-home/ (accessed July 2015).

Vertovec, S. and Wessendorf, S. 2005, *Migration and Cultural, Religious and Linguistic Diversity in Europe: An Overview of Issues and Trends*, ESRC Centre on Migration, Policy and Society, Working Paper 05–18.

Vizcaino, B. 2014, 'What's in a name? Islamic banking rebrands in attempt to go mainstream', *Reuters*, 2 July, at: www.reuters.com/article/2014/07/02/islam-financing-namechange-idUSL6N0PC4SD20140702 (accessed 30 April 2015).

Vogel, F. 2000, *Islamic Law and Legal System: Studies of Saudia Arabia*. Leiden: Brill.

Wajahat, A., Clifton, E., Duss, M., Fang, L., Keyes, S. and Shakir, F. 2011, *Fear, Inc.: The Roots of the Islamophobia Network in America*, Center for American Progress, Washington, DC, at: www.americanprogress.org/issues/2011/08/pdf/islamophobia.pdf (accessed July 2015).

Watson, W. 1974, *Legal Transplants: An Approach to Comparative Law*. London: University of Georgia Press.

Weber, D. 2005, 'The world today: Muslim leaders call for Shariah divorce court', *ABC Online*, 7 April, at: www.abc.net.au/worldtoday/content/2005/s1340348.htm (accessed July 2015).

Wells, J., Lloyd, P. and wires 2012, 'Jones forced to apologise over racist comments', *ABC*, 14 December, at: www.abc.net.au/news/2012-12-13/jones-to-apologise-after-calling-lebanese-muslims-vermin/4426692 (accessed July 2015).

Williams, R. 2008a, 'Archbishop's lecture: Civil and religious law in England: A religious perspective', foundation lecture presented at the Royal Courts of Justice, London, 7 February, at: www.archbishopofcanterbury.org/1575 (accessed January 2010).

Williams, R. 2008b, '"Sharia law" – What did the Archbishop actually say?', 8 February, at: http://rowanwilliams.archbishopofcanterbury.org/articles.php/1135/sharia-law-what-did-the-archbishop-actually-say#sthash.wgCYmlWe.dpuf (accessed January 2010).

Wilson, J. and Grant, J. 2013, 'Islamic marketing – a challenger to the classical marketing canon?', *Journal of Islamic Marketing*, 4 (1): 7–21.

Winters, T. 2008, *BBC Thought for the Day*, radio programme, 11 February, at: www.bbc.co.uk/religion/programmes/thought/documents/t20080211.shtml (accessed February 2011).

Wolfe, C. 2006, 'Faith-based arbitration: Friend or foe? An evaluation of religious arbitration systems and their interaction with secular courts', *Fordham Law Review*, 75: 427–69.

Woodman, G.R. 2001, 'Customary Law in Common Law Systems', *IDS Bulletin*, 32 (1): 28–34, at: www.vanuatu.usp.ac.fj/sol_adobe_documents/usp%20only/customary%20law/woodman.pdf (accessed 16 December 2015).

World Health Organization 2000, *Female Genital Mutilation*. Fact sheet no. 241, WHO, Geneva, at: www.who.int/mediacentre/factsheets/fs241/en/ (accessed 6 April 2016).

Yeo, S.M.H. 1987, 'Ethnicity and the objective test in provocation', *Melbourne University Law Review*, 16: 67–82.

Yeo, S.M.H. 1996, 'Sex, ethnicity, power of self-control and provocation revisited', *Sydney Law Review*, 18 (3): 304–22.

Yilmaz, I. 2003, 'Muslim ADR and neo-ijtihad in England', *Alternatives: Turkish Journal of International Relations*, 2: 117–39.

Yilmaz, I. 2005, *Muslim Laws, Politics and Society in Modern Nation States: Dynamic Legal Pluralisms in England, Turkey and Pakistan*. London: Ashgate.

The Young Review 2014, *Improving Outcomes for Young Black and/or Muslim Men in the Criminal Justice System*, Barrow Cadbury Trust, at: www.youngreview.org/sites/default/files/clinks_young-review_report_dec2014.pdf (accessed 5 December 2015).

Younis, M. 2009, *Muslim Americans Exemplify Diversity, Potential*. Report by the Gallup Center for Muslim Studies, March 2, Gallup, US, at: www.gallup.com/poll/116260/muslim-americans-exemplify-diversity-potential.aspx (accessed July 2015).

Zedner, L. 2007, 'Pre-crime and post-criminology?', *Theoretical Criminology*, 11 (2): 261–81.

Zucca, L. 2012, *A Secular Europe: Law and Religion in the European Constitutional Landscape*. Oxford: Oxford University Press.

Zwartz, B. 2005, 'Australia's Muslims cool on change', *The Age*, 9 February, at: www.theage.com.au/news/world/australias-muslims-cool-on-change/2008/02/08/1202234168549.html (accessed 20 March 2010).